RAISING THE GLOBAL FLOOR

RAISING THE GLOBAL FLOOR

Dismantling the Myth that We Can't Afford Good Working Conditions for Everyone

Jody Heymann and Alison Earle

STANFORD POLITICS AND POLICY
An Imprint of Stanford University Press
Stanford, California

Stanford University Press
Stanford, California

Printed in the United States of America on acid-free, archival-quality paper

Library of Congress Cataloging-in-Publication Data

Heymann, Jody, 1959-
Raising the global floor : dismantling the myth that we can't afford good working conditions for everyone / Jody Heymann and Alison Earle.
p. cm.
Includes bibliographical references and index.
ISBN 978-0-8047-6890-0 (cloth : alk. paper)
1. Employee rights. 2. Labor policy. 3. Labor laws and legislation. 4. Labor economics. I. Earle, Alison. II. Title.
HD6971.8.H49 2010
331.2--dc22 2009029789

Typeset by Bruce Lundquist in 10/14 Minion

To Margaret Mead, for reminding us all of the potential of small groups of people to begin to change the world in ways that matter

To our research team, for living this belief and

To you, for carrying the ball the next yard

The natural distribution is neither just nor unjust; nor is it unjust that persons are born into society at some particular position. These are simply natural facts. What is just and unjust is the way that institutions deal with these facts.

John Rawls (1921–2002)

Contents

Preface

Making Fundamental Rights Count

While the twentieth century was marred by some of history's worst violence—repeated genocides underscoring one group's ability to utterly dehumanize another—and by neglect that led to millions of preventable deaths each year, it was also a century in which people from every nation, religion, and ethnic group around the world came together for the first time to recognize common human rights. Hopes turned into promises. These collective aspirations were embodied in global agreements through the United Nations and other international organizations, but those same bodies had little direct control over translating the dreams of basic rights into daily realities. The responsibility to ensure equal rights irrespective of gender, class, race, ethnicity, or religion; to prevent discrimination on the basis of disability; and to ensure access to health, education, and decent working conditions continues to fall primarily on the shoulders of individual countries.

Have the promises been kept? Little information has been systematically gathered regarding countries' efforts to improve equity. Through human rights organizations and other like-minded institutions, civil society has begun to document and publicize violations of political and civil rights; however, far fewer efforts have been made to track progress in achieving social and economic rights across societies. In the first decade of the twenty-first century, there are few places to which one may turn for readily accessible, easily interpretable information on whether different countries are making critical progress toward providing everyone with the fundamental rights necessary to achieve healthy, productive lives for themselves and their children. At a time when computer search engines can immediately locate any nation's GDP, it is far more difficult to find out how many and which countries have effectively ensured basic rights at work; which nations have genuinely guaranteed equal rights across race, ethnicity, gender, and religion; or how accessible and affordable is quality education—a critical foundation for equal opportunity.

Over the past decade, I have had the great privilege of leading a committed, energetic team of researchers in helping to fill this information gap. Our World Rights Legal Data (WoRLD) center examines the status of economic and social rights in 192 UN nations, with a focus on rights that promote equity. A fruitful dialogue can be had about which measures are most important when it comes to enabling all people to prosper. Is ensuring that everyone has an equal opportunity at achieving success the most critical factor, or ensuring that people's basic needs for safety, food, water, housing, and healthcare have been met? Our work takes as a premise that it is a combination of both of these measures. Regardless of where human beings are born or live and irrespective of their skills and capacities, they should be able to live under decent conditions. Furthermore, the conditions they face as they learn as children and labor as adults should give people an equitable chance at succeeding beyond that floor of having basic needs fulfilled. As a result, this initiative to document rights around the globe includes examining the quality and nature of education that shapes children's life chances; the attributes of working conditions that shape adults' lives and those of their families; the prevention of discrimination that biases outcomes; and the laws that move countries closer to the promise of just, equitable societies. *Raising the Global Floor* is the first book emerging from this major initiative to map constitutions, laws, and public policies around the world that form the foundation for basic guarantees and equal opportunities.

Why Take an Interest in Conditions Worldwide?

Each of us has to decide whether to be concerned with equity in our local community, in our country, or globally. There are two main reasons to care about what countries around the world are doing to address poverty, health, education, working conditions, and other areas that have the capacity to increase or erode equal opportunity. The first stems from a fundamental belief in the equal value of all human lives, irrespective of where people are born. The same sense of compassion and fairness that motivates us to work to prevent children from going hungry locally makes us concerned that children not go hungry elsewhere. Still, far more people share this moral, philosophical, or spiritual premise than act on it—in part because it is easier to ignore devastating conditions that are far away than those that are nearby, and in part out of a sense of futility about solving problems from which we are geographically removed. We hope this initiative will be one of many that helps chip away at barriers to thinking beyond inequalities and injustices just in our local areas, by providing information that makes it harder to ignore and easier to address these disparities globally.

But not everyone believes we have a strong obligation to ensure a decent floor of living conditions and equal opportunity for all human beings. For those who believe otherwise, who feel their primary obligation is only to their neighbors, there is a second reason to take an interest in global conditions. The remarkably rapid globalization that occurred during the twentieth century, the dramatic rise in the speed of transportation, the availability of inexpensive and instantaneous communication, and the relative ease of migration changed the facts about what influences life in Houston and Gaborone alike. The most recent economic crisis should remove all doubt that the world's economies are tightly intertwined. Economic success or failure in one country can rapidly spread and produce major effects on a cascading number of nations. Long before the current economic crisis, it was evident that poor labor standards in one country affected the likelihood of other countries offering decent working conditions. Similarly, the story of global climate change has left as little question about the world's environmental interconnectedness as AIDS left about the world's health interdependence.

Anyone concerned only with their own nation's economic success, high standards of working conditions, health, welfare, or environment needs to address these same conditions globally if they want to succeed at addressing them sustainably at home. To do so requires knowing what the conditions are in the rest of the world—a critical knowledge gap this project begins to fill—regarding policies that help to guarantee a minimum standard of decent living and working conditions, nondiscrimination, and equal opportunity worldwide.

Why Examine Legal Rights?

To examine what countries have done to guarantee basic rights and equalize opportunity, we began by looking at countries' constitutions and laws as these are the mechanisms by which nations formalize their long-term, national commitments to those living within their borders. Unlegislated policies, in contrast, can be unpredictable from one year to the next and are often local rather than national in scope. While individual programs give us a sense of what protections are available in a city or region, they may not be representative of a country's national policies and practices.

While legislation has the advantage of being, on average, more enduring, it is also an imperfect measure because countries can have good laws on the books but poor implementation. We consider it crucial that initiatives that examine legal rights be followed up with assessments of implementation and efforts to hold countries accountable for follow-through.

Why are laws important if there is no guarantee of full implementation? Across countries, having laws on paper does make a difference in practice. Laws lead to change by shaping public attitudes, encouraging government follow-through with inspections and implementation, and enabling court action for enforcement. Even when local enforcement is inadequate, laws may still have an impact by shaping the terms of political debate. Most important, laws that promote equality have led to significant change even in advance of societal norms. Many efforts to increase equal access and equal opportunity—whether across gender, ethnicity, religion, or sexual orientation—have generated resistance historically. Laws are a mechanism by which power can be democratically redistributed, changes in institutions can be created to ensure greater fairness, and a social floor guaranteeing minimum humane conditions can be established.

Why Global Findings Have Been Unavailable Before Now and What Can Be Done With Them

In the past, detailed global comparisons of legal rights have not been available because of the many barriers to performing such comparisons. Finding out what laws are on the books in 192 UN nations requires access to all of the laws in their original languages or in translations, a multilingual team, an immense amount of work to make them comparable, and then countless person hours to sift through all the information. When we began this initiative, we did not fully appreciate the amount of work required to bring this information together in a comprehensible, accessible format.

As we develop this global rights data center, our hope is that the information it contains will not merely sit in a book or in reports, but rather be actively used to promote change. We hope the data will empower citizens worldwide to learn how their own nations measure up when it comes to providing basic guarantees, and where lacking, to press their governments to move toward achieving global standards for the protection of rights.

Raising the Global Floor

The first set of laws this book examines are those pertaining to labor and working conditions. Alison Earle has worked side by side with me since the beginning of this initiative. The most common way for working men, women, and their families worldwide to exit poverty is through work. Education is a ladder out of poverty, because it gives access to better jobs. Jobs define people's income as well as the conditions under which they work and live, which in turn affect their own health, the health of their families, and future opportunities for their children. It is the central role that good working conditions play in addressing poverty, in providing equal opportunities for adults, and in shaping the opportunities of adults and children alike that led us to start with labor.

Jody Heymann
February 2009

RAISING THE GLOBAL FLOOR

1 The Struggle Below the Surface: Declining Working Conditions

THE QUALITY AND THE AVAILABILITY OF WORK dramatically affect the texture of our daily lives. While unemployment lines are lengthening in the United States and around the globe, the number of people who lack work is far exceeded by the hundreds of millions who are employed but lack basic decent working conditions. In national economies gone awry, real wages and benefits among low-skilled workers in many sectors have plummeted. All too frequently people are fired or have little choice but to leave their jobs as a result of the lack of such basic protections as the provision of paid time off to care for their own health or that of their aging parents and newborn infants. Under the threat of companies relocating to nations with lower labor standards, countries have forgone guaranteeing decent working conditions; out of fear of unemployment, workers settle for jobs with poor work protections and benefits. Excerpts from our thousands of interviews with working men and women around the world present some of the consequences of this ongoing struggle below the surface.

Poor working conditions have a profound impact on the health and well-being of individuals:

> At thirty-seven years old, Janet Litvak was a short-order cook in the United States. Like many in the business, she received no paid sick leave. When she caught influenza, she went to work. It did not matter that the Centers for Disease Control and Prevention said stay home; she could not afford to miss a day's wages or risk losing her job. Likewise when she caught gastroenteritis, she knew it was a bad idea to cook for others, but she had to show up at the restaurant.

In the United States, many direct service workers—from those working in food service to nursing homes—lack any ability to take leave. In fact, 43 percent of all private-sector workers are not guaranteed paid sick leave through their employers. As a result, fifty-two million workers in the United States either go to work sick or risk wage or job loss by taking unpaid or unauthorized time off.[1] Over the last twenty years, the number of employers who provide paid sick leave has decreased.[2]

> Gabriela Saavedra worked seven days a week in a Korean-owned sweatshop in Honduras. Her days typically began at 7 A.M. and ended at 6 P.M., but her boss frequently demanded that everyone work until at least 9 P.M. without prior notice. Overtime was not a choice, it was a requirement. Employees were given an ultimatum: either they worked the extra hours or they lost their jobs. Some days Gabriela had gone without sleep because she had been forced to work until 5 A.M. She had little time to eat or go to the bathroom. When she and her coworkers asked for one day off per month, they were told that the factory would simply relocate to China if they complained about their conditions.

According to the International Labour Organization (ILO), this form of extreme mandatory overtime under threat of termination constitutes forced labor.[3] Forced labor captures the lives of more than twelve million adults worldwide,[4] and tens of millions more work under sweatshop conditions "voluntarily" because they have no other way to survive.

The lack of basic workplace protections has severe repercussions for families as well as individuals:

> Nearby in Tegucigalpa, Leti Marta, a twenty-three-year-old bilingual secretary, wanted to breastfeed her newborn daughter. But she had had to return to work immediately after her short forty-two-day maternity leave ended because the baby's father had left them during the pregnancy and it was the only way for her to manage financially. She had tried to express milk at work, but was not able to sustain this practice and was soon forced to stop breastfeeding. Leti's mother, Maria, fed her granddaughter milk "from a can," but having been weaned too young, the child suffered from acute malnutrition, weighing at seven months what she should have weighed at four.

Despite the fact that breastfed babies have a one-and-a-half- to fivefold reduction in infant mortality rates and are significantly less likely to suffer from a wide range of infectious diseases than babies that are not breastfed, nearly one in three nations has no legislation guaranteeing breastfeeding breaks at work. Twenty-seven countries offer less than twelve weeks of leave for new mothers—requiring mothers to return to work earlier than is often healthy to end breastfeeding.

> In the United States, Agnes Charles saw that her two-year-old daughter Katie's asthma was acting up, but she knew that she would risk losing her job if she took her to the doctor and showed up late for work. For fear of losing her family's sole source of income, Agnes had left her sick daughter with a babysitter, who did not always administer her medication properly. If Agnes had been able to stay with her daughter, she would have recognized the symptoms of her worsening condition; the babysitter simply thought the baby was being cranky when she cried more frequently. By the time Agnes picked her daughter up after work, her breathing had gotten so bad that she took her straight to the emergency room, where she was admitted to the hospital for a week. After work, Agnes spent each night in the hospital with her sick daughter.

Only 30 percent of U.S. workers receive paid sick leave that can be used to care for their children. Even fewer have paid leave to care for an adult family member who is ill, leaving at least eighty-six million working men and women in the lurch.[5]

Workers often accept poor working conditions for fear of income and job loss, and the risk of being fired weighs heavily on the choices they make:

> Fifty-two-year-old Viktoriya Danilovna Kozlova worked as a transport dispatcher in Russia while raising her two sons. In an economy where jobs were scarce and where companies provided little support for working parents, she feared getting fired if she took time off to care for her children when they were sick. She explained: "We need money. My child is sick and . . . I cannot even take one day [off] a week because I'm afraid I will be fired."

> Ngo Van Cuong, a young father in Vietnam, was left with few choices when his infant son, Kinh, developed a serious allergic reaction to some food he'd eaten the night before. Because the couple could not afford to lose the money his wife would make selling pots and pans at the market that day, Cuong tried to get the day off to care for their sick son. "I asked my boss to take that day off, but he insisted that I couldn't . . . or else he would fire me." Cuong went to work that morning, but when he returned home on his afternoon break, he saw how sick his son was and decided to stay home to care for him. His boss followed through on his threat, and Cuong was fired.

Families and individuals are ultimately the casualties when there are no decent conditions at work, but countries and companies have the ability to transform the impact of the workplace on human health and well-being:

> Tomasz Nowak, a Polish immigrant in Iceland, worked as an electrical foreman on a construction project. He was earning 400,000 krs per month, the equivalent in dollars of ninefold more than the 2,000 Polish zloty he would have been earning at home. When Tomasz needed a knee operation, the company paid for his hospitalization and for his ten days of sick leave.

Iceland's labor standards guarantee paid leave to all workers—temporary immigrants, long-term residents, and citizens alike.

> Nguyen Thi Sau, a thirty-nine-year-old accountant from Vietnam, reported that her employers were understanding when she had to take three months off work to care for her father at the end of his life. The availability of short-term leave also made it possible for her to provide her aging aunt with essential care, taking her food and medication when she became ill and arranging for a cousin to look in on her.

The company provided what a growing number of countries are guaranteeing: the ability to keep one's job while providing essential care to sick and dying family members.

A Rocky Transformation

The global economy has been dramatically transformed over the past three decades. The size of the international labor force competing for opportunities has doubled and global economic competition has intensified because of the breakup of the Soviet Union and the transition of largely state-controlled economies to capitalism in the Eastern Bloc countries; the opening of the Chinese economy to foreign investment and increased trade in the 1980s and 1990s; and the decreased regulation of the Indian economy, which opened the door to subcontracted labor.

The resulting outsourcing of jobs to lower-wage countries has been frequently lamented in the media and elsewhere across Europe, the United States, and Canada.[6] Following the North American Free Trade Agreement (NAFTA) and other similar treaties, first jobs in manufacturing, in industries from clothing to footwear to machinery, and then those in business services, from customer service to technical support to billing operations, increasingly relocated from the United States, Canada, and Europe to lower-income nations. Manufacturing jobs that first went to Mexico and other middle-income producers subsequently left for China and Vietnam.

Employers have used the threat of relocating jobs and factories to another country as a way to lower wages and working conditions. The fear of job loss, of being "outsourced," and of factory and business closures has left many in the workforce feeling that they have no power to negotiate for better work protections and benefits. This has led to an increase in the prevalence of longer working hours, unpaid overtime, lower wages, and fewer benefits within high-income countries.[7]

On the surface, we see jobs relocating away from countries such as the United States; below the surface, the quality of many of the remaining jobs is deteriorating. These remaining jobs have lower wages and fewer benefits than many of the jobs that left. Moreover, the new jobs emerging in the United States and Europe are increasingly "contingent." A rise in casual, temporary, and part-time employment contracts has been documented in high-income countries across the Organisation for Economic Co-operation and Development (OECD), from North America to Japan to Europe to Australia.[8] While in 1997, one in nine adults in the European Union (EU) had a temporary position, by 2007, one in seven did.[9] The average American born between 1957 and 1969 held nearly eleven jobs by the age of forty-two.[10]

With each job transition, working families face the potential loss of critical work-related benefits. Whereas one year, an American father could take a day of paid leave from work to stay home to care for his sick ten-year-old daughter, ensuring that she took her medicine and got enough rest, the next year, his family could not afford any medication because he had lost his job when his factory relocated to Mexico and he had to take a new job with no benefits. Three months pregnant and facing job loss, a twenty-three-year-old woman in New Zealand will have trouble supporting her new baby, because even if she finds a new job she will not have access to maternity leave due to the year-long job-tenure prerequisite. When his company goes out of business, a fifty-seven-year-old man in Singapore battling cancer can no longer rely on paid sick leave because it was provided through his employer rather than through government social assistance.

The financial crisis of 2008 has heightened the economic instability of families. It is raising the specter of further job loss and worsening working conditions in affluent and developing nations alike. At times like these, the need to guarantee decent work and the possibility of achieving it are, respectively, both more urgent and seemingly more remote. Amid this turmoil, nations often act as though they have no options with respect to ensuring decent working conditions. Some nations contend that in a global economy where countries compete for jobs, mandating good working conditions will lead businesses to move from higher- to lower-income countries and from lower-income countries to the poorest. While there have been some cases of political leaders addressing bad working conditions through speeches or rare legislative proposals, perhaps due to the belief that their hands are tied, nations have often released themselves from the responsibility of guaranteeing a floor of decent working conditions for all of their citizens, leaving individuals to face precarious conditions on their own. Workers have been told that a bad job is better than no job, and that there is nothing that their governments can do to help.

The global failure to respond to poor working conditions is unparalleled. Nations have proven that global efforts can be feasible and effective by coming together to address other widespread societal and public health needs. Although the initial response of national governments and the global community to the AIDS pandemic was inadequate, the scope of efforts eventually grew more effective and wide reaching.[11] If countries have responded both individually and collaboratively to other threats to health and human welfare, why then has more not been done to ensure decent conditions at work? It is as ineffective to tell people to "go find a good job" in order to experience humane working conditions as it is to advise them to "stay away from sick people" in order to avoid illness. Individuals alone cannot change the availability and the quality of work; a societal response is needed to ensure decent conditions for all women and men at work.

This book addresses the fundamental question: Can societies do better at guaranteeing decent work for everyone?

Our Research

More than a decade ago, we started with a deep concern about how to increase equity and address intergenerational poverty and entrenched gender disparities. These fundamental concerns about reducing costly inequalities rapidly led us to assess the impact of work. Around the world, people's living conditions—including their access to adequate housing, water, food, and fuel—are determined by their income. Their income is in turn determined by their work or that of their partners or parents. In many countries around the world, the schools children can attend are likewise determined directly by their families' incomes and indirectly by their parents' work—both by delimiting what they can afford, and by influencing where they live. The details of the daily lives of three billion working adults in the world[12] are defined by the environments in which they spend the majority of their time, which is typically split between their work and their home community.

The nature of available work influences the lifetime opportunities, health, and welfare of employed individuals around the world by affecting the type of labor they are engaged in, the amount of their compensation, the hours they work, and their ability to stay home when sick without risking job loss, among other characteristics. The nature of work also affects the welfare and life chances of family members by determining factors such as the availability of parental leave or flexibility to care for a newborn child, leave for adults to provide essential care to an aging parent, and leave or flexibility for parents to meet children's educational needs or for people to care for a disabled family member.

Given the importance of the quality of work to the quality of our lives and to the foundations of equity both within and across countries, we began over a decade of research to examine how the characteristics of work were distributed across social class, gender, race, ethnicity, and national borders. Our goal was to understand how this distribution influenced people's life chances and how societies can work toward equalizing opportunities.

Our studies included examining the working conditions faced by fifty-five thousand households in seven countries on five continents, conducting in-depth interviews of over two thousand working adults and employers in fourteen countries around the world, and then examining policies in 190 countries.[13]

The first step toward finding solutions is identifying the scope and nature of problems. The following is a summary of some of our main findings.

Inequalities at Work

When both paid and unpaid work are included, around the world women are substantially more likely than men to work long hours, and less likely to have protections at work. For example, in dual-earner households in Mexico, 51 percent of men worked sixty or more hours of paid and unpaid work per week, compared to 84 percent of women. In Brazil, the gap was equally large between the 36 percent of men and 69 percent of women working over sixty hours per week.[14] Data from the United States confirm that this inequitable distribution of paid and unpaid labor is not limited to middle-income nations and continues to be largely due to the dual responsibilities shouldered by working women. Our analysis of data from the Survey of Midlife Development in the United States showed that 78 percent of female working adult caregivers reported performing more household chores than their spouses or partners, while only 15 percent of men reported the same.[15] In addition, working women in the United States are more likely than working men to be caring for a child with a disability or special needs.[16]

In addition to the longer working hours resulting from women's dual work and caregiving responsibilities, women carry these responsibilities with fewer job protections. In the United States, women are less likely than men to receive paid sick leave or annual leave, to be able to decide when to take breaks from work, or to determine their starting and quitting times at work[17]—each important for finding ways to balance caregiving and paid work successfully.[18] Women's disadvantage in working conditions holds true across borders and continents. A study of working men and women in eight European countries found that women are less likely than men to be able to use flexible schedules and to have job autonomy and supervisor support.[19] In our interviews in Botswana, Mexico, and Vietnam, women similarly had less flexibility and worse working conditions than men. Thirty-six percent of women lacked access to paid leave compared to 25 percent of men, and 24 percent of women lacked both paid leave and flexibility compared to 19 percent of men.[20]

Low-income adults, like women, are disadvantaged in their access to nearly every labor protection, from the availability of paid leave to scheduling flexibility. The low-income working adults we studied were less likely to have access to any leave from work than were middle- and higher-income adults, and more important, they were less likely to have access to *paid* leave, which was the only form of leave they could afford to take. Half of low-income working adults in Vietnam, Botswana, and Mexico received paid leave, compared to 81 percent of adults who had middle and higher incomes. The income gap exists in the United States as well. Our analysis of data from the U.S. National Longitudinal Survey of Youth showed that lower-income employees are significantly more likely than middle- and higher-income employees to lack sick or vacation leave, and are more likely to have two weeks or less of combined sick and vacation leave, if they receive any leave at all. Lower-income workers in the United States also had less autonomy and control at their jobs, and they were not able to decide when to take breaks or to choose and change their own schedules. In countries with gaps in protective labor legislation, while better off than the poor, the middle class was also affected by the lack of decent standards.

Our research documented the often devastating impact of the lack of leave for family health needs on working adults and their families. As just one example, 62 percent of parents we interviewed in Vietnam, 48 percent in Mexico, and 28 percent in Botswana reported losing pay or job promotions or having difficulty keeping their jobs because of their need to care for sick children. Across these countries, 76 percent of parents of children with chronic conditions had experienced difficulties at work or had lost pay, jobs, or promotions due to caring for their children.

The lack of labor protections exacerbates gender and income inequalities. Taking the case of caring for family health, 49 percent of women in our study, compared to 28 percent of men, had lost pay or job promotions or had difficulty retaining jobs because of their need to care for sick children. Tragically, families who are in greatest need are most severely affected, and are often driven deeper into poverty: 67 percent of low-income adults, whose earned income was below ten dollars a day, faced a choice between losing pay in order to care for sick children or leaving children home alone.[21]

Many parents who need to work can only find jobs with poor conditions, and they are often unable to find or afford decent childcare. Long, inflexible work hours, evening and night shifts, and the unavailability of childcare often forces families to leave young children home alone or in the care of siblings. Thirty-six percent of the families we interviewed had left a young child home alone, and 27 percent had left a child in the care of another paid or unpaid child. Thirty-nine percent had left a sick child home alone or had sent them to school or daycare while sick. Sixty-one percent of parents who had lost a job or a promotion or had experienced difficulty retaining a job as a result of caring for a sick child had subsequently left a child home alone or in the care of another child.

Unsupervised children risk being victims of violence or injuring themselves without having access to medical advice or assistance. In half of the families we interviewed in Botswana and Mexico and more than a third of those we interviewed in Vietnam, children had suffered from accidents or emergencies while their parents were at work. The associated risks to children's health go beyond physical injuries, as children's development and mental health are deeply affected by their parents' working conditions. Forty-nine percent of families that had been forced to leave young children on their own had a child with behavioral or developmental difficulties; this was double the number of those from families that were able to send their children to formal childcare.

Lacking leave or childcare alternatives, parents sometimes opt to take their children to work rather than leaving them home alone. Twenty-eight percent of parents who were poor and 26 percent of those with a middle-school education or less reported taking their children to work on a regular basis, as did 49 percent of parents working in the informal economy. The results can be devastating for these young children when parents have no choice but to leave them unsupervised at the workplace near hazards, in crowded urban marketplaces, or on busy streets, as occurred for a disproportionately high number of the low-income families, especially those working in the informal economy.

Our research showed that the detrimental consequences of poor parental working conditions for children worldwide persist after they start school. Working parents still need to find caregivers to look after their children during nonschool hours, and their working conditions often reduce their ability to be involved in their children's education. Work-related barriers to helping with homework, participating in school events, and other forms of involvement in children's schooling were reported by 51 percent of parents in Vietnam, 66 percent of parents in Mexico, and 82 percent of parents in Botswana. The most common work-related barriers to parental involvement in children's education were extreme work hours and a lack of paid leave and scheduling flexibility. When parents faced barriers to becoming involved in their children's education, their children were twice as likely to experience behavioral or academic difficulties in school.

The impact of working conditions on the health and life chances of individuals is discussed in greater detail in *Global Inequalities at Work*, which pulls together the findings of researchers and policy makers from around the world.[22] We further describe the impact of working and social conditions on the health and well-being of families on five continents in *Forgotten Families* as well as other books, articles, and reports.[23]

Finding Solutions

Recognizing and understanding these problems is an important first step, but finding economically feasible solutions is essential in order to effect change. This book reports findings from an eight-year study looking at effective ways of improving solutions in the public sector. An accompanying volume, *Profit at the Bottom of the Ladder*, examines solutions from the private sector. In examining the public sector, we chose to focus on policies that have been translated into national legislation that guarantees individuals the right to a floor of decent working conditions.

Although most nations around the world have agreed to a series of international conventions sponsored by the International Labour Organization that set minimum labor standards for all, the ILO has limited power to ensure that promises turn into practice. A country's ratification of these conventions does not in and of itself ensure that its citizens are guaranteed the rights enshrined in these conventions. While a relatively small number of countries attribute the same authority as national laws to United Nations (UN) agreements, most countries require their own parliament, congress, or other legislative bodies to pass laws in order for these minimum standards to be enforceable. Countries that sign ILO conventions agree to self-report on their implementation, and non-governmental organizations (NGOs) have an opportunity to comment on this process, but these conventions are not legally enforceable. Because legally binding social policy is still developed primarily at a national rather than a global level, we chose to examine national laws in all UN countries. Although nearly all governments have important policies that are not legislated, unlegislated policies do not guarantee basic rights, and they can rapidly change from year to year. We therefore opted to focus on countries' longer-term commitments embodied in legislation.

Although we had initially hoped to build on the work of UN agencies and simply analyze the relationship between national laws and economic and human outcomes, we quickly discovered that there was no existing data center of this magnitude. We therefore undertook to build one that would support comparisons of basic working protections in the 192 UN countries. To this end, we recruited a research team with members who were fluent in five of the six UN languages (English, French, Spanish, Chinese, and Arabic), as well as five additional languages. We used labor codes and legislation from around the world as a foundation, as well as data on national social security programs.[24] The methods are described in further detail in the Appendix.

We examined initiatives designed to guarantee that adults would have the working conditions they need to be able to care for their own health and that of their families and to support themselves financially. While numerous public policies could be examined in each of these areas, given our goal of comparing all UN nations, we needed to select a subset of policies that, although not comprehensive, were among those central to human welfare. As protections crucial to workers' health and well-being, we examined the availability of paid sick leave and annual leave, guarantees of at least one day of rest per week, and limits on and wage premiums for night work and overtime. As provisions central to economic outcomes, we examined job protection for illness, one of the most common sources of job loss, and the availability of time off in times of need, the lack of which is frequently associated with wage or salary loss. We would have liked to examine minimum wages across all countries, but sufficient comparable data were not available at the time of data collection.

We also examined public policies that are designed to support the health, development, and economic survival of working women's and men's family members. In particular, we examined the availability of leave to care for the health of children, aging parents, and disabled family members; the availability of maternity, paternity, and parental leave, which have been shown to have crucial impacts on the health and development of infants; and the ability of working mothers to breastfeed, due to its substantial impact on infant and maternal health and child cognitive development. Because children's cognitive and social development extends far beyond the preschool years, we studied the availability of leave or scheduling flexibility to meet children's educational needs and to deal with family emergencies.

This book reports findings on the global availability of each of these labor protections, and it addresses some of the common contentions regarding the perceived barriers to providing decent working conditions. Central to the debate about whether countries can afford to improve working conditions has always been the question of whether they can do so without increasing their unemployment and decreasing their economic competitiveness. While the economic implications of guaranteeing decent work have always been important, they are particularly critical during the economic downturn that began in 2008 and that will likely affect countries around the world for years to come. This book presents the results of unique analyses of the relationship between labor conditions and national competitiveness and unemployment rates. It then examines the impact of legislation on the improvement of working conditions in countries around the world.

In the end, the findings from our global study dismissed many common contentions. Some of the nations with the best working conditions have the lowest unemployment rates, and some of the countries that were rated as the most competitive by global corporate leaders provide the best social support and protections for workers. Although laws may be imperfectly implemented, they do make a difference in rich and poor countries alike.

After presenting the findings of this global study, we examine the requirements for markedly improving the conditions people around the world currently face by addressing the following questions:

- Can countries work alone to ameliorate the working conditions of their populations, or is global action required?
- If global action is necessary, is there any chance of reaching a consensus, or do all nations take a different approach to these issues?
- What are the potential roles of individuals, corporations, civil society, nations, and the global community in achieving change?

To supplement our study of legislation and social insurance in all UN countries, we draw on three other types of research. In one, we interviewed over two thousand working adults in fourteen countries about the impact of their working conditions on their own health and well-being as well as that of their families; in another, we conducted company studies in eight countries, where we interviewed everyone from factory line workers to CEOs; and finally, we developed twelve country studies, in which we examined in detail the contributions of government and civil society to the provision of decent working conditions. While the in-depth interviews of employees, employers, and government leaders are designed to frame the issues, the central feature of this book is the presentation of new evidence regarding the state of global labor legislation and social insurance guaranteeing a floor of humane working conditions. This information is presented in tables and figures examining the relationship between basic rights at work and national employment rates and competitiveness, world maps, and detailed discussions of global patterns of protection.

We hope this book will be of interest and use to those concerned with addressing poverty and gender inequalities, and improving the conditions in which individuals and families live worldwide. In order to make it accessible to readers from a broad range of backgrounds—including individual readers who just want to know how their working conditions relate to others around the world, those who have special expertise in economics and those who do not, policy makers and lawyers, and employers and labor representatives—we have tried to balance the provision of detailed information for those active in the field with the presentation of illustrative examples for those new to these topics.

Overview of Chapters

Part I. Examining the Contentions Feeding Inaction

Chapter 2: The Argument that Humane Working Conditions Lead to Higher Unemployment One of the greatest barriers to improving working conditions has been the claim that laws aimed at protecting workers lead to job loss. Stated simply, the argument contends that guarantees of humane working conditions fuel job flight and that a bad job is better than no job at all. Given the prevalence of this contention, it is remarkable how few data have been brought to bear on the question of whether laws that ensure decent working conditions actually lead companies to relocate. Are high labor standards truly a great source of unemployment?

To date, this question has rarely been addressed with global evidence, perhaps in part due to the lack of a database that includes a comprehensive review of labor laws, employment rates, and other economic outcomes. This chapter reports on the findings from our eight-year study of labor laws in 190 countries. We begin by comparing unemployment rates as reported by the World Bank among countries with and without a series of key labor policies to see if any statistically significant differences emerged. We then look at the relationship between working conditions and unemployment rates in OECD nations to examine the extent to which national guarantees of basic protections, such as the ability to take sick leave or the right not to work sweatshop hours, have any effect on countries' ability to attract jobs. Do countries with stricter labor laws actually have more citizens who cannot find a job or earn a living?

The evidence is clear: there is no relationship between the majority of laws governing leave or humane schedules and the availability of work. Whether looking at paid leave for health needs, paid leave for new mothers, or paid leave for new fathers, good workplace policies are not linked to higher national unemployment rates. Moreover, while these labor laws do not affect the availability of work, they markedly enhance the *quality* of work and improve working adults' ability to keep their jobs while meeting their own needs and those of their families.

Chapter 3: The Contention that Countries Can't Compete if They Protect Working Adults In addition to high rates of employment, countries naturally want their economies to have high rates of growth. Having shown that countries can have many labor protections and still have low unemployment rates, we then assess whether these protections prevent countries from prospering.

This chapter examines the working conditions of countries that have been ranked by business leaders, policy makers, and academics in the World Economic Forum (WEF) as being among the twenty nations with the highest competitiveness rankings in at least eight of the ten years from 1999 to 2008. We then examine the relationship between the labor conditions and the competitiveness of all 131 countries rated by the WEF.

Once again, the evidence dismisses the myth. We found no evidence that providing fundamental forms of leave and livable work schedules makes countries less competitive. In fact, the only sustained relationship between labor laws and economic success is a positive one: nations that guarantee sick leave to care for personal or family health needs are ranked among the highest countries in terms of economic competitiveness.

But how is this possible if there are costs associated with these labor policies? First, workplace benefits constitute only a small fraction of the costs of production. Second, the costs of these benefits are small relative to wages and wage differentials. A week of paid sick leave, for example, entails at most a 2 percent increase in wage costs. Increased productivity due to improved working conditions can rapidly make up for minor costs incurred in implementing these benefits. Third, companies may be drawn to countries that improve the health and well-being of workers and their families at a relatively low cost to business through programs such as public coverage of health insurance, childcare, or sick leave. For example, Toyota announced that some plants were moving from the United States to Canada, where governmental programs protected workers and would save the company money.[25]

Chapter 4: The Myth that Labor Laws Do Not Make a Difference Cynics could argue that the reason that labor laws do not adversely impact employment or competitiveness is that they are infrequently enforced. Alternatively, critics could argue that labor laws are unnecessary in affluent economies because companies voluntarily provide decent working conditions. This chapter presents several in-depth case studies in order to examine whether and how labor laws can improve the conditions people face in diverse political and economic contexts. These case studies seek to address several key questions:

- Do laws make a difference? Are countries able to successfully implement their labor laws even when they do not have unlimited resources for enforcement?
- Are laws necessary? Are good working conditions found in countries with few labor laws?
- Is there a way for nations to provide each other with incentives to reach a minimum level of decent working conditions and to effectively enforce these minimum standards?

Our first case study examines how effectively labor protections have been implemented in Mexico, a country whose population represents the social, political, and economic diversity common to many countries around the world. Mexico has a variety of long-standing, comprehensive social security programs that cover many basic worker protections. The findings were clear that even with relatively limited resources for enforcement, the social security legislation in Mexico has improved the lives of millions of working men and women and their children.

We then turn to a case study that was conducted in Cambodia, a rapidly growing economy undergoing industrialization. The United States–Cambodia Trade Agreement[26] was signed in 1999 and renewed in 2001, giving Cambodia greater access to the U.S. market as long as it improved its implementation of labor laws. An examination of this unique experiment demonstrates that nations can successfully provide incentives to increase the effectiveness and enforcement of labor laws, even in a resource-poor setting.

This chapter then assesses the efficacy of labor laws when it comes to addressing the needs of the considerable number of workers worldwide employed in the informal economy. Examples of steps taken by countries around the world to increase the benefit of labor legislation to informal economy workers are reviewed.

Finally, the chapter looks at the United States, a country with few laws regulating work hours, paid leave, or other working conditions. Many business leaders in the United States argue that most labor legislation is unnecessary because businesses voluntarily provide good benefits, such as sick or vacation leave. This case study examines the validity of this claim and assesses the situation of American workers compared to their counterparts around the world.

Part II. Requirements for Change

Chapter 5: Achieving Global Consensus Just as states and provinces in a federal government can, in the absence of a national consensus, independently make policy changes that affect their citizens, so too can individual countries create national policies without a global consensus. That being said, more people would benefit worldwide if a global consensus on a floor of decent working conditions could be achieved.

Countries are also likely to pass their own legislation much more rapidly as part of a global initiative because global agreements negate the perception that doing so would cause a competitive disadvantage. Furthermore, it would be easier for multinational companies to abide by one set of rules that has been agreed upon and implemented by the majority of countries than to follow scores of different regulations. It would also be easier for NGOs to support the implementation and enforcement of labor standards if certain rights were universal. The major obstacle to achieving a global floor has been the argument that cultures have such different views regarding the nature of decent working conditions that it would be impossible to achieve a global agreement in which the North does not impose its view on the South, or the West on the East.

This chapter examines the question: How different are work experiences and values across cultures? Drawing on analyses conducted as part of the largest study of working families to date, we present the voices and experiences of young and old employees, working mothers and fathers, and adults with elderly parents. The remarkable degree of overlap in their stories speaks to a shared degree of importance placed on certain basic labor protections.

We then examine the public policies of 190 countries around the world to see what each of these nations has done to protect workers. A majority of both low- and high-income nations from a wide range of political and economic contexts have passed legislation guaranteeing basic labor standards. Over 140 countries guarantee one day off every week as well as paid sick leave, paid annual leave, and wage premiums for mandatory overtime. Clearly, a global consensus is possible in many areas.

Chapter 6: Addressing Where the World Lags Behind Have nations achieved consensus and passed legislation on all of the important labor conditions? Here the story is more mixed. The world has come further in addressing needs that first arose with the industrial revolution in the nineteenth century than in addressing needs that arose with the transformations of work, families, and individual lives in the twentieth century.

The nature of work has rapidly evolved over the past fifty years in terms of how, where, and by whom it is undertaken. Gains in gender equality have occurred in nearly every region of the world in areas from education to work and from private life to participation in civic and political life. As a result, more and more children are being raised in households where both parents work outside of the home. The aging population continues to grow in most countries, leaving working adults with additional caregiving responsibilities. At the same time, nations around the globe have entered into increased economic competition and trade across borders and overseas, and work demands have escalated.

These transformations have had an important impact on people's lives and consequently on the needed floor of humane working conditions. Paid sick leave was crucial for the health of individual employees when most families had only one adult in the labor force; today, in a world where in most families all adults work outside of the home while caring for children and dependent adults, leave to care for family members' health is equally essential. At a time when women were expected to be the sole providers for infants and children, paid maternity leave was fundamental; in a world where both mothers and fathers participate more equally at home and at work, paid paternity leave is equally vital.

How have different countries in the world adapted to these changes? While 163 countries provide workers with paid sick leave, only 48 guarantee paid time off to care for children's health and only 33 provide paid leave to care for sick adult family members. Virtually all nations around the globe—177 countries in total—guarantee paid leave for new mothers, and many have had these policies in place for decades. Yet only 74 countries guarantee paid leave for fathers surrounding the birth or adoption of a child. This chapter takes a look at areas where the world lags behind, and where global improvements are needed.

Chapter 7: Moving from Evidence to Action: Raising the Floor of Working Conditions and Equity Improving working conditions for all will require not only knowing that this is a feasible goal and being aware of where the world currently lags behind, but also having a practical plan for how to move forward. Chapter 7 addresses the challenge of implementing change on a global scale without a global government. To date, intergovernmental organizations have had good intentions but limited efficacy. This chapter puts forth some practical short- and long-term steps to be taken by individuals, by nations, and by the global community as a whole.

Major social change starts with the action of concerned individuals. Individual readers have the capacity to make an immense difference where they work, in their civic life, and in the marketplace. This concluding chapter looks at how.

Having demonstrated in Chapters 2 and 3 that individual nations can effectively compete for good jobs and build a prosperous economy while markedly improving working conditions, Chapter 7 details what individual nations need to do in order to accomplish this.

Finally, this chapter examines what international steps are needed to support effective global action. Although the majority of countries have already ratified international agreements guaranteeing basic rights at work through the International Labour Organization or the United Nations, there is no international body that has yet exercised real leverage to guarantee that countries adhere to these commitments. This chapter discusses the potential impact of creating independent, transparent "report cards" rating how countries fare in legislation and implementation and making these reports available to the governments and residents of every nation.

User-friendly, objective evaluations would enable consumers to choose which among similar products to purchase based on the performance of the country in which the product was made. The objective evidence from these evaluations would also empower consumers to pressure companies to source their products from countries with good labor policies that are effectively implemented. At the same time, such a tool would empower nations to pressure employers to follow existing laws. Nations entering into trade agreements can play an important role by insisting on the inclusion of an enforceable clause in these agreements stating that all participating countries will abide by their national labor laws and by the international agreements they have signed, and that a failure to do so would result in the nullification of the treaty and of the trade advantages therein. The report cards would be used to measure compliance.

• • •

Our ability as a global community to reduce inequality, to decrease intergenerational poverty, and to improve everyone's quality of life—including the poor and the middle class, women and men, the young and the old—is dependent on ensuring decent work for all. We hope that this book and the evidence from our research will present new tools for solving these crucial dilemmas.

PART I

EXAMINING THE CONTENTIONS FEEDING INACTION

2 The Argument that Humane Working Conditions Lead to Higher Unemployment

Like many immigrants coming to the United States, Luis Marquez arrived with a handful of dreams, some of which were seemingly ambitious—like being able to record his own music—and others of which were modest, even if more fundamental—like raising and supporting a healthy family. Due to the working conditions he encountered, even the latter became next to impossible.

A single parent, Luis was raising his two young children alone in Boston, far from his extended family in the Dominican Republic. When his marriage dissolved, he rapidly abandoned his dream of establishing a musical career in order to focus on caring for his children, five-year-old Yolanda and eight-year-old Carlos. With little formal education, the best job Luis could find was working as a security guard. His low wages were barely sufficient to cover even the most basic daily living expenses for food, rent, and clothing.

The firm that hired Luis offered no form of paid leave, flexibility, or time off. As a result, he could rarely visit his children's school because each visit meant losing income and facing more trouble paying the bills. On one rare trip to the school, he was reminded of the challenges his children faced as he stood at the fence near the playground and watched the children playing outside:

> This bunch of kids—young boys . . . between the ages of five and six— . . . had this girl in the corner and they were all spitting on her. Spit, all over! And . . . if you see the look on this girl: she was humiliated . . . And I called the teacher, and [I said], "Look what they're doing to her!" And [the teacher was]

> talking to someone else. And I felt like doing something because . . . I felt so bad for [the young girl].
>
> What if it had been Yolanda? What developmental and emotional issues were his own children facing, and how would he find out about or address them if he was so limited in his ability to be involved at their school?
>
> Like many children in school, Yolanda and Carlos were often sick when they were young. They caught strep throat from other children at school and their common colds turned into ear infections. Every time his children got sick, the school called Luis at work and asked him to come pick them up. Without paid sick days, vacation, or personal days, Luis had to miss work without pay. He always feared that this would reflect poorly on his job performance and lead to his dismissal. He also had to take unpaid time off when his children had holidays from school because there was no one else to care for them. The lack of paid sick days, the lack of leave to meet his children's educational needs, and the lack of employer- or state-provided after-school care took its toll on Yolanda and Carlos's well-being and exacerbated Luis's concerns about losing his job.
>
> After budgeting for his children's food, clothing, and after-school childcare and making the payments for the car he needed to get to work, the remaining money did not even cover the rent in public housing. Luis therefore decided to switch from the day to the night shift so that he could earn an extra dollar an hour and work overtime when the family needed more money. Working the night shift in theory also meant that he could be more available for his children during the day to help them with homework or care for them if they were too sick to go to school. In reality, though, he could do so only if he went without sleep and did not have to work overtime. Moreover, finding night care for his children was extremely difficult; the many childcare providers he visited and spoke with all worked only during the day.

Poor working conditions had profound and potentially long-lasting effects on Luis and his family, as they did on many of the low-income parents we interviewed. Luis was always struggling to get by. Without leave from work, he could not care for his children when they were sick or be involved with their education while earning enough money to pay the rent. Without childcare provided by his employer or by the government, he could afford to use only the cheapest childcare providers; these unregulated caregivers were not always reliable and often offered substandard care. Although his presence would have helped his growing children's emotional and intellectual development, his grueling schedule left him little time to spend with them.

> Viktor Kowalski's experience could hardly have been more different. An electrician and a father of two, Viktor had immigrated to Iceland from Poland in order to take advantage of the higher wages. He worked for the Bechtel Construction Company in Fjardaal, building an aluminum smelter for Alcoa. The 2,000 to 2,500 Polish zloty (US$735 to US$919)[1] per month he would have earned in Poland paled in comparison to the 300,000 krs (US$5,009)[2] per month he earned at Bechtel.
>
> When Viktor was sick for five days, he had no problem taking leave and the sickness benefit fund paid his wages. He happily took advantage of the optional English classes the company offered to improve his job skills and marketability. Living a four-hour flight from home, the job also ensured him time off every three months which he could use to go back to Poland.

The Most Common Argument Against Humane Working Conditions: A Bad Job Is Better than No Job

Few dispute the fact that good wages and the ability to take sick leave or leave to care for family are valuable to all working adults. Although workers and their families—mothers, fathers, children, spouses, and disabled family members—could all benefit from adults having good conditions at work, the argument against guaranteeing a humane floor of working conditions often falls back on the notion that it would lead to higher national unemployment rates. The contention goes as follows: if businesses incur the expenses of offering higher wages or paid leave, they will hire fewer workers. According to this theory, even in the absence of globalization, if businesses have to pay higher wages to the person flipping burgers, the cost of the burgers will increase. Consequently, the demand for burgers will decrease and businesses will hire fewer people. It is worth noting that this argument ignores the reality that raising wages also increases the amount of cash that consumers are able to spend.

Economists have studied the impact of raising wages on employment for over three decades, generating a range of theoretical estimates.[3] On one side are the traditional economists who argue that there is some evidence that raising minimum wages leads to higher unemployment rates and that the question is not *if* it increases job loss, but rather *for whom* and *by how much*.[4] Most argue that teenagers experience stronger disemployment effects than other groups.[5]

On the other side are economists who review similar sources of evidence and argue that no statistically significant impacts on employment exist.[6]

A similar argument is used against offering benefits such as paid leave. If businesses have to cover the costs of hiring and training new workers to temporarily replace employees on parental leave, or pay employees overtime for doing extra work to compensate for employees away on sick leave, the costs of their goods or services will increase, the demand will decrease, and they will hire fewer employees.

Looking at the Facts

By analyzing the relationship between unemployment rates and the guarantee of a floor of decent labor conditions in a wide range of countries around the world, we were able to assess the validity of the argument that links labor protections to job loss.

The Global Picture

Using our global data on national labor legislation, we began by comparing unemployment rates as reported by the World Bank among countries with and without a series of key labor policies to see if any statistically significant differences emerged.[7] The basic protections we looked at included the availability of paid leave for both men and women around the birth or adoption of a child, time during the workday to breastfeed an infant, paid time off to care for personal or family health needs, annual leave, at least one day of rest per week, limits on work hours, protections against mandatory overtime, time off for important life events, and protections regarding night work.[8] No relationship existed between any of these labor protections and national unemployment rates.

Whereas the global competitiveness rankings we will examine in the next chapter are provided by an independent source, the global unemployment figures provided by the World Bank are nationally reported, meaning that countries relay their own data. While some countries have extensive statistical capacities to evaluate their actual unemployment figures, other nations have few resources to do so. Moreover, governments may underreport unemployment due to political pressures. Given this context, we thought it important to further examine the potential existence of any relationship between job availability and decent working conditions using only unemployment rates that are rigorously measured and externally verified.

A Closer Look at the OECD

We looked at the relationship between working conditions and unemployment rates in OECD nations because these countries have independent verification of the accuracy of their data and hold excellent track records for effectively implementing their labor legislation. The Organisation for Economic Co-operation and Development is currently composed of thirty nations, including twenty-two European countries, the United States, Canada, Australia, New Zealand, Japan, Republic of Korea, Mexico, and Turkey.[9] These largely advanced economies in North America, Europe, and Asia have gathered unemployment data using a consistent definition that takes into account participation in both the formal and informal economies.[10] As a result, comparable and reliable unemployment rate data have been collected for OECD member states.

We selected the countries that were ranked among the OECD countries in the lower half of unemployment rates in at least eight of the ten years from 1998 to 2007. Looking at the thirteen countries with consistently low unemployment rates for a decade, we examined which of these nations guaranteed:

- Paid leave for new mothers[11]
- The right of mothers to breastfeed new infants during working hours for at least six months
- Paid leave for new fathers[12]
- Paid leave to meet the personal health needs of working men and women
- Leave (paid or unpaid) to address family members' health needs
- Paid vacation leave once a year
- A day of rest every week
- Restrictions on the amount of mandatory overtime
- Increased pay for overtime hours
- Paid leave for events such as marriages and funerals or for other personal circumstances
- Increased pay for night work

None of these protections prevented countries from having low unemployment rates.

Nearly every low-unemployment country guarantees paid leave to new mothers (see Table 2.1). The only exception is the United States. The duration of maternal leave provided by some countries is quite substantial: nine months or more in Luxembourg and Denmark, and over a year in Norway, Japan, the Republic of Korea, and Austria. Among those that offer shorter durations, Switzerland and the Netherlands still offer over three months, and Mexico offers twelve weeks. All low-unemployment countries—whether they ensure twelve weeks or one year of paid leave—far outshine the United States.

More than two-thirds of low-unemployment countries also guarantee that mothers can breastfeed new infants during working hours for at least six months (see Table 2.2).

While paid leave for new fathers is less universal, the majority of low-unemployment countries guarantee substantial leave for men (see Table 2.3). Fathers can have access to leave specifically through paternity leave or through parental leave, which can be used by either parent. When combining the leave

TABLE 2.1 Low-unemployment countries:
Do they guarantee paid leave to new mothers?

Country	*Paid leave for mothers*	*Duration of paid leave (weeks)*	*Wage replacement rate*
Austria	Yes	81–146	100%, flat
Denmark	Yes	50–58	80–100%
Iceland	Yes	26	80%
Ireland	Yes	26	80%
Japan	Yes	58	30–60%
Korea, Republic of	Yes	60	100%, flat
Luxembourg	Yes	42	100%, flat
Mexico	Yes	12	100%
Netherlands	Yes	16	100%
Norway	Yes	90–100	80–100%, flat
Switzerland	Yes	14	80%
United Kingdom	Yes	39	90%
United States of America	No	NA	NA

NOTES: Using employment rates from the OECD, we examined policies for the countries that had below the median unemployment rates in at least eight of the ten years from 1998 to 2007.
"Flat" wage replacement rate indicates that all employees receive the same set cash payment. When both a percentage and a flat rate are indicated, part of the leave is paid at a flat rate and part at a percentage of the employee's wages.
Above notes apply to all tables in Chapter 2.
We present data on the maximum amount of leave available to a mother if she takes all of the maternity leave available to women and all of the parental leave available to either parent. For Austria, Denmark, and Norway, we report the minimum and maximum duration of leave to reflect each country's policy of providing parents with a choice between taking a shorter leave with a higher (percentage or flat rate) benefit or a longer leave with a lower benefit.

TABLE 2.2 Low-unemployment countries: Do they guarantee breastfeeding breaks?

Country	*Guaranteed breast-feeding breaks*	*Age of child when breaks end*	*Breaks are one hour or more per day*
Austria	Yes	For duration of breastfeeding	Yes
Denmark	No	NA	NA
Iceland	No	NA	NA
Ireland	Yes	6 months	Yes
Japan	Yes	1 year	Yes
Korea, Republic of	Yes	1 year	Yes
Luxembourg	Yes	For duration of breastfeeding	Yes
Mexico	Yes	For duration of breastfeeding	Yes
Netherlands	Yes	9 months	Yes
Norway	Yes	For duration of breastfeeding	Yes
Switzerland	Yes	1 year	Yes
United Kingdom	No	NA	NA
United States of America	No	NA	NA

TABLE 2.3 Low-unemployment countries: Do they guarantee paid leave to new fathers?

Country	*Paid leave for fathers*	*Duration of paid leave (weeks)*	*Wage replacement rate*
Austria	Yes	63–130	flat rate
Denmark	Yes	34–42	80–100%
Iceland	Yes	26	80%
Ireland	No	NA	NA
Japan	Yes	44	30–40%
Korea, Republic of	Yes	52	flat rate
Luxembourg	Yes	26.4	100%, flat
Mexico	No	NA	NA
Netherlands	Yes	0.4	100%
Norway	Yes	87–97	80–100%, flat
Switzerland	No	NA	NA
United Kingdom	Yes	2	90%
United States of America	No	NA	NA

NOTE: We present data on the maximum amount of leave available to a father if he takes all of the paternity leave available to men and all of the parental leave available to either parent. For Austria, Denmark, and Norway, we report the minimum and maximum duration of leave to reflect each country's policy of providing parents with a choice between taking a shorter leave with a higher (percentage or flat rate) benefit or a longer leave with a lower benefit.

available through both paternity and parental leave, men have access to half a year or more in Luxembourg, Denmark, and Iceland; and over a year in Austria, Norway, and the Republic of Korea.

Nearly all low-unemployment countries provide employees with access to paid leave to meet their personal health needs (see Table 2.4). Only the United States and the Republic of Korea provide no such guarantees. With the exception of Switzerland, which provides at least three weeks of sick leave,[13] all other low-unemployment countries guarantee at least a month or more of paid sick leave, and just over half of these countries ensure that this benefit begins on the first day of illness.

While it is not always paid, the vast majority of low-unemployment countries, eleven out of thirteen, also provide leave to address family members' health needs (see Table 2.5). The Netherlands, Norway, Denmark, Iceland, Ireland, Japan, Luxembourg, and Austria provide paid leave to care for children's health needs, while Switzerland, the United Kingdom, and the United States ensure that workers have some unpaid leave. Leave to care for adults' health needs is ensured in the Netherlands, Norway, Denmark, Austria, Ireland, Japan, the United Kingdom, and the United States.

With the exception of the United States, all of the low-unemployment countries guarantee all workers a period of vacation leave with pay at least once a year (see Table 2.6). The amount of paid annual leave ranges from between one and two weeks in Mexico and Japan to four weeks or more in Iceland, the Netherlands, Norway, Luxembourg, Austria, Ireland, Switzerland, the United Kingdom, and Denmark.

Every low-unemployment country except the United States guarantees workers a day of rest every week (see Table 2.6).

Although they have chosen different strategies, the majority of low-unemployment countries address the issue of overtime (see Table 2.7). Mexico, Norway, Switzerland, Austria, Denmark, and the Republic of Korea restrict the amount of overtime; and Mexico, Norway, Switzerland, Luxembourg, Austria, Denmark, the Republic of Korea, Japan, and the United States mandate increased pay (premiums) for overtime hours.

Restrictions on night work for certain categories of workers are common among the low-unemployment nations. Eleven countries restrict or ban night work for children, pregnant or nursing women, or workers who have health issues that make night work harmful. Norway generally restricts night work: employees' representatives must be consulted before night work can be required. The Republic of Korea, Switzerland, Luxembourg, and Japan require the payment of a premium for night work (see Table 2.8).

TABLE 2.4 Low-unemployment countries: Do they guarantee paid sick leave?

Country	*Paid sick leave*	*Duration of paid sick leave (days)*	*Paid leave available for 26 weeks or until recovery*	*Wage replacement rate*	*Benefits begin on first day of illness*
Austria	Yes	31 or more	Yes	50–100%	Yes
Denmark	Yes	31 or more	Yes	100%, flat	Yes
Iceland	Yes	31 or more	Yes	100%, flat	Yes
Ireland	Yes	31 or more	Yes	flat rate	No
Japan	Yes	31 or more	Yes	60%	No
Korea, Republic of	No	NA	NA	NA	NA
Luxembourg	Yes	31 or more	Yes	100%	Yes
Mexico	Yes	31 or more	Yes	60%	No
Netherlands	Yes	31 or more	Yes	70%	Yes
Norway	Yes	31 or more	Yes	100%	Yes
Switzerland	Yes	11–30 days	No	80%	Yes
United Kingdom	Yes	31 or more	Yes	flat rate	No
United States of America	No	NA	NA	NA	NA

NOTE: A number of nations adjust benefits during lengthy sick leaves. In the above table these variable benefit amounts are represented by ranges in percent of wages paid and by payment of a percent of wages followed by a flat rate benefit.

TABLE 2.5 Low-unemployment countries:
Do they guarantee leave to attend to the health needs of a family member?

Country	*Leave to care for children's health needs*	*Leave to care for adult family members' health needs*
Austria	Yes	Yes
Denmark	Yes	Yes
Iceland	Yes	No
Ireland	Yes	Yes
Japan	Yes	Yes
Korea, Republic of	No	No
Luxembourg	Yes	No
Mexico	No	No
Netherlands	Yes	Yes
Norway	Yes	Yes
Switzerland	Yes	No
United Kingdom	Yes	Yes
United States of America	Yes	Yes

TABLE 2.6 Low-unemployment countries:
Do they guarantee paid annual leave and a weekly day of rest?

Country	*Guarantee of paid annual leave*	*Duration of paid leave (weeks)*	*Guarantee of a weekly day of rest*
Austria	Yes	5.0	Yes
Denmark	Yes	5.5	Yes
Iceland	Yes	4.4	Yes
Ireland	Yes	4.0	Yes
Japan	Yes	1.8	Yes
Korea, Republic of	Yes	2.7	Yes
Luxembourg	Yes	4.5	Yes
Mexico	Yes	1.1	Yes
Netherlands	Yes	4.0	Yes
Norway	Yes	4.2	Yes
Switzerland	Yes	4.0	Yes
United Kingdom	Yes	5.1	Yes
United States of America	No	NA	No

TABLE 2.7 Low-unemployment countries:
Do they limit or provide compensation for overtime work?

Country	*Ban or limit on overtime*	*Overtime premium*
Austria	Yes	Yes
Denmark	Yes	Yes
Iceland	No	No
Ireland	No	No
Japan	No	Yes
Korea, Republic of	Yes	Yes
Luxembourg	No	Yes
Mexico	Yes	Yes
Netherlands	No	No
Norway	Yes	Yes
Switzerland	Yes	Yes
United Kingdom	No	No
United States of America	No	Yes

TABLE 2.8 Low-unemployment countries: Do they limit or provide a premium for night work?

Country	*Premium for night work*	*Broad restrictions on night work*	*Ban or restriction for children*	*Ban or restriction for pregnant or nursing women or medical reasons*
Austria	No	No	After 8 p.m.	After 10 p.m.
Denmark	No	No	After 8 p.m. for children under age 18	After 10 p.m.
Iceland	No	No	No	No
Ireland	No	No	No	After midnight
Japan	After 10 p.m.	No	At 8 p.m., but later depending on age and gender	After 10 p.m. for pregnant and nursing women
Korea, Republic of	After 10 p.m.	No	After 10 p.m.	After 10 p.m.
Luxembourg	After 10 p.m.	No	After 8 p.m.	After 10 p.m.
Mexico	No	No	After 10 p.m. for children under age 16	After 10 p.m.
Netherlands	No	No	No	After midnight
Norway	No	Yes	After 8 p.m. for children under 15	No
Switzerland	After 11 p.m.	After 9 p.m.	After 8 p.m.	After 1 a.m.
United Kingdom	No	No	After 11 p.m.	After 11 p.m.
United States of America	No	No	No	No

In summary, many OECD countries were able to achieve low unemployment while guaranteeing important labor protections. Although some countries, such as Slovakia, have good working conditions and *high* unemployment, an equal or greater number of countries have good working conditions and *low* unemployment, such as Ireland, Norway, Mexico, and Austria. Clearly this combination is viable.

Countries' Successful Strategies

While many manufacturing jobs left the United States, Canada, and Europe for lower-income countries from Central America to Southeast Asia, national unemployment in these high-income countries did not rise consistently during the period when manufacturing jobs relocated. Moreover, it is far from clear that sacrificing basic benefits is a good way to get jobs back or to guarantee low unemployment. It is easy to illustrate the reason by examining one country that has gained garment manufacturing jobs—Bangladesh—and one that has lost them—Canada. The lowest provincial minimum wage in Canada (US$1,342.30 per month) is over fifty times the minimum wage in Bangladesh (US$25.00 per month),[14] and this is what drove the movement of these manufacturing jobs. If Canada were to stop guaranteeing all workers two weeks of annual leave, the difference between minimum wages in Canada and in Bangladesh would still be more than fiftyfold. Effective competition has to occur on different grounds. In order to see how decent working conditions and low unemployment can coexist, it is worth taking a closer look at a few countries' achievements in this area.

Norway

Norway's experience between 1998 and 2007 could be described in two very different ways. One tells the story of a country that profited from a unique set of circumstances: abundant natural resources, particularly oil and natural gas, which have facilitated the creation of social supports. The other tells the tale of a nation, government, and people that developed in such a way as to enable good working conditions and economic success to coexist in a reciprocal relationship; the country's social policy contributed to its economic success, just as its economic success contributed to its social policy.

We started off believing the first story—that a unique set of circumstances had been most influential in shaping Norway's enviable balance of strong working conditions, social supports, and a thriving economy. However, the more time we spent examining nations around the world—ranging from economic successes to marked failures and from those providing decent working conditions to those allowing sweatshop conditions—the more we grew to recognize a common set of ingredients.

Indeed Norway does have natural resources, but no more so than other countries where the benefits are far less equitably shared, such as the United States or the Congo. Angola has reaped billions of dollars from oil annually, yet the majority of its population remains unemployed and destitute; and in Europe, Russia exports more natural gas than Norway without being as economically successful.[15]

And yes, Norway is a smaller country, but its size can be seen either as a challenge or as an advantage in terms of its ability to compete economically. The extent to which its size facilitates governance is also not entirely convincing. The majority of large countries—from India with its population of over a billion, to the United States with the world's largest economy—have state and local governments that have a similar advantage of being smaller than their national counterparts when it comes to building bridges across constituencies. Moreover, large economies are in a far more favorable position than smaller ones when it comes to negotiating terms of trade.

So if these factors alone do not account for Norway's competitiveness, what has enabled its achievements? Like all countries, Norway faces challenges, including the repercussions of the 2008 global economic downturn. However, the country's history of impressive employment statistics is not a product of chance, but rather the result of several effective policy decisions and strategies.

Strategies for Success Five key factors underlay Norway's success and that of other countries we studied in providing abundant high-quality work:

1. Developing an effective mechanism for setting a floor of decent labor conditions that protected workers while increasing productivity.
2. Investing in improving the access and quality of postsecondary education, which helped create a highly skilled workforce.
3. Providing access to early childhood care and education, which improved long-term educational outcomes while increasing parents' ability to work effectively.
4. Investing in retraining employees between jobs, thereby enabling workers to keep up with rapid developments in the global economy.
5. Strategically developing certain sectors by building on their existing competitive advantages and skill sets.

Establishing a Floor of Decent Working Conditions Each of the countries we examined that succeeded in having good working conditions and low unemployment had made a conscious effort to achieve this through a combination of legislation and social policies. Norway built a floor of decent working conditions through a series of legislative guarantees and a system of negotiated wages and benefits that covered the majority of the population. Through its legislation, Norway guarantees paid sick leave of up to one year with full wage replacement; twenty-five days of paid annual leave; a 40 percent wage premium for overtime hours; for mothers nine weeks of maternity and fifty-two weeks of childcare leave, for fathers six weeks of paternity and fifty-two weeks of childcare leave, in addition to guaranteeing thirty-nine weeks of leave that can be taken by either mother or father; and family leave to care for children and other family members when ill or injured.

Beyond these legislative guarantees, the majority of the country is covered by the results of collective bargaining between labor and employer representatives. The International Labour Organization measured the coordination of benefits and wages in fifty-one countries and found that Norway had among the most coordinated collective bargaining systems, meaning that unions negotiated for more than their individual members.[16] A high level of coordination can but does not necessarily result in final agreements that are economically difficult for companies. At its core, coordinated collective bargaining levels the playing field in terms of wages and benefits at companies within a country, decreases the incentive for competing within a country by lowering compensation, and increases the necessity to arrive at wages and benefits that all companies can sustain.[17]

But neither the legislation to ensure a floor, nor mechanisms of collective bargaining that cover the majority of the population would lead to improved working conditions with low unemployment, *unless* companies were able to achieve strong profit rates at the same time.[18] Norway's investments in education and in labor standards that increase productivity were essential to its higher profit rates.

Many of the elements of the labor standards floor contributed to productivity as well as to quality of life. Adults who come to work sick are far less productive than those who do not. Guaranteeing an adequate amount of sick leave decreases the extent to which adults with infectious diseases spread their conditions to other workers. Moreover, even with noninfectious diseases, sick leave provides the ability of working adults to recover more rapidly and spend more productive time at the workplace. This does not mean that sick leave should not be implemented in a way to avoid misuse or abuse. Rather, it simply means that when used appropriately, sick leave can be productivity enhancing (as will be discussed further in the next chapter on competitiveness).

The same applies to working conditions that increase adults' ability to work while caring for their family members. Adequate parental leave and public funding and provision of early childhood care and education have been shown internationally to increase women's attachment to the workforce, meaning that they are more likely to stay in the workforce once they have entered it. This not only enhances family incomes while decreasing gender inequalities, it also increases national competitiveness.[19]

While not all labor protections necessarily increase productivity in situations where benefits to society outweigh costs, it has been important to the success of countries such as Norway that many of their labor policies have led to economic benefits, thereby helping to offset the costs associated with their implementation.

Investing in Higher Education Norway's investments in human capital and in the development of a highly educated workforce have been central to its ability to compete economically while providing good wages and benefits. Around the world, highly educated workers generally receive higher earnings and better benefits in the workplace. Norway has displayed a long-term commitment to supporting higher education by making it affordable and accessible to the majority of the population. In 1947, the State Educational Loan Fund (Lånekassen) was founded with the goal of "remov[ing] inequality and . . . promot[ing] equal opportunities so that the pursuit of education is possible regardless of geographical conditions, age, sex and economical and social positions."[20] Loans and grants are available for basic education, vocational training, and higher education in both public and private schools in Norway, as well as abroad. The majority of student loans are interest free for the duration of schooling.[21]

Norway's levels of educational attainment have continued to rise in recent decades, with the country's ongoing investments in education.[22] While the country's overall unemployment rate of 2.8 percent in 2007 was below the OECD average of 5.8 percent,[23] adults in Norway with higher educational attainment[24] had an even lower rate of unemployment (1.8 percent in 2007).[25]

There is strong political support within the Norwegian parliament for ongoing, high-level investments in education. A 2007 report prepared for the OECD by the Norwegian Directorate for Education and Training revealed that the Norwegian national education budget constituted 7.6 percent of the country's GDP, which was significantly higher than the OECD average of 5.5 percent.[26] Norway is among the eight OECD countries that do not charge tuition for postsecondary studies at public institutions.[27] As a result of the free access provided by government investments, Norway has the eighth-highest entry rate into tertiary education among OECD countries.[28] Moreover, the trend in Norway is for an increasing number of young adults to seek postsecondary education. In 2006, nearly 42 percent of Norwegian workers aged twenty-five to thirty-four had a postsecondary education, which was markedly higher than the OECD's average rate of 28 percent for the same age group.[29]

Providing Access to Early Childhood Care and Education Recognizing the benefits of providing early childhood care, Norway has ensured that preschool education is available to children throughout the country. More than two-thirds of the costs of this care are borne by the Norwegian government, with parents' contributions varying between 22 percent and 30 percent. In 2004, the government introduced a maximum cap on parental contributions to early childhood care fees, which prevented parents from having to pay more than NOK 2,330 (US$340) per child per month.[30] Moreover, costs were further alleviated, as adults are provided with a family allowance of NOK 11,640 (US$1,695) per year per child under eighteen.[31] As a result of funding by national and municipal governments, approximately 80 percent of Norwegian children receive an early childhood education. The government's goal is to eventually have all children taking part in early childhood education and to ensure through legislation sufficient preschool slots for all children.[32]

The high level of access to early childhood care and education in Norway has greatly increased Norwegian children's school readiness. The evidence is abundant that early childhood care and education improve primary and secondary school outcomes, as well as long-term outcomes, including those pertaining to health and employment. Research has shown that children who have attended preschool display a larger vocabulary and better reading skills at age six than their brothers and sisters who have not had an opportunity to attend preschool.[33] Such children are less likely to need remedial education.[34] Studies on numerous early childhood programs have demonstrated a wide series of gains for children, including improved achievement test scores, a decreased need for special education services, decreased rates of being held back a year in school, and higher rates of high school graduation.[35] At the same time, the availability of affordable, high-quality early childhood care increases maternal labor force participation rates. This can be seen in the Norwegian economy, where almost 80 percent of adult women are in the labor force.[36]

In addition to providing for preschool and day care in early childhood, the Norwegian government has required schools to provide programs for school-aged children—again both providing immediate gains in terms of parental employment and contributing long term to improved educational outcomes and a more competitive labor force. Since 1999, all municipalities in Norway have been legally obligated to provide appropriate before- and after-school programs for children in grades one through four. For children with special needs, this period can be extended up to grade seven. These facilities are designed to ensure that children get the chance to play and develop in a safe environment and engage in development activities suited to their age group while their parents are at work.[37] While parents have to pay fees for their children to attend,[38] Norwegian parents receive a child benefit providing resources to do so. In 2007, over 33 percent of students in grades one to seven—a total of 143,947 children nationwide—were enrolled in after-school care programs.[39]

Investing in Retraining Adult Workers While Norway's investments in preschool, primary school, secondary school, and university have helped prepare future generations to enter the workforce; the country's investments in providing adults with additional skills have helped adult workers adapt to the rapidly evolving globalized economy. Although it is essential that children receive good training, the skills they acquire in their first pass through school are unlikely to be sufficient to carry them through a fifty-year career. Ongoing training has always been important to maintain a highly skilled workforce, and it has become increasingly important as the pace of technological advances has accelerated.

In Norway, when a person loses his or her job,[40] the government provides the terminated employee with an annual compensation of 62.4 percent of his or her previous salary for one year.[41] The incentive to return to the workforce is strong, but the safety net is there in the interim. During this period of receiving unemployment insurance, the worker is expected to obtain the necessary training to reenter the workforce. Like other educational pursuits in Norway, this training is virtually free of charge. Local colleges and vocational schools around the country provide courses that are adapted to meet the needs of local companies. For example, when a petrochemical company laid off technicians with skills in polymer chemistry, these workers were given the opportunity to receive training at the local college in order to adapt their skills to the growing biomedical industry. Retraining is also available for lower-skilled workers; for example, factory workers were retrained from older plants to work in the expanding renewable-energy field.

Strategically Developing Certain Sectors Norway's success has been accelerated by its ability to use its highly skilled workforce to strategically develop industries in which it had a substantial competitive advantage. Norway has been a leading country at sea for centuries, and although ships have evolved a great deal since the Viking era, ocean-going vessels have remained central to trade. Norway took advantage of its historical leadership in shipping to develop modern industries with which to compete in the global economy. The Norwegians have become recognized as leaders in the development of navigation systems, and Norway produces among the most advanced and versatile training simulators. These simulators allow captains-in-training to experience guiding a small boat or large ship into port in a variety of settings; they simulate the arrival of unexpected traffic and weather conditions, including typhoons and hurricanes, and provide a nearly 360–degree view along with the appropriate vibrations. Although Norway no longer produces ship hulls due to the high labor intensity involved, it continues to design, manufacture, and install complex electronic equipment into the hulls that are brought in from Romania. While most ships are registered in other nations due to taxation, liability, and other financial issues, Norway remains among the five nations in the world managing the greatest number of ships. It has developed various subsidiary services and manufacturing industries, including shipping insurance, brokerage, banking, and financing, which greatly contribute to the nation's economy and employment. Norway is among the world's three most prominent countries in conducting ship-safety evaluations and certifications. Norwegians also adapted their high-tech skills in nautical equipment to other uses, such as manufacturing medical and vehicle safety equipment. For example, Norway produces the triggering mechanism for automobile airbags. This strategic approach to competition led to further job creation and earnings.

Norway was equally resourceful when it came to developing its fishing industry in such as way as to enable the nation to compete in an evolving global economy. While many countries with historically strong fishing industries were depleting their natural stocks, Norway developed an immensely competitive fish farming industry off its coastal shores. By 2007, Norwegians were farming salmon and trout and were working to develop competitive sole and halibut farming industries. Norway's salmon and trout prices have been so competitive that the EU has accused it of "dumping." In fact, its competitiveness in this area is in large part due to its ability to improve the yield of fish per pound of fish food and to address challenges that are central to all aqua cultures, such as reducing the impact of pestilence. As a result, Norway's fish farming industry, which has developed over the last three decades, is now on the same order of magnitude as manufacturing and is so productive that its primary challenge is getting access to sufficient markets.[42]

Strengths and Challenges Norway's high floor of working conditions and its investments in education and social supports have paid off in health, developmental, and economic outcomes. Norway ranked second in the UN's 2007/08 Human Development Report (HDR),[43] and has consistently been ranked among the top seven nations ever since the HDR reporting began in 1990, holding the number-one spot for six consecutive years from 2001 to 2006.[44] Norway has an average life expectancy at birth of 79.8 years, and at three deaths per thousand live births, it has one of lowest infant mortality rates in the world. Its combined gross enrollment ratio for primary, secondary, and postsecondary education is 99.2 percent, remarkably close to 100 percent.[45]

As in all countries, certain populations within Norway continue to face challenges. Like much of North America, Europe, and Japan, Norway is struggling to find the best way to support healthy aging in the workplace as the average age of the population rises and the age of retirement decreases. The nation also struggles with issues common to immigration. Although immigrants who are legal residents have the same benefits as citizens, and asylum seekers receive health care and education while their cases are under review,[46] social disparities in employment opportunities and earnings remain between immigrant and Norwegian-born populations. Companies often hire immigrants at a fraction of the wages they pay to Norwegians. These issues, although not unique to Norway, still merit attention from policy makers and labor experts.[47]

Despite facing these ongoing challenges, Norway has demonstrated the feasibility of maintaining high employment rates and economic competitiveness while providing good working conditions. Its achievement of this goal has had a remarkably important impact on the lives of its workers. Although some have argued that Norway's success has been based merely on its good fortune in having rich natural resources, particularly oil and gas, the world is resplendent with examples of nations with equally large reservoirs of natural resources but that fail to provide a floor of quality working conditions or social supports. Moreover, Norway uses a relatively small fraction of the wealth generated by its natural resources to support public and social services. The government has limited itself to using the interest on the capital generated from these resources, while investing the capital itself internationally in order to avoid the rampant inflation that would result from local spending or investment of large sums of capital. Such restrictions in spending can be considered the economic equivalent of sustainable development and could be adopted by the large number of nations with significant natural resources.

Norway succeeded uniquely well in creating and competing for good jobs, and it achieved this by adopting several practical strategies that could be implemented by other nations: by restricting the practices that undercut labor standards; by promoting labor policies that both improve lives and raise productivity; by increasing postsecondary education, with its long-term benefits; by investing in preschool education and postlayoff training, with their immediate payoffs; and by competing strategically. But Norway is only one example of a country that has abundant work while guaranteeing workers decent wages and conditions. The core features of its approaches to economic success are common among the other countries in our study that managed to maintain strong working conditions concurrently with low unemployment rates relative to their region. These common features stretched from the Caribbean and Latin America to Europe, Asia, and beyond.

Barbados, Mexico, and Beyond

The palm trees on the Barbadian coast could hardly seem farther from the snow-covered, evergreen forest in the hills of northern Norway, nor could the twenty-four-hour nights and the summer midnight sun above the Norwegian Arctic Circle seem more distant from Barbados's year-round, even-keeled tropical days. However, Barbados has more in common with Norway than one might initially suspect.

Ranking third in the Human Development Index for the Americas as of 2007, behind the United States and Canada, Barbados had a higher GDP per capita than many of the neighboring islands. At US$12,687 a year, it was higher than St. Kitts and Nevis to the north and more than four times higher than Jamaica and Dominica to the west.[48] In addition, Barbados had lower unemployment than most countries in the Caribbean.[49]

The route to success of each country is uniquely carved out by different historical and political factors, making the story of Barbados distinct from that of Norway. Yet there are some undeniably strong common elements across countries, regions, and histories. Like the other nations, Barbados's success was profoundly shaped by its investment in education, by the existence of legislation to promote good working conditions, by a "flexicurity" system that balanced workers' need for protection against unemployment with businesses' need to adapt to economic cycles, and by a true dialogue between labor and management.

By 1970, Barbados already had a primary school enrollment rate of 87 percent. Strong investments in secondary school led to a notable increase from 73 percent in 1970 to nearly 88 percent enrollment in the year 2005.[50] Over this same period, GDP per capita grew from US$800 to US$10,560 (in 2008 dollars).[51]

The growth in education and GDP were deeply linked. In 1963, the average real wage was 3,500 Barbadian dollars per year. With advances in secondary and technical education, the average real wage had more than doubled by 1990 to 7,800 Barbadian dollars per year. Barbados had markedly increased its role in the financial sector, and it could only have done so by increasing the educational attainment of those living and working there.[52]

Labor laws provided basic protections such as holidays with pay, a minimum wage, workplace safety, and the right to unionize. All of this was done in the context of flexicurity. A national insurance scheme provided workers with income during periods of maternity leave, illness, injury, unemployment, and retirement. Severance is paid when workers are fired as a result of downsizing, but companies have a great deal of freedom in ensuring that the hiring and firing process meets their ability to compete and meets the needs of the economic environment. Barbados's commitment to these protections is long-standing. Pensions were first introduced in 1937 and severance pay was enacted in 1973. Business, labor, and government are brought together under a national productivity council to structure the social insurance program.

Mexico provides another example. While coming from a very different geographic and socioeconomic context than Norway, Mexico's 2008 unemployment rate of 3.7 percent was significantly below the regional average and low even by OECD standards.[53] At the same time, Mexico has legislated a floor of decent working conditions that includes twelve weeks of paid leave to new mothers with 100 percent wage replacement, at least an hour or more of breastfeeding breaks every day for mothers until the baby is weaned, up to a year of paid sick leave with 60 percent income protection, and over a week of paid vacation time. Many of the features highlighted in the Norwegian and Barbadian cases played a role in achieving this balance in Mexico, such as investing in both early and advanced education for its population and approaching economic competition strategically. For decades private employers in Mexico have been mandated to provide early childhood care and education as a part of Seguro Social (Social Security). Mexico currently has a commitment to expand early childhood care and education beyond formal-sector jobs to the entire country. Its investment in widely affordable tertiary education is long-standing. At the same time, the nation has competed strategically using the resources it has, including signing the North American Free Trade Agreement in order to build on its proximity to the large U.S. economic market. The Mexican economy, as in most nations, is far from perfect, nor is the national educational system without problems. But the successes yielded from economically productive social benefits are readily apparent in Mexico and many of the countries that are ranked as low in unemployment in this chapter and high in competitiveness in the next, while maintaining strong working conditions. The reason that these nations have been able to have higher labor standards and lower unemployment rates is that workers are more productive when federal laws support education across the life course, and when they have a chance to care for their own health and that of their families while succeeding at work.

The Fork in the Road

Our data on labor protections in 190 countries around the world make it clear that there is no single relationship between national employment rates and working conditions. By taking a look at the experiences of individual countries, it becomes clear that low labor costs alone are not enough to secure low unemployment rates. For example, Bangladesh, where garment workers are among the lowest-paid workers in the world,[54] had a low official unemployment rate of 4.2 percent but an underemployment rate of 24.5 percent in 2006; in addition, 35.1 million (41 percent) adults and youth were considered to be "out of the labor force" as they were no longer actively looking for jobs.[55] Bangladesh's low investment in human capital and its reputation for abusive working conditions have markedly decreased businesses' willingness to locate jobs there.

At the other end of the spectrum, Norway has an even lower unemployment rate, averaging 3.7 percent over the ten years from 1998 to 2007, and far less underemployment while providing generous guarantees of paid annual leave, sick leave, leave for new parents, public holidays, unemployment benefits, accident pay (such as workers' compensation), and pension plans. At NOK 126, the minimum wage in the Norwegian construction sector is over US$19 per hour, using 2009 exchange rates.[56] Compare this to the United States, which has a considerably higher unemployment rate and a considerably lower minimum wage of $6.55 per hour across the majority of sectors, and where there are no guarantees of paid sick days, paid annual leave, a day of rest, maternal or paternal leave, or many other basic provisions.

The lack of social protections in the United States has taken its toll on American society; with six deaths per thousand infants, the country ranks thirtieth in terms of infant survival, among the worst in high-income countries. It ranks seventeenth in education and twenty-ninth in overall life expectancy. In contrast, Norway has among the world's lowest infant mortality rates, the highest human development indicators, and the second-highest life expectancy.[57] Its economic strategy and investment in human capital have enabled it to attract jobs and to compete at the high end of the economic spectrum. We are not arguing that companies never profit or that countries never attract jobs through a race to undercut labor standards; indeed, many companies and a number of countries have flourished economically while minimizing workers' benefits. In order to compete simply by providing the lowest wages, countries need not invest in the infrastructure and human capital required to attain higher levels of quality and productivity. Nevertheless, this chapter illustrates the feasibility of a very different strategy for success by demonstrating how countries and companies can compete for jobs while ensuring a floor of decent working conditions. Nations do not have to force their citizens into jobs with poor conditions or abandon existing protections of humane work in order to keep jobs within their borders.

There are clearly two very different paths to choose from. Which one will we decide to follow?

3 The Contention that Countries Can't Compete if They Protect Working Adults

"PROTECTING WORKERS WOULD BE NICE, but it is simply unaffordable if you want to stay competitive in a global economy." Such arguments regarding competitiveness continue to dominate labor policy debates in diverse economies and political regimes around the world. Policy makers and business leaders frequently contend that nations must choose between protecting their workers and competing effectively in the world economy, presenting these two options as being mutually exclusive.

Fears about the loss of competitiveness are almost as diverse as the countries in which they originate. High-income countries fear their competitiveness is at risk because their wages are already higher than those in developing economies. Adding new benefits such as guaranteeing a decent amount of vacation leave, additional wages for night work, or paid leave to care for a new infant or an elderly parent has a higher dollar cost in countries where wages and salaries are higher to begin with. At times leaders in advanced economies also fear that their nations will be further disadvantaged if they implement labor standards when developing economies do not.

The irony is that while high-income countries have traditionally argued that their relatively high labor standards have put them at a disadvantage, it is low-income nations that now most often contend that they cannot compete if labor standards are globally imposed. Unlike advanced economies that are able to compete on the basis of capital and infrastructure, developing economies note that their competitive advantage comes from their low-cost labor.

In some cases, their roads, ports, transportation systems, broadband Internet, and other communication systems may not be on a par with those of some advanced economies, and their budgets may not yet allow them to invest in as much advanced technology or capital for manufacturing and services, but they contend that their labor can remain cheap as long as its costs are not increased by imposed international labor standards.

Is it possible that both advanced and developing countries' claims that decent labor standards thwart competitiveness could be wrong, and that global labor standards would in fact improve all workers' well-being without undermining economies?

In this chapter, we introduce some of the most common arguments against improving working conditions, and we assess the accuracy of these contentions by looking at the evidence. We examine the labor policies of some of the world's most competitive nations in order to evaluate the feasibility of remaining competitive while legislating a floor of decent working conditions, and we then broaden the scope of our analysis to include the study of policies in countries ranging economically from the weakest to the strongest. Does having strong labor protections affect a nation's overall competitiveness ranking? After presenting data proving the viability of being economically competitive while protecting workers, we examine what makes this possible. We conclude the chapter by presenting some critical steps toward achieving this end.

Popular Debates Around the World

Before turning to the economic data, we begin by establishing the prevalence of economic concerns in labor policy debates worldwide, demonstrating how leaders, groups, and individuals within the same society uphold completely opposing views on this critical and contentious issue.

Australia

In its policy brief *Forward with Fairness* released in the spring of 2007, the Australian Labor Party proposed changes to labor law that would increase scheduling flexibility at work, augment the amount of time employees would have for themselves and their families, and reach a compromise on how readily employers could fire employees. Specifically, the proposals included four weeks of annual leave for full-time workers and ten days of leave for personal or family health and other needs. Part-time workers would benefit from improved conditions as well in the form of "part-time parity"; they would receive paid annual leave and sick days prorated by the percentage of time they worked. Parents of preschool children would have the right to request flexible work arrangements, but employers would be allowed to refuse these arrangements on reasonable business grounds. A balance was reached in regard to companies' ability to fire people: small firms that employed fewer than fifteen people would be allowed to dismiss employees without cause during their first year of employment. While this would provide more flexibility for employers who might find it costly to comply with the regulatory requirements for documenting the grounds for dismissal, it would provide more security for employees than the policies put in place by the Howard government in 2005. Introducing a set of five minimum work standards referred to as the Australian Fair Pay and Conditions Standards, *WorkChoices* allowed companies of up to one hundred employees to dismiss without cause for up to six months.

How would the enactment of the *Forward with Fairness* policies affect the nation's economic competitiveness? As in most industrialized countries, business interests in Australia are represented by a chamber of commerce. The Australian Chamber of Commerce and Industry (ACCI) argued that the impact of the reforms could only be negative and that Australian workers would end up losing out to lower-cost workers abroad. The Chamber's media release from April 28, 2007, described the proposed policy as:

> a harsh and unnecessary hit that will damage the Australian economy. It is hard to see how the policy will create one new job in Australia. Mr. Rudd promised business on 17 April that he would ease the regulatory burden, however his industrial relations policy has done the very opposite by imposing a triple whammy of new regulation on employers (new legislative obligations, new award obligations and new collective bargaining obligations). Each level of regulation increases business costs, reduces flexibility in employing staff, adds red-tape and compromises business efficiency.[1]

The Labor Party won the elections in November of 2007. The new federal government, led by Prime Minister Kevin Rudd, introduced new workplace relations legislation consistent with and based on the policies put forth in *Forward with Fairness*. The question remains: Who is right regarding the economics?

Indonesia

In Indonesia, employees have been dealing with a similar tension between perceived employee and business interests. In 2003, Indonesia passed a labor law to provide workers with increased protections both by shortening the time required to become a permanent employee and by improving the rights associated with this status. Business groups were opposed to these protections. Indonesian Footwear Association chairman Harijanto told the *Jakarta Post*: "Investors are reluctant to come here because as soon as they arrive here they are faced with labor regulations that could jeopardize their businesses." Apindo (Indonesia's employers association) secretary-general Djimanto has said that the 2003 labor law "requires that employers give a severance and service pay to dismissed workers equivalent to thirty times their monthly salaries . . . As a comparison, China provides severance pay equal to ten times the monthly salary and Vietnam five times."[2] Business groups argued in favor of reforming the 2003 law, contending that "the revision of the [2003] labor law is vital to provide a more stable labor system that would lead to more jobs from the expected inflow of labor-intensive investment."[3]

In 2006, the government proposed to amend the protections. The 2006 law would extend the length of time that companies could hire and use temporary workers from three years up to five years. Already disadvantaged by not having the rights of regular employees, temporary workers would also be in a worse position to negotiate for their salaries and benefits; although they could form unions, more workers would be required in order to do so than in the past. Firing would be made easier, and severance pay would be decreased. Employee groups raised concerns that the "proposed amendments, including measures making it harder to strike and reducing generous severance packages, would chip away at their job security."[4]

In 2008, the two sides were still at odds with one another. The Indonesian government continues to publicly support the current regulations,[5] employers' associations continue to call for reforms,[6] and the opposition parties and labor unions maintain their vocal opposition to such reforms.[7]

China

In China, foreign companies took on an active role in the ongoing legislative debate. In 2006, the country sought to revise its labor laws in an effort to improve the lives of low-income workers who were increasingly migrating to the country's coastal cities and inland magnets. The Labor Contract Law was proposed to ensure that contracts were in place to provide migrant and other workers with clear rights. In particular, the new law would restrict the duration and use of probationary periods in an effort to protect temporary workers, and it would address the conditions under which employment could be terminated.

The proposed legislation was published in March of 2006. The European Chamber of Commerce in China supported the new legislation and the goal of improving the work environment and working conditions: "A more mature legal environment should be considered as an advantage in attracting foreign investment."[8] In contrast, the U.S.-China Business Council argued that "the Draft Law may also reduce employment opportunities for [People's Republic of China] workers and negatively impact the PRC's competitiveness and appeal as a destination for foreign investment."[9] The vast majority of responses from business associations were negative, explicitly or indirectly hinting at the possible departure of foreign investment, foreign-owned plants, and jobs. The monthly magazine of the American Chamber of Commerce in Shanghai, which represents 1,300 U.S. companies, said that the new law is "like going twenty years backward."[10] The *New York Times* reported:

> many multinational corporations had lobbied against provisions in an earlier draft of the labor law. The early draft, circulated widely in business and legal circles, more sharply limited the use of temporary workers and required obtaining approval from the state-controlled union for layoffs. Companies argued that the rules would substantially increase labor costs and reduce flexibility, and some foreign businesses warned that they would have little choice [but] to move their operations out of China if the provisions were enacted unchanged.[11]

The direct response by the Chinese People's Congress to such concerns demonstrates the prevalence and strength of the belief that labor standards could harm global competitiveness in both trade and foreign investment. The Associated Press reported:

> Xin, deputy chairwoman of the law committee of the legislature's Standing Committee, tried to assure foreign investors they will not be hurt by the new rules. "If there is some bias in the application of the law, it would be in favor of foreign investors because local governments have great tolerance for foreign investors in order to attract and retain investment," Xin said. "Even if [companies] violate labor law, [officials] are still hesitant to [confront] them."[12]

The new Labor Contract Law came into force on January 1, 2008. Although it introduced significant "pro-worker" regulations in an attempt to enhance employees' bargaining power and working conditions, its restrictions are considerably more modest than they were in the original draft, and it remains to be seen how the new regulations will be enforced.

In December of 2007, the Standing Committee of the National People's Congress passed the Labor Arbitration Law, which granted employees the right to initiate labor disputes against their employers and provided workers with free access to a much more efficient and expeditious arbitration process. The Labor Arbitration Law came into effect on May 1, 2008.

United States

The year after China began considering improvements to protect its domestic migrant workers, across the globe the United States was considering the Healthy Families Act. The U.S. Senate Committee on Health, Education, Labor, and Pensions held hearings on the bill in 2007. The Act was designed to ensure that—for the first time in history—all Americans would receive at least a small amount of paid leave from work when they or their family members got sick. The proposed seven days of paid sick leave was modest by any global standard.

In opposing this legislation, business representatives argued that improving labor standards in the United States—even in a minor way—would pose a threat to the country's international competitiveness. In his written testimony, G. Roger King, business lobbyist and partner of the Jones Day law firm, wrote: "Employers in this country are already burdened by numerous federal, state and local regulations which result in millions of dollars in compliance costs. These mandated and largely unfunded 'cost of doing business' requirements in certain instances not only hinder and impede the creation of new jobs, but also inhibit our nation's employers from competing globally."[13] Brian Phillips, president of a human resource services company, contended, "If small companies are hit with employees who feel they are entitled to paid time off, it could lead to staffing issues and ultimately impact business productivity or customer satisfaction."[14]

Business associations echoed these arguments. Marc Freedman, director of Labor Law Policy for the U.S. Chamber of Commerce, said, "The U.S. Chamber of Commerce is strongly opposed to this legislation . . . We view it as a costly mandate on businesses that would eliminate the flexibility employers require to design leave policies that meet their employees' needs while still preserving the employer's interest in having a reliable, stable workforce in place."[15]

Even though workers in most other parts of the world already had guaranteed sick leave, business arguments about the unaffordability of such leave for Americans went beyond misgivings about the leave being *paid*. Similar arguments were made against the *unpaid* leave in the United States. The Family and Medical Leave Act (FMLA), which covers half of American workers, requires employers to provide twelve weeks of unpaid leave every twelve months in the event of the birth or adoption of a child or a serious medical condition experienced by the worker or an immediate family member. A 2005 hearing of the U.S. Senate Committee on Health, Education, Labor and Pensions examined whether the FMLA's unpaid leave, passed into law in 1993, should become more restricted. Representing the auto industry, Patrick Lancaster, executive vice-president and chief administrative officer of American Axle and Manufacturing (AAM), argued, "the U.S. automotive industry is undergoing a structural change caused by global competition, customer demands for global pricing and rising domestic production costs. One of AAM's domestic cost drivers is the significant increase in absenteeism caused by abuses of the FMLA."[16]

European Union

Meanwhile, Europe took a very different stance when it engaged in a process of reviewing working conditions in the face of changes unleashed by the global economy. In March 2000, the member countries of the European Union met in Lisbon to discuss how to reach a goal shared by many of their international counterparts: to become "the most competitive and dynamic knowledge-driven economy by 2010."[17] In seeking to reconcile this ambition with the practical changes it would require, in November 2006 the European Commission (EC) released a report on "Modernising labour law to meet the challenges of the 21st century."[18] The report called on European nations to ensure a "floor of rights" to protect those working under precarious conditions, such as subcontracted and temporary workers, while providing training that would benefit both employees and business leaders and responding to employers' needs for flexibility in hiring and firing. The business community across Europe contested these objectives, which were designed to be balanced, arguing that the cost burden of any increased protections for employees would be too high.

In the United Kingdom, Susan Anderson of the Confederation of British Industry told Parliament: "[Our publication *Lightening the Load*] looks at European and national legislation on employment issues . . . In this report [we calculated] the cumulative cost of employment legislation and looked at the total cost from 1998 to 2006 . . . The total cost was just a shade over £37 billion. That is quite a considerable cost."[19] She went on to say that new policies that reduce employers' flexibility could negatively affect the United Kingdom's competitiveness due to investors' perceptions in the global market.

In all the debate about labor conditions, there was remarkably little discussion about what would bring both the global and national economies to their knees in 2008— the lack of transparency, oversight, regulation, and judgment of financial institutions.

Academic Debates

Divergent opinions about the economic affordability of raising labor standards are not limited to the popular press and policy makers. The voices of academics, and of economists in particular, can be heard on both sides of the debate.

Arguing against labor standards, some economists have contended that the establishment of global labor standards is simply another case of inappropriate market interference, which will have the unintended consequence of harming the group it aims to help—low-wage, developing nations where conditions are worst.[20] They argue that countries' low labor standards provide them with a comparative advantage in producing and selling goods relative to other nations with higher standards, to the extent that the lower labor standards are reflected in lower export prices.[21] Implementing labor standards would negate this comparative advantage, thereby reducing these nations' ability to attract jobs and grow.

Those in favor of labor standards have argued that labor standards can be justified through improvements in economic efficiency and productivity, which contribute to competitiveness.[22] When labor standards encourage firms to invest in training their workers, the firm's overall productivity and income rise in the long run, although in the short run the firm may incur costs. Labor standards can also lead to greater employee retention, which in turn gives companies incentive to invest in firm-specific training and productivity-enhancing technology. The overall impact if all firms or all countries were to raise standards would be an increase in global human capital, resulting in higher productivity levels and ultimately greater wealth.[23]

Without a doubt, the debate on the economic impact of improving global labor conditions is in full swing, with the opposing camps clear on their positions and the logic behind them. But what about the evidence to test the claims of leaders, policy makers, and academics from around the world?

Previous Evidence on Labor Standards and Competitiveness

Opponents of labor standards commonly contend that Europeans cannot compete economically due to their labor laws, ranging from sick leave to meet personal or family health needs, to restrictions on work hours, to guaranteed annual leave. They point to the 1980s and a good part of the 1990s, when European countries had higher unemployment rates than the United States, which experienced an almost unparalleled period of economic growth. Yet in a review of the empirical evidence in favor and against the "case of social protection," labor economists Rebecca Blank and Richard Freeman concluded that there was little support for the claim of a large trade-off between providing social protections and macroeconomic performance.[24] Moreover, in the 1990s, Europe recovered economically while fundamentally maintaining its public policies and supports for workers and their families. By the end of 2002, the Euro was stronger than the U.S. dollar.

Prior to the new studies we report in this volume, valuable global research on these issues had been conducted but was largely limited in its scope of labor protections examined. Researchers had examined the important relationship between foreign investment and the allowance of the worst types of labor abuses. The studies examining the relationship between the incidence of child labor and forced labor and foreign direct investment (FDI) flows revealed that higher labor standards did not lead to lower FDI.[25] Research examining the impact of restrictions on child labor, the prevention of forced labor, and the promotion of unionization rights in eighty-seven countries found that each of these protections had a positive effect on FDI flows.[26] Moreover, countries that tolerate gender discrimination experienced a reduction in their "comparative advantage in unskilled-labor-intensive goods."[27] Studies using multiple measures of labor standards, focusing on the freedom of association and on collective bargaining rights, also provided strong evidence that basic protections improve economic outcomes.[28] Studies focusing on EU, OECD, or industrialized economies, including a meta-analysis of more than one thousand studies, found no economic losses associated with collective bargaining and unions.[29] Similarly, a study of a wide range of nations within and outside of the OECD showed no relationship between core labor standards and trade performance.[30]

New Global Research on Labor Standards and Competitiveness

While these studies conclusively showed that guaranteeing the core labor standards defined by the ILO[31]—banning forced labor, child labor, and discrimination and guaranteeing the right to organize—did not impede foreign investment, they limited their investigations to the provision of these few basic labor standards. Our research, detailed below, is the first to look worldwide at the relationship between better working conditions and competitiveness.

Working Conditions in the Most Competitive Countries

We examined data on global working conditions to see whether countries that legislate a floor of decent working conditions above and beyond the core labor standards are prospering or struggling economically. Each year, the business-led World Economic Forum ranks countries in terms of economic competitiveness and publishes its rankings in its Global Competitiveness Report. Country rankings are based on a series of indicators deemed to be the key drivers of economic growth and competitiveness.[32]

We classified the following countries as "highly competitive," meaning they ranked among the twenty countries with the highest competitiveness rankings in at least eight of the ten years from 1999 to 2008: Australia, Austria, Canada, Denmark, Finland, Germany, Iceland, Japan, the Netherlands, Norway, Singapore, Sweden, Switzerland, the United Kingdom, and the United States. We then analyzed labor legislation in these nations.

We found that the evidence clearly contradicted the rhetoric voiced by business lobbyists with respect to the feasibility of countries being competitive while guaranteeing a set of valuable minimum labor standards. In fact, guarantees of good working conditions are common among the most competitive economies. The question is not *whether* they have adequate labor protections such as paid sick leave and paid parental leave, but rather *how many* protections they have, *how long* each type of leave lasts and *how much* income is guaranteed.

We found that all of the fifteen highly competitive nations have some form of sick leave for people dealing with health issues (see Table 3.1). In fourteen of the countries, this leave is paid; the only competitive country that limits the guarantee to unpaid leave is the United States of America. Strikingly, in eleven of the fifteen most competitive countries, paid sick leave is offered for a month or more.[33] Ten of the countries offer paid leave for six months or more, or until the employee fully recovers.

TABLE 3.1 Highly competitive countries: Do they guarantee paid sick leave?

Country	*Paid sick leave*	*Duration of paid sick leave (days)*	*Paid leave available for 26 weeks or until recovery*	*Wage replacement rate*	*Benefits begin on first day of ilness*
Australia	Yes	7–10	No	100%	Yes
Austria	Yes	31 or more	Yes	50–100%	Yes
Canada	Yes	31 or more	No	55%	No
Denmark	Yes	31 or more	Yes	100%, flat	Yes
Finland	Yes	31 or more	Yes	70–100%	Yes
Germany	Yes	31 or more	Yes	70–100%	Yes
Iceland	Yes	31 or more	Yes	100%, flat	Yes
Japan	Yes	31 or more	Yes	60%	No
Netherlands	Yes	31 or more	Yes	70%	Yes
Norway	Yes	31 or more	Yes	100%	Yes
Singapore	Yes	11–30	No	100%	Yes
Sweden	Yes	31 or more	Yes	80%	No
Switzerland	Yes	11–30	No	80%	Yes
United Kingdom	Yes	31 or more	Yes	flat rate	No
United States of America	No	NA	NA	NA	NA

NOTES: Using the World Economic Forum's rankings on the Global/Growth Competitiveness Index, we examined policies for the fifteen most competitive countries. These countries were selected because they ranked among the world's top twenty competitors in at least eight of the ten years from 1999 to 2008.

"Flat" wage replacement rate indicates that all employees receive the same set cash payment. When both a percentage and a flat rate are indicated, part of the leave is paid at a flat rate and part at a percentage of the employee's wages.

Above notes apply to all tables in Chapter 3.

A number of nations adjust benefits during lengthy sick leaves. In the above table these variable benefit amounts are represented by ranges in percent of wages paid and by payment of a percent of wages followed by a flat rate benefit.

Fourteen of the most competitive countries guarantee annual leave from work with pay (see Table 3.2). In the majority of these countries, annual leave is provided with full wages and is substantial in duration. For example, the United Kingdom and Denmark each offer over five weeks of paid leave, and Austria, Finland, Germany, Iceland, Norway, and Sweden ensure that all employees receive over four weeks per year. Among the most competitive nations, the only country with no guarantee of paid annual leave is—once again—the United States.

A majority of nations further guarantee a weekly day of rest. Only the United States and Australia fail to provide this basic protection (see Table 3.2).

Guarantees of adequate leave for new mothers are equally common. Thirteen of the top fifteen most competitive countries provide leave with income for new mothers (see Table 3.3). Only the United States offers no paid maternity leave, no paid parental leave, and no payment for new parents, except for the unpaid leave guaranteed through the FMLA, which covers only half of working Americans. Australia, the other industrialized nation often highlighted for its penurious policies for new parents, already surpasses the United States by providing mothers with twelve months of unpaid job-protected leave and a "baby bonus" worth approximately AUS$5,000[34] or equivalent to just over a month's worth of average annual earnings in 2008[35] to families with an adjusted taxable income of AUS$75,000[36] or less. Moreover, the government announced they would begin paid parental leave in 2011.

TABLE 3.2 Highly competitive countries:
Do they guarantee paid annual leave and a weekly day of rest?

Country	*Guarantee of paid annual leave*	*Duration of paid leave (weeks)*	*Guarantee of a weekly day of rest*
Australia	Yes	4.0	No
Austria	Yes	5.0	Yes
Canada	Yes	2.0	Yes
Denmark	Yes	5.5	Yes
Finland	Yes	4.4	Yes
Germany	Yes	4.4	Yes
Iceland	Yes	4.4	Yes
Japan	Yes	1.8	Yes
Netherlands	Yes	4.0	Yes
Norway	Yes	4.2	Yes
Singapore	Yes	1.3	Yes
Sweden	Yes	5.0	Yes
Switzerland	Yes	4.0	Yes
United Kingdom	Yes	5.1	Yes
United States of America	No	NA	No

TABLE 3.3 Highly competitive countries: Do they guarantee paid leave to new mothers?

Country	*Paid leave for mothers*	*Duration of paid leave (weeks)*	*Wage replacement rate*
Australia	No*	NA	NA
Austria	Yes	81–146	100%, flat
Canada	Yes	50	55%
Denmark	Yes	50–58	80–100%
Finland	Yes	164	25–90%
Germany	Yes	66–118	33–100%
Iceland	Yes	26	80%
Japan	Yes	58	30–60%
Netherlands	Yes	16	100%
Norway	Yes	90–100	80–100%, flat
Singapore	Yes	14	100%
Sweden	Yes	69**	80%, flat
Switzerland	Yes	14	80%
United Kingdom	Yes	39	90%
United States of America	No	NA	NA

NOTE: We present data on the maximum amount of leave available to a mother if she takes all of the maternity leave available to women and all of the parental leave available to either parent. For Austria, Denmark, Germany, and Norway, we report the minimum and maximum duration of leave to reflect each country's policy of providing parents with a choice between taking a shorter leave with a higher (percentage or flat rate) benefit or a longer leave with a lower benefit.

*In May 2009, the Australian government announced plans to begin providing parental leave on January 1, 2011 to all adults earning up to AUS$150,000 for 18 weeks paid at the federal minimum wage.

**Sweden's parental leave policy also allows parents to take part-time leave with partial benefits for a longer duration.

In all of the most competitive countries except for the United States and Australia, the maximum leave available to new mothers—when combining maternity and parental leave—is at least the fourteen weeks recommended by the ILO. In the majority of the highly competitive countries, including Austria, Canada, Denmark, Finland, Germany, Iceland, Japan, Norway, Sweden, and the United Kingdom, the amount of leave for new mothers is six months or more.

Paid leave for new fathers is nearly as widespread (see Table 3.4). Only Switzerland offers paid leave to new mothers but not to new fathers.

Regarding allowing time for breastfeeding breaks, these countries are fairly evenly split (see Table 3.5). Austria, Germany, Japan, the Netherlands, Norway, Sweden, and Switzerland all ensure women the right to breastfeed while working.

All of the highly competitive nations make it possible for parents to take at least unpaid leave from work to address their children's health needs (see Table 3.6). When adult family members need help with healthcare, a clear majority—twelve out of fifteen—ensure that workers can provide this assistance.

Sweden and Denmark guarantee leave for children's needs, including education, while Switzerland requires employers to ensure work schedules that enable parents to attend to educational needs for children up to age fifteen. Singapore allows parents to take leave for education as part of broader leave for family needs.

In some protections, the most competitive nations differ in the approaches they take. Although a significant number of countries, including Austria, Denmark, Finland, Norway, Singapore, Sweden, and Switzerland, have remained

TABLE 3.4 Highly competitive countries: Do they guarantee paid leave to new fathers?

Country	*Paid leave for fathers*	*Duration of paid leave (weeks)*	*Wage replacement rate*
Australia	No*	NA	NA
Austria	Yes	65–130	flat rate
Canada	Yes	35	55%
Denmark	Yes	34–42	80–100%
Finland	Yes	154	25–70%
Germany	Yes	52–104	33–67%
Iceland	Yes	26	80%
Japan	Yes	44	30–40%
Netherlands	Yes	0.4	100%
Norway	Yes	87–97	80–100%, flat
Singapore	Yes	2	100%
Sweden	Yes	67**	80%, flat
Switzerland	No	NA	NA
United Kingdom	Yes	2	90%
United States of America	No	NA	NA

NOTE: We present data on the maximum amount of leave available to a father if he takes all of the paternity leave available to men and all of the parental leave available to either parent. For Austria, Denmark, Germany, and Norway, we report the minimum and maximum duration of leave to reflect each country's policy of providing parents with a choice between taking a shorter leave with a higher (percentage or flat rate) benefit or a longer leave with a lower benefit.

*In May 2009, the Australian government announced plans to begin providing parental leave on January 1, 2011 to all adults earning up to AUS$150,000 for 18 weeks paid at the federal minimum wage.

**Sweden's parental leave policy also allows parents to take part-time leave with partial benefits for a longer duration.

TABLE 3.5 Highly competitive countries: Do they guarantee breastfeeding breaks?

Country	*Guaranteed breast-feeding breaks*	*Age of child when breaks end*	*Breaks are one hour or more per day*
Australia	No	NA	NA
Austria	Yes	For duration of breastfeeding	Yes
Canada	No	NA	NA
Denmark	No	NA	NA
Finland	No	NA	NA
Germany	Yes	For duration of breastfeeding	Yes
Iceland	No	NA	NA
Japan	Yes	1 year	Yes
Netherlands	Yes	9 months	Yes
Norway	Yes	For duration of breastfeeding	Yes
Singapore	No	NA	NA
Sweden	Yes	For duration of breastfeeding	Yes
Switzerland	Yes	1 year	Yes
United Kingdom	No	NA	NA
United States of America	No	NA	NA

competitive while restricting overtime, others have implemented no restrictions but instead have mandated pay premiums (see Table 3.7).

In some areas the most competitive countries offer less consistent protection. While Finland, Norway, and Sweden have demonstrated that it is clearly possible to be competitive while maintaining broad restrictions on night work; and Germany, Japan, and Switzerland provide a wage premium for those who are required to work at night; other nations provide protections only for perceived vulnerable groups: children, pregnant or nursing women, or employees who are deemed through a medical exam to be unfit for work at night. Over half of the most competitive countries, including Austria, Canada, Denmark, Germany, Japan, the Netherlands, Norway, Switzerland, and the United Kingdom, ban or restrict night work for these groups (see Table 3.8).

In short, basic protections for all people at work—from the right to annual leave, sick leave, and a day of rest to paid parental leave—are solidly in place in

TABLE 3.6 Highly competitive countries:
Do they guarantee leave to attend to the health needs of a family member?

Country	*Leave to care for children's health needs*	*Leave to care for adult family members' health needs*
Australia	Yes	Yes
Austria	Yes	Yes
Canada	Yes	Yes
Denmark	Yes	Yes
Finland	Yes	Yes
Germany	Yes	Yes
Iceland	Yes	No
Japan	Yes	Yes
Netherlands	Yes	Yes
Norway	Yes	Yes
Singapore	Yes	No
Sweden	Yes	Yes
Switzerland	Yes	No
United Kingdom	Yes	Yes
United States of America	Yes	Yes

TABLE 3.7 Highly competitive countries:
Do they guarantee an overtime premium?

Country	*Ban or limit on overtime*	*Overtime premium*
Australia	No	No
Austria	Yes	Yes
Canada	No	Yes
Denmark	Yes	Yes
Finland	Yes	Yes
Germany	No	Rest or premium
Iceland	No	No
Japan	No	Yes
Netherlands	No	No
Norway	Yes	Yes
Singapore	Yes	Yes
Sweden	Yes	Rest or premium
Switzerland	Yes	Yes
United Kingdom	No	No
United States of America	No	Yes

TABLE 3.8 Highly competitive countries:
Do they limit or provide a premium for night work?

Country	*Premium for night work*	*Ban or broad restrictions on night work*	*Ban or restriction for children, pregnant or nursing women, or medical reasons*
Australia	No	No	No
Austria	No	No	Yes
Canada	No	No	Yes
Denmark	No	No	Yes
Finland	No	Yes	No
Germany	After 11 p.m.	No	Yes
Iceland	No	No	No
Japan	After 10 p.m.	No	Yes
Netherlands	No	No	Yes
Norway	No	Yes	Yes
Singapore	No	No	No
Sweden	No	Yes	No
Switzerland	After 11 p.m.	No	Yes
United Kingdom	No	No	Yes
United States of America	No	No	No

the overwhelming majority of highly competitive economies. There is no evidence that these protections in any way detract from these countries' ability to compete in the global economy. Given that a number of these countries even have additional protections in place, such as wage premiums for and restrictions on night work, it is clear that it is not only possible but entirely realistic for countries to be competitive while maintaining good working conditions.

The Relationship Between Labor Protections and Competitiveness on a Global Scale

In addition to examining the working conditions in the world's most competitive countries, we compared the labor protections in over 120 countries ranked according to their competitiveness by the WEF.[37] The results are equally striking: none of the labor legislation we analyzed that guaranteed a basic floor of good working conditions is linked to lower levels of competitiveness. In fact, countries demonstrated that they could be very competitive with great working conditions as well as with poor ones. Likewise, countries could be uncompetitive for a vast array of reasons that had little to do with their working conditions.

Importantly, one area in which improved working conditions are consistently associated with increased competitiveness was investment in adults' ability to care for their children and families. As nearly all nations guarantee paid leave for new mothers, we examined whether there was any link between a country's economic competitiveness and the duration of its maternal leave. Countries that provide a longer duration of paid leave for new mothers, at least fourteen weeks, are more likely to be ranked in the top third of the competitive countries (see Figure 3.1). The average duration of paid leave available to mothers in the most competitive nations is forty-three weeks, compared to twenty-five weeks in the least competitive nations.

As there is far greater variability in the existence of paid leave for new fathers, we analyzed whether new fathers had access to *any* paternity or parental leave (see Figure 3.1). Again, highly competitive nations are significantly more likely to offer paid leave for new fathers: 67 percent of the most competitive nations offer paid leave for new fathers, compared to 33 percent of the least competitive nations.

The positive relationship between national competitiveness and investing in parents' ability to care for their children's health holds true for children well beyond infancy as well (see Figure 3.1). While two-thirds of the most competitive nations provide leave to care for children's health, just over one in four (27 percent) of the least competitive nations do so.

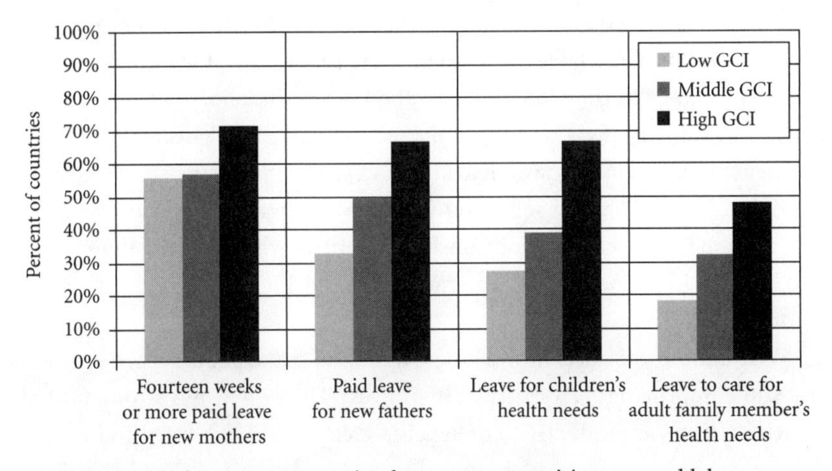

FIGURE 3.1 Is there any connection between competitiveness and labor protections for personal and family needs?

NOTE: GCI refers to the World Economic Forum's Global Competitiveness Index rankings.

There are logical reasons why each of these labor standards may contribute to enhanced long-term national competitiveness: they enable the development of a healthier, better-educated labor force over the long term. While cross-sectional data alone cannot demonstrate that these investments in workers' ability to care for their children were the cause of these nations being more competitive, it is certainly clear that investing in working adults and their families in no way endangered these countries' competitiveness. Moreover, all of the surrounding evidence argues that labor provisions supporting the health and development of children and families, like other investments in children and youth, are strong drivers of a society's ability to compete.

Countries that are more competitive are also significantly more likely to provide leave to care for adult family members, with the most competitive countries providing this type of leave two and a half times as often as the least competitive countries (see Figure 3.1).

Competing Economically While Ensuring Good Working Conditions

Many nations are competing in the global economy while ensuring basic labor protections. What enables them to do so? Why don't the costs of providing time off for illness or for birth or adoption and offering wage premiums for night work reduce a nation's GDP or a company's profits? Why don't these apparent increased labor costs make it harder to compete for and maintain jobs? The short answer is that allowing employees to work a decent number of hours and giving them the time they need to care for their own health and that of their families enables them to be more productive at work.

At the center of the global race to the bottom in labor standards is the belief that the cost of goods and services can be lowered by decreasing wages and benefits. Costs can, however, also be lowered by increasing employee productivity. The reason that some countries have been able to sustain successful economies and remain enormously competitive while offering high wages and benefits in a globalized economy with increasing free trade is that their labor forces are more productive.

Why and how do decent working conditions make people more productive while improving the quality of their lives? The evidence is strong for the positive effects on productivity of benefits such as paid sick leave and conditions such as reasonable work hours.

Studies have repeatedly demonstrated the large degree to which illness leads to lost productivity.[38] Factory production slows down, services are hampered, and sales are diminished when employees are absent due to illness. Productivity also declines when employees go to work when they are sick. The lost productivity associated with "presenteeism" has been demonstrated for health problems ranging from migraines and depression to infectious diseases such as mononucleosis.[39] In fact, recent studies have documented that the costs that companies incur due to sick employees coming to work often surpass the costs of employees staying home when they are ill.[40] As a result, paid sick leave can lead to real dollar savings for employers.[41]

Paid sick days are associated with a number of positive workplace outcomes. First, they give working adults the time to care for their own health needs, to rest and recuperate, and to avoid aggravating health problems that could result in additional lost work days in the future.[42] Employees recover more rapidly when they have time to consult a doctor and attend to their illnesses. With a shorter total period of illness, they have more healthy days at work. Second, paid sick days decrease the likelihood that infectious employees will come to work and spread illnesses to coworkers,[43] thus increasing the loss of productivity due to both absenteeism and presenteeism. Third, as detailed previously, when employees are sick at work, they may reduce their own productivity as well as that of colleagues who rely on them.

Limits on the total number of overtime work hours are another part of a basic floor of decent working conditions that can lead to enhanced productivity. While productivity rates can increase as employees build skills during a reasonable work week, productivity per person, per hour declines when work hours are markedly extended. The relationship between work hours and productivity has long been recognized. Two examples from an earlier age of global economic transformations are illustrative. In the late 1800s, in the midst of the industrial revolution, an optical works firm in Germany reduced daily work hours from nine to eight, and saw a 3 percent rise in production over the course of the year. Around the same time, a Manchester, England, engineering company stopped all overtime and early morning work and reduced weekly hours from fifty-three to forty-eight, and experienced lower absenteeism with no reduction in production levels.[44]

Recent studies continue to highlight that long hours are associated with lower productivity. Researchers who examined eighteen manufacturing industries in the United States over a thirty-five-year period found that productivity declined between 2 and 4 percent for every 10 percent increase in overtime hours.[45] While the declines were not large in the context of the American forty-hour work week, they would presumably be substantially larger in countries where the base work week is already significantly longer or in sectors where work weeks frequently surpass eighty hours in duration. Moreover, even at the rate observed in the United States, these findings demonstrate that, depending on the skill level of the employee and on the regularity and the amount of overtime required, higher productivity may be achieved by hiring additional workers rather than repeatedly depending on extensive overtime hours.

The productivity benefits are not unique to one country or sector. Construction workers in Canada and the United States have similarly detailed that while occasional overtime can benefit projects, regular amounts of significant overtime lead to lower productivity.[46] The experience in Japan, a country known for frequently having long work hours, is similar, with adults reporting lowered productivity as hours rise.[47]

The economic benefits of reasonable work hours go beyond the direct link to productivity. When workers work extensive overtime, the risk of costly accidents and injuries rises dramatically.[48] In one study, the risk of injuries or accidents rose by 16 to 28 percent for those working fifty- and sixty-hour weeks instead of forty-hour weeks.[49] Overtime and long hours also have been shown to have a detrimental effect on health, which, as we have delineated, in turn affects productivity. Studies from Canada and the European Union have documented increased risk of high blood pressure, cigarette and alcohol consumption, heart disease, weight gain, and mental health problems, as well as mortality.[50] Finally, over one hundred studies across North America, Europe, and the Pacific all found that extended daily working hours were linked with increased absenteeism.[51]

It is reasonable to ask whether good working conditions that benefit the competitiveness of individual employers will be equally effective at contributing to a country's competitiveness when they are implemented on a national scale. When the working condition improves productivity of employees, as described above for well-structured sick leave policies and limiting excessive overtime, the benefits are readily scalable to nationwide. Similarly, policies that reduce unnecessary "job churning" benefit countries as well as companies by increasing productivity. By aiding the development of employees' firm-specific skills, the increased productivity often makes up for any costs incurred for the higher compensation put in place to increase retention.[52] (The kinds of policies whose competitive advantage is not scalable are those whose *only* benefit to a company resides in its ability to attract employees over a neighboring firm.)

An important example is the evidence of economic gains from policies such as paid parental leave. A series of studies have shown that women who receive paid maternal leave are significantly more likely to return to the same employer after childbirth.[53] Improved employee retention not only allows firms to harness the higher productivity of more experienced workers, but it also reduces hiring and training costs.

Although individual companies would not benefit in relation to their competitors in the recruitment of new employees if these policies were nationally adopted, national policies can still lead to less overall movement of employees between companies. Because workers gain job-specific skills and expertise with tenure, their ability to retain jobs can improve the efficiency and productivity of the national economy overall. Clearly, job mobility can be beneficial to all concerned when job transitions are made to improve the match between employee skills and interests and company needs. The problem lies in the fact that much of the job transition related to parenting has been unrelated to the needs of either employees or firms. In the absence of job-protected paid maternal leave, if women have on average two children, they will have two additional job searches and transitions that are not related to skills, interests, or commitments of the women or their employers and therefore not efficiency enhancing.

Finally, improved working conditions can make countries as a whole more competitive by lowering societal costs such as healthcare expenditures or improving societal outcomes such as children's development. Long-term national gains in parental leave can be seen in terms of improvements in child health and development, as well as educational outcomes that shape the next generation's competitiveness. Numerous studies have demonstrated that parental availability to take part in curative care is critical to ensuring children's physical and mental health,[54] particularly for children with chronic health and developmental conditions.[55] Parents' presence has been shown to reduce hospital stays by 31 percent, resulting in savings in hospital costs.[56] Parents with either paid sick or vacation leave are 5.2 times more likely to stay home to care for their sick children as parents who lack these benefits.[57] Studies have also shown that family support improves the health of adults, providing them with better health outcomes from conditions such as coronary disease,[58] myocardial infarction,[59] and strokes,[60] as well as improving longevity[61] and mental health outcomes among the elderly.[62] The resulting lower societal costs provide a critical reason, in addition to rising productivity, explaining why countries adopting decent labor standards can grow more economically competitive.

While these policies can contribute to competitiveness, the way they are structured also affects their impact. Two examples follow. It is important to set the duration of parental leave in a way that balances the need to ensure that parents have sufficient time with their newborn and newly adopted children with that of also seeking to avoid differential gender uptake and to minimize incentives for gender discrimination at work. Similarly, the amount of leave should take into consideration maximizing the benefit of decreased turnover while minimizing the cost to firms of having to cover positions and time periods that are difficult to fill. Similarly, sick leave compensation, duration, and procedures need to be structured in a way that facilitates men and women taking the time off they need to address health problems while minimizing potential abuse, supporting timely return to work, and providing accommodations to encourage full participation at work of employees with chronic or recurrent health conditions.

Moving Forward

There is no reason that individual countries and the global community as a whole could not afford to ensure everyone the floor of decent working conditions described in this chapter, from paid annual leave to paid sick leave to paid maternal and paternal leave to paid breastfeeding breaks. Establishing this basic level of benefits would cost only a small fraction of wages and would in no way affect countries' ability to compete against each other. To the extent to which one believes that lower labor costs are a way for poorer countries to compete while strengthening their economies, the gaps in wages between countries are what drive the amount that is paid for labor, and this combined with productivity contributes to production costs. These policies have a small impact on relative labor costs but a large impact on people's lives. Moreover, many of their costs are offset by productivity gains.

While it will inevitably be a great challenge to address wage and income inequalities, it is essential to do so. Working toward a global minimum wage that is relative to the median income or living wage in each country would be a natural first step in this process. It would eliminate the worst abuses that leave people working around the clock without making enough money for their families to survive. The establishment of a relative minimum wage would not erase the ability of countries to use wage differentials to their advantage for economic growth.

Advanced economies are able to compete effectively while ensuring high wages because their histories of human capital and infrastructural investments contribute to higher productivity levels. A global commitment to ensuring that resources are available to low-income countries striving to develop their own infrastructures and educational systems is the only way to ensure that these nations get a chance to compete as higher-wage countries in the future. This shift is essential for achieving greater equity and for improving the conditions under which the worst-off live worldwide. In the long run, raising the lowest global wages will protect poorly paid workers in countries in the North, South, East, and West alike.

Different Equilibria

Companies and countries can reach two quite different equilibria. One equilibrium entails low wages for the majority of workers and few labor protections, benefits, or training opportunities. In this equation, people lose their jobs when they are absent for routine illnesses or when they miss work to care for family members. People work longer but less effectively because, as noted earlier, research has demonstrated that weak labor standards lead to greater inefficiency and lower productivity.[63]

The other equilibrium entails higher-costing but much more productive labor. It includes protections such as restrictions on mandatory overtime so that employees work long-enough hours to gain skills and expertise but not so long as to denude their lives or impede their productivity. When workers get sick with routine illnesses, they stay home on paid leave, see healthcare providers as needed, get well sooner, protect their coworkers from infection, and return to work refreshed and recovered. This equation involves free or affordable preschool and after-school educational programs, freeing parents up for work, enhancing educational outcomes, and thus enabling young people to be more productive when they enter the workforce as adults.

The path we choose could not have more profound implications for the quality of all our lives. Economic growth can occur in either scenario, but only the latter will enable the majority of the world to gain from the distribution of the benefits of that growth.

4 The Myth that Labor Laws Do Not Make a Difference

IRONICALLY, the two major arguments against getting better labor laws passed around the world take opposite positions. The first argument assumes that labor laws matter so much that they overwhelm the effect of other economic policy, and that guaranteeing decent working conditions inevitably leads to higher unemployment and lower competitiveness. The findings presented in the previous two chapters address this concern. They clearly document that countries with decent labor laws have been able to compete at the highest levels, and that legislating a floor of decent labor conditions has not prevented countries from achieving low unemployment rates.

The second argument contends the opposite: that labor laws do not matter and are thus not worth passing. Those supporting this view contend that laws have little economic effect because they are so infrequently enforced, particularly in low- and middle-income countries, and that workers in affluent countries do just as well without legislation. By examining in greater detail the experience of implementation of labor laws in several low- and middle-income countries as well as the experience of working conditions in a high-income country with few legislated labor standards, this chapter demonstrates the importance of labor laws for improving worker conditions while still allowing countries and companies to be economically successful.

The Value of Labor Laws Even When Resources Are Not Abundant

While it may be clear that labor laws can make a difference in the lives of men and women in countries that have ample resources to enforce those laws, the question remains: Can national governments implement labor laws even when resources are scarce? In political circles in affluent countries, some of the discussions about working protections in middle- and low-income countries have sparked the response that laws are irrelevant in these cases because they are rarely implemented. Do such assumptions speak to any real differences or are they merely the next generation of stereotypes about countries?

While any number of countries could be used as examples of where labor laws have been implemented in spite of low or moderate resources, we begin with Mexico because it is a country that shares important commonalities with many nations. As a middle-income country that has had an imperfect democracy, Mexico is improving in its openness to multiple parties in real elections. In recent years, political leadership at local and national levels has come from both the left and the right. Mexico is home to millions who live in extreme poverty, but also to some of the world's most affluent individuals. It has within its borders the social, political, and economic range and diversity of many different countries around the world.

Importantly, the country has many good labor policies on its books. Working conditions in the private sector are governed by social security legislation. The Mexican Social Security Institute (IMSS) was founded in 1943, not long after the United States passed the Social Security Act in 1935. Unlike the American Social Security system, however, the Mexican system provides a range of workplace protections and benefits to those employed in the formal economy. Working men and women who are covered by the IMSS are guaranteed paid sick leave, paid disability, health insurance, childcare, and pensions.[1] Instituto de Seguridad y Servicios Sociales de los Trabajadores del Estado (ISSSTE), or the State Employees' Social Security and Social Services Institute, provides a parallel set of programs for government employees.

From 1999 to 2002, we conducted in-depth interviews of working families, employers, teachers, and childcare and healthcare providers in Mexico as part of the Project on Global Working Families.[2] We spoke with many working adults who were eligible for IMSS benefits. Did eligible individuals know about the benefits and could they in practice receive the assistance and support that the laws were supposed to guarantee, or did the laws have little impact because they were not followed? While sufficient childcare slots were not always available, and as in any system, policies such as paid leave were not perfectly implemented, respondents repeatedly described in confidential interviews away from their work sites how both the legislated labor protections and mandated services were successfully provided in practice, as well as the magnitude of the difference these protections made in their lives.

Parents told us time and again how important the Mexican social security's legal guarantees of healthcare, childcare, and paid leave were to their families' health, their children's development, and their ability to earn a living. Those who received IMSS coverage through their formal-sector employers were provided with paid sick leave coordinated with the provision for healthcare and childcare. Paulina Vasquez illustrated the effectiveness of this system as she described the times when her son became sick with common childhood ailments:

> When he's been sick, [the daycare staff have] called me right away at my work. They would tell me that the baby was sick. I would ask for permission at my work—we can ask for permission in these cases—and go to the daycare center. The doctor would tell me what was wrong and give me a referral sheet for medical consultation. With that sheet I would go to the clinic the same day, because there they would get his fever under control or stop his diarrhea. They would suspend the baby from the daycare center for several days, but they would do the same thing to me. Thus, both of us were protected. They would give me a three-day permission not to go to work, which is usually the time it takes for the child to get better. When he was stable again, he would go back to his center and I would go to work.

The case of IMSS demonstrates not only that implementation is possible in a middle-income country, but also that less-than-perfect implementation can still lead to substantial and meaningful differences in people's lives. While the Mexican social security system did not cover everyone in the country who worked, and at the time of the study it did not provide enough childcare spaces for all who sought them, millions were effectively covered by IMSS. The impact it had on the lives of working adults in Mexico and their children was inestimable.

Seventy-five percent of the formal-sector workers we interviewed reported that they were able to make use of paid leave. This is in great contrast to the informal economy,[3] where only 24 percent of workers reported having access to paid leave.

Evidence of Mexico's successful implementation of its social security program can be seen in the marked effect the program has had on social inequalities. Paid sick leave benefits guaranteed through IMSS have significantly narrowed the gaps in basic benefits available to lower- and higher-income workers. In the informal economy, where workers are not covered by IMSS, there was a 41 percentage point gap in the access to paid leave between higher- and lower-income workers we interviewed. In the formal sector, where paid sick leave is provided by law through IMSS, the gap was markedly smaller at only 15 percentage points.[4] Similarly, disparities in access to formal childcare across income levels are striking in many nations, and Mexico is no exception. However, the IMSS mandated provision of childcare for children aged six weeks to four years effectively reduces the gap between rich and poor workers. In the informal economy, a 50 percentage point gap was found in center-based childcare between higher- and lower-income workers, in contrast to the formal sector, where the gap was only 10 percentage points.[5]

The impact of these enormous improvements in equity can often be best understood by looking at some of the stories behind the statistics:

> Liany Rivera Barrios was raising two preschool children with the help of her mother. The father of her older son was killed in a car accident within months of their son's birth, and the father of her infant had left her. Her family was surviving on the income she made as a cashier in a restaurant. If not for the childcare provided by Mexican social security, Liany could not have enrolled her children in a daycare center. She earned 350 pesos (US$38) every two weeks. Two weeks' attendance at a private daycare center in her area costs 400 pesos (US$43).

> Amalia Montoya could no more afford private childcare than Liany. She too was raising an infant son alone. In contrast to Liany, working as a housecleaner Amalia was not covered by social security, and private childcare was far beyond her economic means. Amalia therefore had no choice but to take her infant son to work with her. "It was really difficult because it's not the same as being in your own house. When he began to cry because he was hungry, I couldn't tend to him at the same time as working." Her son gradually became malnourished, which placed

him at a higher risk of illness. He was frequently sick during the early months of his life, and this made caring for him while working even more difficult.

In summary, there is no doubt that the labor protections and supports provided by Mexican laws were effectively reaching many of the eligible working adults, and that many employers understood and followed the laws. Equally clear is the evidence that the system of supports makes a very real difference in the lives of working adults and their children. While more resources for increased implementation would undoubtedly increase the impact of these laws, to argue that low- and middle-income countries have no implementation is to slip into stereotypes that make it sadly easy to dismiss the crucial benefits that millions of their citizens are already receiving.

Mexico's experience also provides an important example of the role of labor policies in reducing inequities. Mexico has good labor legislation, including protections for paid leave during illness and childcare. The implementation of these laws has led to a substantial narrowing of the gap between rich and poor in terms of access to benefits that play a crucial role in ensuring the healthy development of adults and children alike.

The Role of Governmental Agreements and NGOs in Creating Incentives to Implement Labor Laws

Governments across the globe play an important role in implementing their own domestic labor laws. While individual nations clearly must enforce their own labor laws, once a country has adopted labor legislation, implementation can be influenced by the actions of its trading, investing, and purchasing partners. Cambodia provides an important example of how bargaining between a foreign and local government can lead to increased implementation of a country's own labor laws.

The apparel industry in Cambodia exploded after the fall of the Pol Pot regime, as the nation began to recover from many years of war and oppression and the economy began to regenerate. While previously clothing produced in Cambodia was barely an exportable product, the industry rose to become 50 percent of Cambodia's total exports during the 1990s.[6] With 90 percent of its exports destined for the United States, Cambodia was overwhelmingly producing for the U.S. market. This new trade relationship was developing just as the American public was becoming increasingly concerned about several aspects of globalization. Americans were worried about the ability of low-wage countries to undercut the cost of production in the United States and about the consequent loss of manufacturing jobs in America. People increasingly believed that labor abuses in poor countries were contributing to this job loss. The movement to boycott goods produced with child labor was only one of the outcomes of this growing awareness. There was also mounting public ambivalence between a desire to diminish trade barriers in order to lower product costs and an urge to increase trade barriers in order to protect jobs.

NGOs concerned about sweatshops and child labor, together with unions preoccupied with protecting American jobs, formed a coalition to limit the access of Cambodian apparel makers to the U.S. market. With its rapidly expanding niche in the garment manufacturing industry, Cambodia was interested in reaching an agreement that would facilitate rather than impinge on its access to the U.S. market. In 1999, the United States–Cambodia Trade Agreement was signed. Renewed in 2001, this agreement granted Cambodia greater U.S. market access as long as it improved its working conditions. Under the agreement, for the duration of the global Agreement on Textiles and Clothing, Cambodia could increase its exports to the United States by 6 percent per year or more if it showed improvements in its working conditions. Two programs were developed as part of the United States–Cambodia Trade Agreement to improve implementation of Cambodia's labor laws: Better Factories Cambodia and an Arbitration Council.

Better Factories Cambodia was created as a voluntary program under which those companies that agreed to have their factories monitored by an outside observer would receive a larger proportion of Cambodia's export quota to the United States.[7] In the end, all factories that exported apparel registered to become part of the Better Factories program.[8] Under this program, each factory was visited by external monitors who assessed working conditions for compliance with a list of up to five hundred regulations. Recommendations for improvements were provided to the management, and companies were given the opportunity to address inadequacies before the reports were made public.[9]

While the implementation of labor policies was imperfect, the system of independent monitoring demonstrated important overall improvements in labor conditions among participating factories. Our research group analyzed data available from the monitoring reports in Cambodia and found that when health and safety problems were identified, factories generally responded and improved the conditions before the monitoring team's next visit. Implementation was less effective when it came to limiting mandatory overtime and providing guaranteed daycare. That being said, the number of factories with these problems still declined as a result of the monitoring.

The second mechanism set up under the United States–Cambodia Trade Agreement, the Arbitration Council, was a mediating body created to settle disputes between labor and management. Disputes first went to the government's Ministry of Labor, but if a ministry solution was not achieved, all parties were required to go to the Arbitration Council. In the process, one arbitrator was chosen by workers and another was chosen by employers. These two arbitrators would select the third from a Ministry of Labor list.[10] While parties were obligated to participate in arbitration, the results were not binding unless both the workers and management agreed ahead of time to make them so.

Even though labor leaders noted that the effectiveness of the Arbitration Council was limited by its nonbinding nature, and although business leaders continued to be unwilling to make it binding, more than two-thirds of the cases brought to the Council ended in an agreement or a settlement.[11] The Arbitration Council effectively brought increased transparency to the nature and resolution of disagreements. All findings were publicly recorded, and the selection process of the arbitrators left parties feeling that the process was far more balanced than the courts had been previously in addressing cases. Transparency was important because it not only helped in individual cases where workers sought to ensure that rights were implemented, but on a larger scale it also helped ensure that unions could safely organize and that NGOs could effectively work for better implementation of labor rights. Previously these actions had led to job loss.

The programs at the center of the trade agreement worked in favor of Cambodian companies and the Cambodian economy because they enabled increased access to the U.S. market. Cambodia received a bonus for its improved working conditions and was awarded an increase in access to the U.S. market of 9 percent annually from 2000 to 2002, 12 percent in 2003, and 18 percent in 2004, increasing every year as the implementation of its labor laws improved.[12] As Cambodia's working conditions improved, there was a concurrent increase in the demand from the private sector for apparel manufactured there. As the country's reputation improved due to the Better Factories Program, name-brand companies such as Nike chose to keep their production in Cambodia.[13] Recognition of the improvement of Cambodian working conditions also attracted more investment from large multinationals such as the Gap, which wanted to demonstrate that they sourced their goods from factories with decent labor conditions. In fact, four out of five investors cited this factor as being central to their decision to be in Cambodia.[14]

What made it possible for this program to succeed was that Cambodia, like many countries, had an excellent foundation of existing labor laws and equal rights provisions. These laws covered minimum wages, maximum weekly work hours, overtime pay, annual leave, maternity leave, and breastfeeding breaks, and they protected essential rights such as the right to earn equal pay for equal work, the right to unionization, the right to education, and the rights of children and the disabled. These rights were guaranteed in the Cambodian constitution in 1993 and in the Labor Code in 1997, and they were reaffirmed in Cambodia's ratification of international conventions.[15] Ensuring that workers received these rights in practice was not cultural imperialism or protectionism by foreign companies and NGOs. The Cambodian government had independently committed to them. Rather, the United States–Cambodia Trade Agreement, the Better Factories program, and the Arbitration Council together increased implementation of existing Cambodian laws.

While the Cambodian case demonstrates how trade agreements between countries may be used to improve implementation of existing labor laws while stimulating, not hindering, economic growth, in other cases the drive for improvements in working conditions has been led by international consumer groups, local or foreign NGO watchdogs, or the investors themselves.

The experience of the Nike Corporation, one of the leading brands in the footwear and apparel industry and one of the first companies targeted for its abuse of workers and egregious disregard for labor laws across different factories in Asia, is a case in point of how consumer pressure on individual multinational companies has improved factory labor conditions and labor law enforcement. Going back to 1996 and earlier, Nike was publicly criticized for sweatshop conditions including forced overtime, below-minimum wages, physical and sexual abuse on the job, refusal to meet workers' basic human needs such as access to drinking water and bathrooms, and the lack of health and safety protections that resulted in illness and disease.[16] Vietnam Labor Watch, a San Francisco–based advocacy group founded in response to reports of worker abuses in Nike shoe factories, demanded that Nike implement a series of reforms. Other advocacy and non-governmental organizations became involved in lobbying Nike to change its practices, including

Press for Change, Global Exchange, Campaign for Labor Rights, the Clean Clothes Campaign, and the Living Wage Project. The reforms these advocacy groups demanded from Nike included revealing factory locations in order to facilitate inspections and independent monitoring, adopting a fair living wage, eliminating physical and sexual abuse and corporal punishment, adhering to local health and safety regulations, and repaying wages lost due to violations of minimum-wage laws.[17] In response to growing media coverage documenting sweatshop labor conditions and the threat of a boycott of its products,[18] Nike took a series of actions to improve working conditions in its contracting factories and to fundamentally alter the company's reputation. Nike created a department for labor practices and established a Code of Conduct to be followed by its contractors.[19] Steps taken to improve labor conditions included hiring the Ernst and Young accounting firm to conduct independent audits and making the findings public. Audit findings included a report documenting that one-quarter to one-half of Nike's Asian factories prevented workers from using the bathrooms and/or taking water breaks during their shifts.[20] Nike was one of the first multinational corporations to disclose factory locations and independent audit results, and it succeeded in transforming the association of its brand with terrible labor violations to an affiliation with conscientious and committed implementation of labor protections.

Ways to Protect Workers in the Informal Economy

The previous case studies compellingly demonstrate the difference that having labor laws can make in workplace conditions. They show that effective implementation of labor laws is possible even in low- and moderate-resource settings, that even if implementation is imperfect the impact on workers' lives can be marked, and that trading partners and consumers can encourage and achieve better implementation of a nation's labor laws. Despite the potential for improvement in working conditions suggested by these case studies, an important concern is that law-based approaches historically have had an important gap: not all workers are covered by labor legislation. To make a difference in the lives of all working men and women, a strategy for protecting those working in the informal economy is needed.

Workers may not be covered by labor laws for a variety of reasons. For example, countries may exempt small companies from their laws, effectively excluding workers in those enterprises from labor protections. Certain forms of labor, such as selling goods as a street vendor or working as a childcare provider in an individual's home, are rarely recognized or regulated by governments; these workers are part of the informal economy and are considered to be "self-employed." Similarly, part-time work, temporary or casual positions, and jobs that are subcontracted or precarious in other ways are less likely to be covered by labor laws.

The same factors that limit the likelihood of these jobs being covered by legislation also often make it more difficult to accurately estimate the number of people affected by the lack of protections. As a result, there is a wide range of estimates of the number of people in the informal economy. We focus here on countries in Latin America, Africa, and Asia where the informal economy is often considered to be particularly large.

Estimates of the size of the informal economy vary widely. Two common ways to estimate its magnitude are to count workers employed by small firms (because labor laws often cover only larger firms, and the smallest firms are almost always the most difficult to effectively regulate) and to count workers who lack social security coverage. When measured by enterprise size, estimates suggest that 48 percent of the workforce in El Salvador is informally employed. When measured by social security coverage, that number jumps to nearly 63 percent. Parallel numbers from Mexico regarding the size of the informal sector are 31 percent using enterprise size and 43 percent using social security status, and from Peru they are 58 percent and 62 percent, respectively.[21] Estimates for Brazil find that, based on enterprise size, 49 percent of workers are in the informal economy and based on social security status, nearly the same number, 50 percent, are considered informal laborers.[22] In North Africa the ILO estimates that 50 percent of Tunisians and 55 percent of Egyptians who are not in the agricultural workforce are employed in the informal economy; the parallel numbers for Sub-Saharan Africa are 72 percent in Kenya and 51 percent in South Africa. The size of the informal economy is estimated to be highest in India, representing an estimated 83 percent of working adults.[23] Despite the difficulty in obtaining precise evaluations, it is clear that the informal economy is large in many low- and middle-income countries around the world. This leads naturally to the questions: What can be done to improve the working conditions of those in the informal economy? And, does the existence of labor laws for the formal economy help or harm those in the informal economy?

Policy makers have a range of options available for improving working conditions in the informal sector. For example, labor legislation can be extended to cover small enterprises and subcontractors. Workers in the informal economy can be permitted channels for collective bargaining for the same rights as workers in the formal economy. Social security supports such as sick leave insurance and childcare can be provided through mechanisms other than employment and thus be made available to everyone. Governments can also facilitate the ability of workers to obtain and retain formal-sector jobs when they so choose.

Many countries have taken a more direct approach and enacted labor legislation that affords equal protections to all workers, including those who traditionally would have been in the informal economy. For example, occupational health and safety legislation in Japan, Republic of Korea, Nepal, and Vietnam applies to all workers, irrespective of whether they work independently or have an employer. India, Sri Lanka, South Africa, Morocco, Malawi, Dominican Republic, Indonesia, and Thailand have ensured that a number of their labor laws, beyond those governing occupational health and safety, apply to all workers.[24] Countries such as Argentina, Chile, Mexico, Venezuela, the Philippines, Cameroon, Uruguay, Iran, and the United States have also passed legislation requiring firms to hold subcontractors responsible (to varying degrees) for their compliance with labor and safety laws.[25] Even standards governing minimum wages may be translated to piecework through estimations of how much work (how many pieces) can safely be done per hour. India, which has one of the largest informal economies, has set up a commission with the goal of ensuring that the basic labor rights legally enshrined for the formal sector extend to all workers.[26]

Other countries have taken the approach of making it easier for small firms to register and thus be incorporated into the formal economy. In Shanghai, China, the municipal government has set up technical assistance, guaranteed bank loans, and facilitated work with government bureaus in order to encourage small firms to join the formal economy.[27] There is no reason why only large firms can comply with most labor laws. Small employers can economically succeed while ensuring that employees have annual leave and paid short-term sick leave, and that they do not work sweatshop hours.

A complementary approach is to provide all citizens with national social security supports such as childcare, insurance for parental leave, and long-term sick leave. These supports need not necessarily be bound by workplace or type of employment. In Mexico, Seguro Popular (Popular Security) was created in 2001 as a pilot program in five states in order to extend social security coverage to the over half of the population—including workers in the informal economy—not covered by IMSS, ISSSTE, or private insurance. In 2002, legislation was passed to make Seguro Popular available across the country. It now covers over five million people and has the goal of covering the complete uninsured population within a decade. The program is partially subsidized by the government and partially by annual fees paid by workers, who receive access to the same care and coverage as IMSS and ISSSTE.

The Value of Labor Laws in Afffluent Countries

Labor legislation clearly can be an immensely effective mechanism for raising the standard of working conditions, particularly for poor and marginalized women, men, and their families. But is legislation necessary?

In the countries where most basic human rights in the workplace are not guaranteed by law, those who oppose passing labor laws often argue that such laws are unnecessary because the overwhelming majority of companies voluntarily implement labor protections without being required to do so by law. This argument is commonly used in the United States, a country that is unique among advanced economies in how few protections it guarantees its workers. Is the business lobby in the United States correct when it argues that labor laws are simply not necessary because American companies voluntarily take care of all those who work for them? In order to better understand what America's lack of labor laws has meant for workers in practice, we examined the workplace protections discussed in this book. We found that workplace practices place the American experience in sharp relief against those of other nations.

Paid Sick Leave

Most European workers have a month or more of paid sick leave. In Austria, workers have sick leave paid at their full salary for the first twelve weeks. Social security subsequently provides paid leave with partial wage replacement for up to a year. Norway similarly guarantees paid sick leave at full salary for up to fifty-two weeks beginning with the first day of illness for all workers employed by a firm, and paid leave at nearly two-thirds of the regular salary for self-employed workers. In Switzerland, even new employees can take up to three weeks of paid sick leave.

Outside of Europe, Canada ensures income from the third through fifteenth week of illness at 55 percent of usual earnings. Even Australia and New Zealand, which have historically been less generous in their labor policies than other industrialized countries, guarantee at least some sick leave. New Zealand mandates five sick days per year at full pay and allows these days to accumulate to a maximum of twenty days if unused. In Australia, employees are guaranteed ten days of paid personal sick leave.[28] In short, even in these relatively parsimonious countries, a minimum of at least five days of sick leave are guaranteed. These benefits stand in stark contrast to the United States, which guarantees none.

While Americans are no different from people in other countries in their need for paid sick leave, there is no federal legislation guaranteeing any paid leave when they are ill or injured, and private provisions do not reach anywhere near European standards. Barely half (57 percent) of all private-sector workers in the United States, or about 52 million workers, have paid sick days.[29] Less than one-third are entitled to paid days off when their children are sick, and even fewer receive paid days off when aging parents are ill, which means that 86 million workers do not have paid leave to address family health needs.[30] These aggregated figures mask the disparities by income. Nearly three-quarters of workers living at or below the poverty line lacked paid sick leave some or all of the time they worked over a five-year period.[31] Only one in five private-sector workers in the bottom income quartile has paid sick leave, whereas almost three-quarters of workers at the top of the pay scale have access to this type of leave.[32] When combining this fact with the lack of national health insurance in the United States, it should not be surprising that major illness is one of the leading causes of bankruptcy and home loss in the nation.[33] In short, as a result of well-implemented labor laws, European, Canadian, Australian, and New Zealand workers fare far better than their American counterparts.

Annual Leave

A European Union policy ensures workers in Europe a minimum of four weeks annual leave per year. A substantial number of workers in EU nations actually have access to even more leave because of the higher unionization rates in Europe. In six of the European countries for which reliable, recent data are available, the majority of workers are union members, and in another five, a third to half of workers are unionized (two to three times the U.S. rate).[34] As a result, the majority of workers in Norway, Belgium, Finland,

Sweden, and Denmark receive more than the mandated four weeks, acquiring between five and six weeks per year.[35]

Compared to other industrialized countries, the American private-sector approach to labor has left its citizens working longer hours with fewer paid days off. Just as paid sick leave is not guaranteed in the United States, there is also no guarantee of any annual leave or days of rest. As a result, the average annual leave for a full-time private-sector worker in the United States is less than two weeks.[36] Moreover, low-wage workers are markedly disadvantaged compared with higher-paid workers. Fifty-seven percent of workers below the national poverty line lacked paid leave some or all of the time over a five-year period.[37] Overall, one in four U.S. workers was employed in a job with no paid days off in 2008.[38]

In practice, the voluntary, private-sector solution in which virtually no labor protections are enshrined in law has not resulted in broad coverage of leave policies. Instead, it has left U.S. workers far behind their international coworkers. EU regional directives, national legislation in all European countries, and negotiated agreements together have ensured that European workers receive substantially more paid annual leave than workers in the United States.

Leave for New Parents

Looking at leave for new mothers also is illustrative. Finland, for example, offers new mothers over three years of paid leave, including eight weeks before birth and 156 weeks of parental and "childcare leave." Women in France are guaranteed sixteen weeks of paid leave for each of their first and second children, twenty-six weeks of paid leave for their third and subsequent children, and at least thirty-four weeks for multiple births, as well as full-time or part-time leave with a childcare allowance for an additional six months for the first child and until the child is three for subsequent children. Germany provides all new mothers with sixty-six weeks of leave paid at their full salary for fourteen weeks and at 67 percent of their salary for the remainder.

The bare-bones policies in the United States—in the rare instances when laws exist—also pale in comparison to non-EU and less wealthy countries. Cuba offers eighteen weeks of maternity leave paid at 100 percent of earnings as well as forty weeks of parental leave paid at 60 percent. In Peru, new mothers have fifteen weeks of leave paid at 100 percent of earnings. Morocco guarantees fourteen weeks, also paid at 100 percent of earnings. In Latvia, new mothers receive sixteen weeks of paid leave with 100 percent of wages (eight weeks before birth and eight weeks after) plus forty-four weeks with 70 percent of wages.

New fathers in Europe also get to enjoy time off around the birth of a child. Austria, Finland, the Czech Republic, Norway, and Sweden guarantee a year or more of paid leave (combined paternity and parental leave) to new fathers. Fathers in Denmark and Italy receive six months or more. Outside of Europe, Canadian fathers have thirty-five weeks of paid parental leave available to them. Even Spain, at the low end of the spectrum, allows fathers to take four weeks at full pay.

Women and men in the United States are far worse off than those in other nations in terms of leave around the birth or adoption of a new baby. No form of paid maternity, paternity, or general parental leave is provided. As noted earlier, the only leave legally guaranteed to new parents in the United States is unpaid. While business representatives have argued that companies would voluntarily provide paid parental leave, obviating the need for any public guarantees, private efforts by employers have not filled the void.

A minority of American workers have access to fully paid maternity, paternity, or parental leave. A number of studies confirm that only a small number of firms provide their workers with paid leave around the birth or adoption of a child. In a 2000 survey of both small (fewer than 250 employees) and large (more than 250 employees) companies, only 12 percent reported providing paid maternity leave other than temporary disability insurance, and only 7 percent reported providing paid paternity leave.[39] Here again, the theory that workers will be provided with good working conditions in the absence of adequate paid leave laws falls flat.

In short, the United States lags drastically behind its global counterparts in providing a floor of decent conditions that includes paid sick leave, paid parental leave, and other fundamental protections that are standard in most affluent nations. The lack of these protections at work has taken a great toll on the lives of women and men and their families in the United States. We have described the cost of this omission to the health and income of adults, and to the health and human development of their children and disabled dependents, elsewhere in great depth.[40] The statistics provided here illustrate how far the United States lags behind other advanced economies in providing labor protections because of its use of a largely voluntary model with little labor legislation.

Where Do These Examples of the Impact of Labor Laws Leave Us?

In summary, the studies that we and others have conducted convincingly demonstrate a series of facts. First, in the absence of legislation, even the wealthiest country on the planet—the United States—has not been able to ensure decent working conditions for the majority of its citizens. Second, middle- *and* low-income countries have been able to implement their labor laws to a degree that makes a difference in the lives of those living within their borders. Third, when a country's legislation is in place, outside governments and consumers can help ensure that local citizens have their rights met in practice and not just on paper. Fourth, when policies are well designed, working conditions and economic competiveness may be improved simultaneously. Fifth, the number of people and sectors targeted by labor laws varies markedly by country, yet men and women in both the formal and informal economies can reap benefits from legislation that guarantees good work standards.

Labor laws can dramatically improve working conditions for all workers, particularly for the most marginalized, in at least two ways. The first is through effective enforcement by governments, and the second is by setting standards that lead companies to change their minimum provisions through moral suasion and social pressure, even in the absence of perfect enforcement mechanisms. This latter method may play as large a role as the first in some settings. Having examined labor laws in all UN nations and worked on the ground on all six inhabited continents, we are convinced that having labor laws in place improves working conditions in practice across a wide range of economic, political, and social contexts. We hope that the series of case studies presented in this chapter have effectively illustrated this point.

That being said, passing legislation is only the first step. Countries around the world vary widely in their degrees of implementation. While these differences do not always conform to stereotypes about which nations perform better or worse, it is essential to work to improve the level of implementation in all countries. Measuring what is occurring in workplaces has to be central to the efforts to improve practice on the ground.

Yet, in spite of the importance of measuring outcomes, neither the public sector nor the private sector has rigorously analyzed the extent to which labor laws are followed in different countries around the world. This is an indicator of how far we still remain from ensuring decent working conditions for all people. The private sector has created transparency indices to measure financial transactions and corruption, but it has developed no equivalent reporting system for worker protections. Through the International Labour Organization, the public sector has spent nearly a century negotiating agreements on labor conventions, but only countries' self-reports and nonsystematic feedback from non-governmental organizations on the implementation of those conventions have been collected. The ILO itself does not measure implementation of labor laws in all countries. It has not sent objective, outside teams to evaluate compliance with conventions in countries in all regions, nor has it funded NGOs to examine all nations systematically. The regular evaluation of labor protection enforcement in all countries is an urgent matter, and these findings must be made publicly available.

PART II
REQUIREMENTS FOR CHANGE

5 Achieving Global Consensus

Although Gabriela Saavedra had spent all of her nineteen years within a thirty-mile radius of her one-room shack made of scrap wood and cardboard in a slum in Tegucigalpa, the capital of Honduras, her life could not have been more dramatically defined by the global economy. She had briefly worked at a German-owned factory that manufactured car parts, where the wages were low but livable. She worked full-time but was still able to see her nineteen-month-old daughter, Ana Daniel, in the evenings. The hour-long commute to work was the only time Gabriela had for herself. After only a few months at this job, however, the German manufacturer began losing business and was forced to shut down several of its factories. Both Gabriela and one of her best friends, Alicia, lost their jobs. While Alicia and her children could survive on her husband's wages, Gabriela's husband and mother had both died, and she was the sole provider for her young daughter. She therefore had no choice but to take on any work she could find.

Wearing a sweatshirt emblazoned with the Nike trademark, Gabriela made us feel welcome in her one-room home, offering us water and telling us about her new job at a Korean-owned factory. She was now sewing nightgowns destined for North America, and her new schedule consisted of working fifteen to twenty-two hours a day, seven days a week. She was desperately conflicted about her situation. Her daughter, Ana Daniel, was the light of her life. If Gabriela kept her job at the sweatshop, either Ana Daniel would have to be left home alone, or Gabriela's ten-year-old half-sister would have to drop out of school in order to care for her. Neither option was safe, but there was no way that Gabriela could afford to pay for childcare with the sixteen dollars a week left over from her earnings after the company subtracted the cost of her one meal a day. With the little care she was receiving, Ana Daniel had already begun to get sick more often, and Gabriela was not able to take leave from work to take her to the doctor. Gabriela had only two alternatives: either she could endure these poor working conditions or she could quit her job, but she had no idea how she would pay for basic necessities, including food, if she resigned.

Fighting for better working conditions seemed futile. The factory owner had made it clear to all of his workers that if they started complaining, he was ready to move to China on a moment's notice in order to find cheap laborers who were willing to work under sweatshop conditions. He had left South Korea when working conditions had gotten too good there, and he had chosen to move to Honduras due to its limited labor protections. South Korea had started to legislate and implement a set of basic protections for workers, including mandating that companies provide at least twenty-four hours of rest per week to all of their employees; guarantee higher pay or premiums for overtime work equal to 150 percent of wages; provide paid maternity leave as well as paid parental leave that could be used by either mothers or fathers; ensure fifteen days of annual leave; and provide wage premiums for night work. Workers in Honduras were not as well protected. While they were supposed to receive at least twenty-four hours of rest each week, they were guaranteed only ten days of annual leave, a fraction of the maternity leave received by South Koreans, no parental leave, and only half of the value of overtime and night-wage premiums that were guaranteed in South Korea. Moreover, the government in Honduras had done less to ensure that all foreign-owned factories followed Honduran laws than South Korea had done to ensure that local companies followed local labor laws.

The fight for a global floor of humane working conditions is at least a century old, dating back to the emergence of the International Labour Organization, the first such global association, shortly after World War I.[1] The ILO was formed on the heels of an earlier period of rapid economic globalization when people around the world became acutely aware of the degree to which the quality of their working conditions was interlinked and affected by economic transformations. Yet, over the course of this past century, many arguments have been raised against creating a global floor of decent working conditions. This chapter will address these arguments, focusing in particular on the claim that people's experiences differ so much from one country to the next that a common approach to improving working conditions is not viable, and that cultural and political differences would prevent the achievement of a global consensus.

Is It Possible to Establish a Truly Global Floor?

The 192 countries around the world incorporate up to one hundred language groups, five thousand ethnic groups, nineteen major religions, and at least eleven forms of government. Given this diversity, it is not surprising that questions have arisen regarding the feasibility of reaching a global consensus on working conditions, how these conditions affect people's lives, and what role governments should play in improving them.

How can we develop a set of global labor standards that apply to both industrialized and developing nations if Swedish writer Johan Norberg is correct in contending that standards are determined by a nation's stage of development? Norberg argues that poor working conditions must be endured until a nation develops its infrastructure, technology, and productivity: "Sweatshops are a natural stage of development. We had sweatshops in Sweden in the late 19th century. We complained about Japanese sweatshops 40 years ago . . . One mistake that Western critics of globalization make is that they compare their current working standards to those in the developing world."[2]

Even when there is strong local support for improving working conditions, opponents often argue that labor standards are somehow culturally foreign. For example, public commentary reported by *Business Week* during Japan's amendment of its Labor Standards Law in 1987 accused the government of "embracing the Western notion of a five-day workweek" when they "amended the 40-year old Labor Standards Law to make the 40-hour workweek official," cutting it back from the formerly standard forty-eight-hour workweek.[3]

Other opponents question whether large suppliers of low-cost labor, such as China, would ever participate in the process of setting a global floor. According to the U.S.-China Business Council, "China has a virtually inexhaustible supply of migrant workers, most of whom are ignorant of their rights under Chinese law and are willing to work under any conditions without protest."[4] Some, like business school professor Peter Navarro, present cultural as well as socioeconomic arguments: "In the absence of any union representation, many Chinese workers are forced to endure some of the most dangerous, repetitive, and oppressive working conditions in the world. Part of the problem is a form of corporate organization that has its roots in the commune structure and a culture in which many Chinese have grown up under Communist rule."[5]

Some academics concur that there is a fundamental difference in labor protections and in their acceptance in developed and developing countries. The legitimacy of a double standard—where what is acceptable in developing nations is different than what is tolerated in the industrialized world—is aptly summarized by Pranab Bardhan, an economics professor at the University of California:

> [A]pparel jobs are among the lowest paying manufacturing jobs in our country, but they are among the best paying in poor countries . . . It is certainly true that working conditions in less developed countries can strike Western observers as unacceptable if not appalling. But two points need to be considered. First, wages and working conditions are likely to be even worse in non-trade-oriented sectors, such as services and subsistence agriculture, sectors that have been largely untouched by globalization. Second, poor working conditions in those countries are not a new development but have always been a chronic fact of life.[6]

The implication is that because these conditions are "chronic" they are accepted as part of the value system of poor Asian economies, such as Bardhan's native Bangladesh.

The viability of establishing global labor standards is often challenged as part of a broader argument about the implausibility of establishing a set of core human rights that transcends borders. This view maintains that because values and morals vary so much by nation, there is also variation in beliefs regarding the basic, humane working conditions that should be protected.

In short, the arguments against establishing a global floor of decent labor conditions have fallen into three categories:

- Life and work experiences around the world are so different that countries could never agree on the components of a global floor.
- Even if all countries could agree on which protections all human beings should have a right to, some countries could afford to offer these protections while others could not.

- Even if a global floor were agreed upon and legislated, there would be no way to ensure that the rules would have an impact on the lives of most workers.

Our goal throughout this book is to look at the evidence base—or the lack thereof—for each of the common arguments against improving working conditions. Most of this chapter will be devoted to the crucial questions of whether human experiences at work have enough in common across countries that we *should* have the same basic work protections in place across borders, and whether there are enough shared beliefs across cultures and political and economic systems that we *could* ever reach an agreement as a global community about how to proceed. Before focusing on these issues, we will address the affordability of a universal set of labor standards.

The economic argument is fundamentally different from the cultural one in that it is based on the belief that all peoples will eventually be able to obtain better working conditions, but that such standards are currently unaffordable and thus unattainable for poor countries. Policy makers have contended that sweatshop hours and conditions are necessary in order for countries to be able to uphold their competitive advantage. In the first two chapters of this book, we demonstrated how feasible it is to compete and have high employment rates along with good working conditions. That being said, we understand that meeting this objective can be easier for nations with more highly trained workforces and well-established infrastructures in place, than for those that lack these features.

The strong numeric evidence is often ignored when assessing whether it is financially feasible for poor countries to ensure that all workers can have a day off a week, some form of annual leave to spend with their families, and leave to care for their sick parents or children. Providing one week of paid sick leave, for example, costs employers 2 percent of wages in low- and high-wage countries alike. For each of the leave policies, the costs are scaled to each country's income. As a result, these protections are affordable for companies in both high- and low-income countries. Moreover, many basic protections such as a limit on the number of work hours and on mandatory overtime, and the provision of a day of rest actually lead to increased productivity per hour, rendering these policies even more readily affordable in low-income countries. The establishment of a decent wage floor is a more difficult, yet still-viable process if it is set relative to a country's own median wage or cost of living. While the wages in Bangladesh would still be much lower than those in France, reasonably set national minimum wages would enable women and men to earn their way out of poverty. At the same time, lower-cost countries could continue to benefit from this competitive advantage while training their workforces and building more competitive infrastructures.

Even if global labor standards are clearly economically feasible, the case could be made that they would be undesirable if work experiences around the world have little in common. Moreover, even if the experiences of workers in different countries are similar, global standards may be practically unachievable if national governments' approaches are completely different. Do people's work experiences differ completely depending on the country they live in? Understanding whether there are real commonalities in human experiences at work will help highlight the extent to which we could reasonably expect to come to an agreement on a global scale on certain issues.

How Much Do Individuals' Experiences at Work Have in Common Around the World? A Look at the Evidence

We developed a research program with the goal of gaining a better understanding of men and women's experiences at work around the world. As part of our efforts in over twenty-five countries from diverse parts of the world, the Project on Global Working Families combined the analyses of large, nationally representative surveys of more than fifty-five thousand households with in-depth interviews of over two thousand working women and men and employers from fourteen countries on six continents.

Here we invite you to be the judge of the evidence and decide how similar these people's experiences were. We offer a set of quotes detailing the experiences of men and women from around the world, and ask you to determine whether it is easy to identify the country each quote is from. (The answers can be found at the end of the chapter, but we recommend you try doing this exercise before looking at the answer key.) In order to simplify this task, we have limited the countries of origin of these quotes to five: the United States, Vietnam, Botswana, Russia, or Mexico.

COMPARISONS—PART 1

Experiences with Health Problems

"I force myself to work. I can't do anything else . . . Like I said, when I am absent from work, I don't get paid—like for today. Because I keep coming to the hospital, I get less money than I was counting on. At the end of the month, I am not able to do all the things I wanted to do."
Country: ______________________________ (1)

"I was afraid if I were to take time off when I am sick and also take time off when my daughter is sick, I would be taking too much time off. The people above me [my supervisors] at the company will disapprove. So when I am sick, I try to go to work. It is only when my daughter is seriously sick, then I would take time off." Country: ______________________________ (2)

"When I have an episode, I feel dizzy and I have a pain in my chest and bones. My heart beats faster and faster. I feel so tired. Sometimes I feel like sleeping. Unfortunately, my employer does not give me permission to go and rest, even when I have these pains. She tells me to just do things slowly, but she never gives me time to go and rest." Country: ______________________________ (3)

"[Illnesses are] unscheduled, you don't know your kid is going to get sick. You try not to get them sick but they go to school, and there's other sicknesses . . . One morning, [my son] didn't want to go [to school because he was sick] . . . I made him go, and because I made him go, I had to come and get him—the school wouldn't let him walk home . . . [My supervisor] told me to get someone else to do it [even though] I was able to be back in an hour . . . Who did she want to do it, some stranger?"
Country: ______________________________ (4)

"[My daughter] was sick back in the fall. She got real sick. It was a combination of asthma and just a real bad cold. I remember I had to get in [to work] and so I left her [at home] . . . And then I ended up spending almost the whole day at work . . . just calling [home] . . . She needed me here, but I felt like I had to be at work." Country: ______________________________(5)

"If I have an appointment with the doctor, I asked for permission . . . They let me leave 15 minutes before such and such hour . . . And if I wasn't there at the end of the hour, they called on the phone. And that is what caused me to leave. Because I felt like a slave." Country: ______________________________ (6)

Experiences with Work Hours

"My employers were not very nice. I would [work] without [having] lunch and the hours were very long. I worked without eating and it was very hard . . . The main thing that drove me to leave the job was that I was working long hours without food. I really felt it was impossible for me to work so hard without eating anything." Country: ______________________________ (7)

"I start work at seven in the morning and I leave at six at night. It's all day but I take my daughter with me. Sometimes my husband leaves at six at night and there's no food ready for him, but like I said: I work."
Country: ____ (8)

Experiences Working at Night

A twenty-seven-year old mother worked the night shift at a grocery store, leaving her three children aged two, four, and six alone at home: "I feel worried, even though I make sure to close the gas pipes in the house . . . My neighbors told me [that the children had wandered onto the street alone]. It's a big risk, because a car could run over them or someone could kidnap them." Country: ______________________________________ (9)

"As . . . [my husband] was not working, I worked day and night, until nine or ten at night. I was so tired that I just fell asleep, unable to take care of anything else. In the morning I took [the kids] to school, then I went to work. Days went by, a year went by like that. If I did not work, how could I provide for the children?" Country: ______________________________(10)

"No, I do not like it. . . . Because I always have to ask someone to take my child from the kindergarten, take care of her, feed her, and sit with her. Either my husband or I could not make it and we do not know whom we can ask. I [would] like [to have a] working day until 6 P.M.—for example, from 9 A.M. to 6 P.M.—in order for me to have time to take my child from the kindergarten and to be at home the whole weekend. . . . I work until 10 P.M., plus an additional thirty minutes to get home." Country: ____________________________ (11)

Were you able to guess which country each quote was from? Most people find it difficult to do so. Experiences are indeed mirrored across national borders when it comes to what it means to get sick at work, to have family members get sick and to lack the necessary leave from work to be able to care for them, and for adults to have to work evenings or nights when family members are depending on them. The facts simply do not support the argument that human experiences are too different around the globe to ever reach an agreement on the basic minimum standards needed at work.

Do Countries Take Divergent Approaches to Similar Problems? A Look at the Evidence

The second common argument against global standards contends that even if the problems people face are similar, high- and low-income countries will predictably take different approaches to address these issues. Is this true?

Can we guess which countries have laws to protect working men and women from the worst abuses in the workplace? Which nations have the most generous guarantees of paid leave? Are they easily distinguished from the countries that offer few protections to their workers? Are these differences based on the countries' incomes and resources? Here again we ask you to critically appraise the evidence, this time assessing the approaches taken by different governments. To help make this easier, we provide the countries and we ask you to match them with their policies.

COMPARISONS—PART 2

Paid Annual Leave

1. Azerbaijan	a) 14 days of leave after one year of service
2. Benin	b) 6 days of leave after one year of service, increasing annually to a maximum of 12 days
3. China	c) 1 day of leave for every 20 days worked during the previous year
4. India	d) At least 21 days of leave
5. Mexico	e) 28 days of leave
6. Pakistan	f) At least 4 weeks of leave for those aged 21 and over, and at least 5 weeks for those under 21
7. Paraguay	g) 5 days of leave after 1 to 9 years of service, 10 days after 10 to 19 years, and 15 days after 20 years or more of service
8. Russia	h) 12 consecutive days of leave after up to 5 years of service, 18 consecutive days after 5 to 10 years, and 30 consecutive days after 10 years or more of service
9. Switzerland	i) None
10. United States	j) 2 days of leave for each month of work

Leave for New Mothers

1. Brazil	a) 18 weeks of leave at 100 percent of earnings, and 40 weeks of childcare leave paid at 60 percent of earnings
2. Canada	b) 22 weeks of leave at 70 percent of earnings, and unpaid "baby care" leave until the child turns 3
3. Cuba	c) 12 weeks of leave at 100 percent of earnings
4. Finland	d) 15 weeks of leave at 55 percent of earnings for childbirth, and 37 weeks of childcare leave
5. India	e) At least 8 weeks of leave at 100 percent of earnings every 3 years

6. Malawi	f) 17.5 weeks of leave paid at 25 to 90 percent of earnings (with higher percentages paid to lower-wage earners) for childbirth, 26 weeks of paid parental leave, and paid "childcare leave" until the child is 3 years old
7. Mexico	g) 6 weeks of leave before childbirth and 6 weeks after childbirth, paid at 100 percent of earnings
8. Mongolia	h) 120 days of leave paid at 100 percent of earnings
9. United Kingdom	i) 12 weeks of unpaid leave
10. United States	j) 6 weeks of leave paid at 90 percent of earnings, and 33 weeks paid at a flat rate or at 90 percent of earnings, whichever is lower

Sick Leave

1. Eritrea	a) Up to 180 days; paid at 50 percent of earnings for the first 20 days and at 66.6 percent thereafter, payable after a 3-day waiting period
2. Guatemala	b) 12 weeks of unpaid leave for a serious health condition
3. Iceland	c) Until recovery; paid at 80 percent of full earnings from days 2 to 14 with a ceiling on payments after day 15
4. Italy	d) 26 weeks paid at 66.6 percent of earnings, payable after a 3-day waiting period
5. Mexico	e) 6 months; paid at 100 percent of earnings for the first month, 50 percent for the next 2 months, and unpaid thereafter
6. Seychelles	f) 52 weeks paid at 60 percent of earnings, payable after a 3-day waiting period
7. Spain	g) 190 days; paid at 100 percent of earnings for the first 60 days and at a flat monthly rate thereafter
8. Sweden	h) 52 weeks in a 24-month period, paid at 100 percent of earnings for the first 14 days and at a flat rate thereafter

9.	Tanzania	i)	126 days; paid at 100 percent of earnings for the first 63 days and 50 percent thereafter
10.	United States	j)	12 months; paid at 60 percent of earnings for days 4 to 20 and 75 percent thereafter, with a possible extension to 18 or 30 months for special cases

Breastfeeding Breaks

			Mothers can take:
1.	Belarus	a)	Two half-hour breaks per day or reduce work hours by one hour per day
2.	Dominican Republic	b)	Two one-hour breaks per day in the child's first year
3.	India	c)	Two half-hour breaks per day
4.	Italy	d)	One half-hour break every 3 hours in the child's first 3 years; women with two or more children under 3 years of age are entitled to one-hour breaks
5.	Jordan	e)	Two breaks per day in the child's first 15 months
6.	Mexico	f)	No breastfeeding breaks
7.	Norway	g)	One hour per day in the child's first year
8.	Spain	h)	Three 20-minute breaks per day in the child's first year
9.	Syria	i)	One hour of absence from work per day in the child's first 9 months, which can be divided into two breaks, or a half-hour reduction of the workday
10.	United States	j)	One hour-long break per day in the child's first year

How did you do? Most of us who have tried this brainteaser have found that it destroys many stereotypes that are based on assumptions about how predictably a country's wealth or geography determines its policy approach. Still, a reasonable question remains about a global consensus: Will a different picture of the evidence of global similarities and differences in national approaches emerge if all countries are examined?

Evidence on the Degree of Consensus from the Global Data

As described in Chapter 1, we launched a multiyear program to analyze labor legislation from countries that make their laws available in any of five of the six UN official languages, in original or in translation, or in any of five additional languages for which our team had functional fluency. This enabled us to examine labor policy for 190 of the 192 countries in the United Nations.[7]

In this section, we let the countries' actions speak for themselves by presenting the laws passed by nations around the world. While laws on the books do not guarantee implementation, they dramatically increase the probability of implementation as well as raise countries' ability to enforce regulations. Moreover, written laws are the closest representation of individual countries' views on the importance of certain policies.

The results were striking: while a great variability exists in the ways in which different rights are constructed, an exceptional degree of consensus prevails about people's rights to certain basic protections. Below are details on sample policies on which there is remarkably clear global consensus.

Guarantee of a Day of Rest

There is a clear consensus about the fact that people should not have to work nonstop, without a break or a day off during the week. International agreement was reached nearly a century ago regarding the importance of all adults having breaks or rest from work. Shortly after its formation, the International Labour Organization passed a convention to ensure that workers receive a full twenty-four hours of rest each week. Passed in 1921, the ILO's C14 Convention was created in response to profound concerns about the sweatshop hours that had emerged with industrialization. To date, 119 countries have ratified this treaty.[8] This was not the only agreement that recognized the importance of time away from work. The Universal Declaration of Human Rights was adopted unanimously by the United Nations in 1948 and has been reaffirmed by 171 countries in the Vienna Declaration of 1993, including the United States, which has

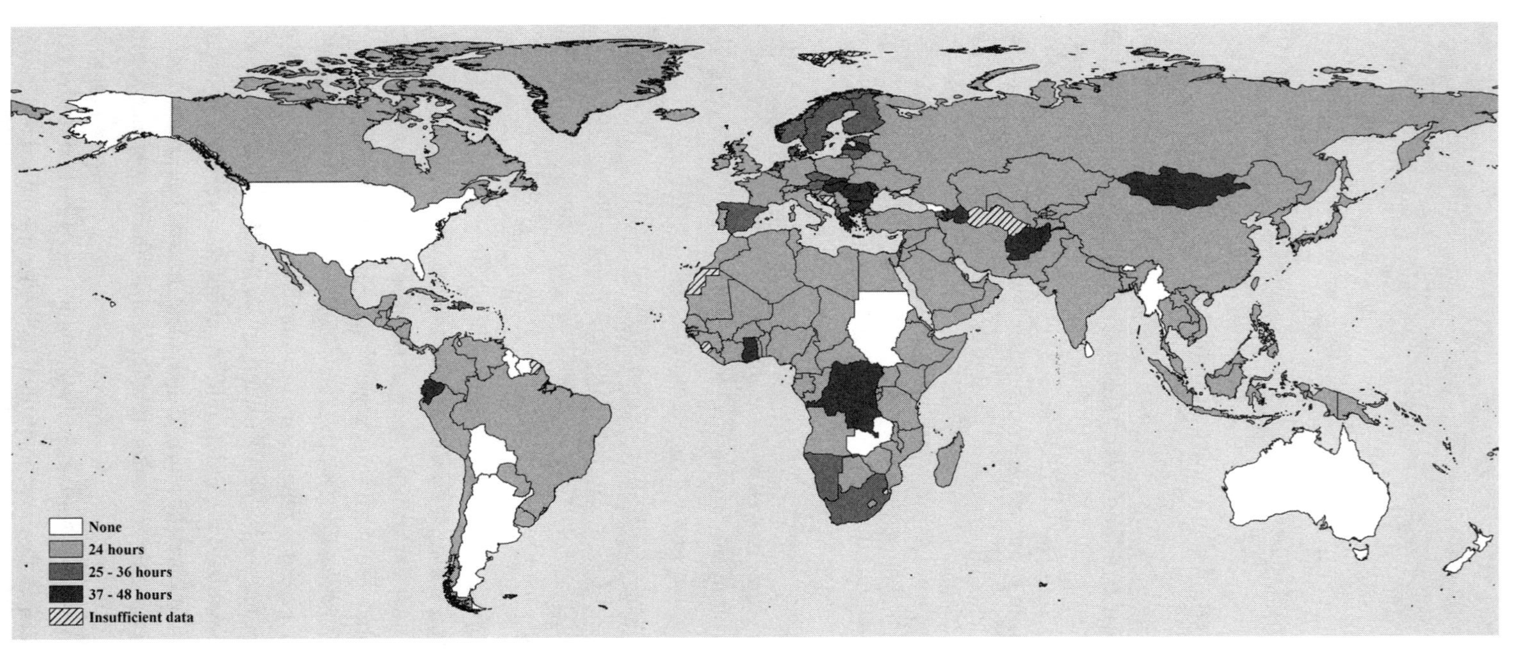

MAP 5.1 Global Availability of a Weekly Day of Rest

signed relatively few international agreements.[9] Article 24 states that "everyone has a right to rest and leisure, including reasonable limitation of working hours and periodic holidays with pay."[10] There is no ambiguity in these affirmations.

Guarantees of a weekly day of rest have been widely adopted in legislation by countries around the world as well as agreed upon in international conventions. One hundred fifty-seven nations have passed legislation requiring all employers to give workers at least one day off every week (see Map 5.1). These laws have been passed by many of the world's largest economies, including all of the countries in the European Union. Notable omissions are the United States, Australia, and New Zealand, which find themselves in the company of a small number of far poorer nations, including Myanmar, Sudan, Zambia, and Bolivia.

Consensus regarding the importance of providing workers with at least one day of rest per week transcends rich and poor countries. Eighty percent or more of countries in each income quartile guarantee at least twenty-four hours of rest each week. Guarantees of longer rest periods of between twenty-five and forty-eight hours in duration are slightly more frequent in high-income countries (26 percent) than in upper-middle-income nations (22 percent), while they are provided by 14 percent of lower-middle-income and 8 percent of low-income countries.

Limits on Mandatory Overtime and Guarantees of Overtime Wage Premiums

A widespread consensus regarding the importance of ensuring reasonable work hours is similarly reflected in international treaties. The UN's International Covenant on Economic, Social and Cultural Rights (ICESCR) declares that all countries should "recognize the right of everyone to the enjoyment of just and favorable conditions of work which ensure, in particular . . . reasonable limitation of working hours and periodic holidays with pay, as well as remuneration for public holidays."[11] One hundred fifty-seven countries have accepted the ICESCR.[12]

In order to address the need for reasonable work hours and to minimize excessively long shifts, a significant number of countries have passed legislation to limit overtime. Other nations guarantee a wage premium for overtime work, meaning that wages for overtime hours are paid at a higher rate than regular hours (see Map 5.2). Overtime premiums are offered in 149 countries, and the majority mandate premiums of between 126 and 150 percent of usual wages. Some nations have adopted a dual-approach by both limiting mandatory overtime and offering premiums for overtime hours. Other nations provide workers

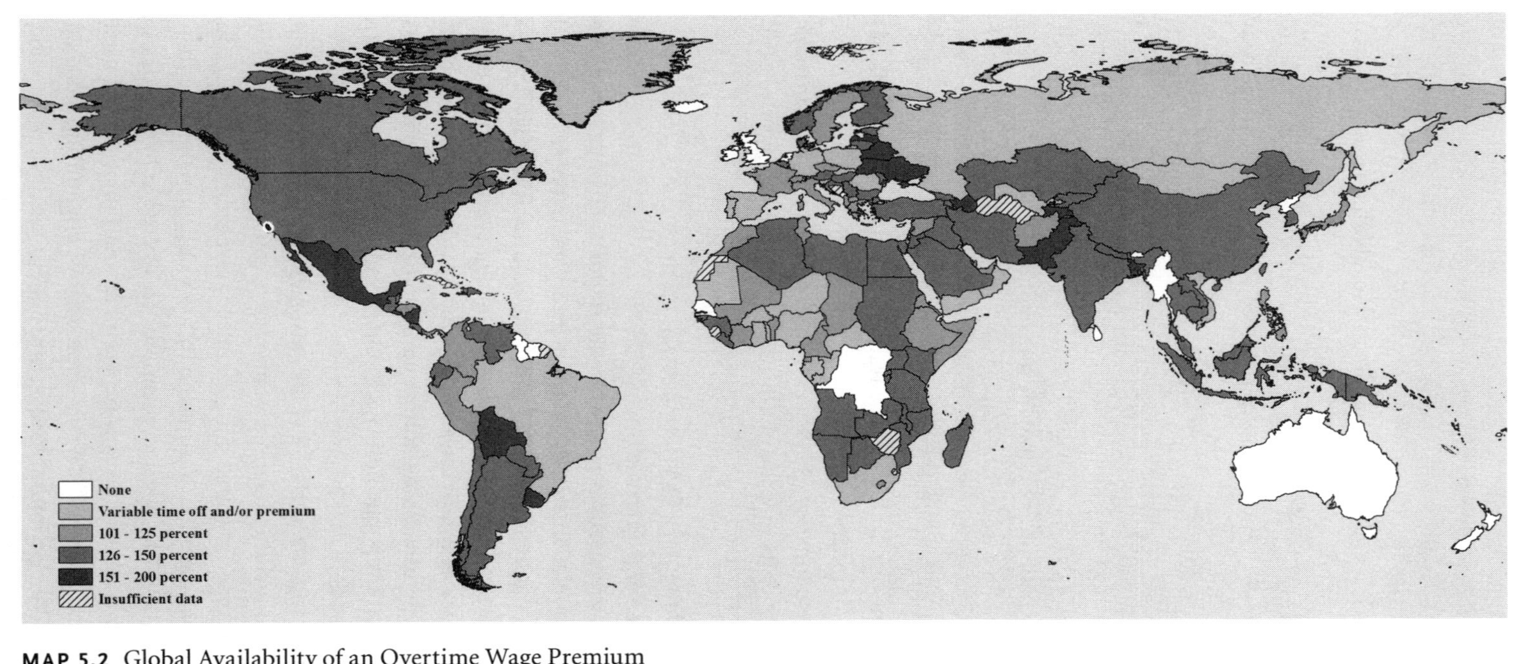

MAP 5.2 Global Availability of an Overtime Wage Premium

NOTE: "Variable time off and/or premium" indicates that overtime is remunerated with compensatory time off and/or a premium, which can be determined by legislation, by decree, or by collective bargaining.

with compensatory time off. Still others ensure that workers have a choice between taking compensatory time off or a wage premium, and in Yemen, workers get both compensatory time off and extra compensation for overtime.

Guarantee of Paid Annual Leave

As with the provision of a day of rest and of overtime pay, the recognition of people's need for leave from work each year to spend time with family and friends or to care for themselves is reflected in national legislation as well as international agreements. As noted above, 157 nations have agreed upon the importance of annual leave in the ICESCR, and all countries in the UN have agreed to abide by the Universal Declaration of Human Rights, which recognizes the importance of annual leave for all workers.

Paid annual leave is mandated in the national legislation of 164 countries in all geographic regions around the world and at all economic levels (see Map 5.3). This includes countries as diverse as the Bahamas and Botswana, the Republic of Korea and Kuwait, Somalia and Syria, and Cambodia and Cuba.

Consensus is widespread across countries with differing income levels that everyone has a right to annual leave. Paid annual leave is guaranteed to workers in 96 percent of low-income nations, 90 percent of lower-middle-income nations, 94 percent of upper-middle-income nations, and 90 percent of high-income nations.[13] The only middle- and high-income nations that do not ensure paid annual leave are the United States, Brunei, Liechtenstein, Guyana, Suriname, and the island nations of Trinidad and Tobago, St. Lucia, St. Vincent and the Grenadines, Jamaica, Tuvalu, and Kiribati.

Considerable consensus holds that the minimum standard of paid annual leave should be at least two weeks.[14] Nearly all (91 percent) of the nations guaranteeing annual leave for which we had duration data ensure at least two weeks. Over half of the nations guaranteeing leave exceed this two-week standard, with 20 percent providing three weeks and 38 percent providing four weeks or more.[15]

Guarantee of Paid Sick Leave

Although, remarkably, no international convention guarantees workers the ability to take leave from work when they are sick, the global consensus around the right to sick leave is as prevalent as that concerning the right to reasonable work hours and rest. There is strong evidence that paid leave is crucial to employees' ability to meet their own health needs, to rest and recuperate, and to avoid taking longer periods of time off in the future due to

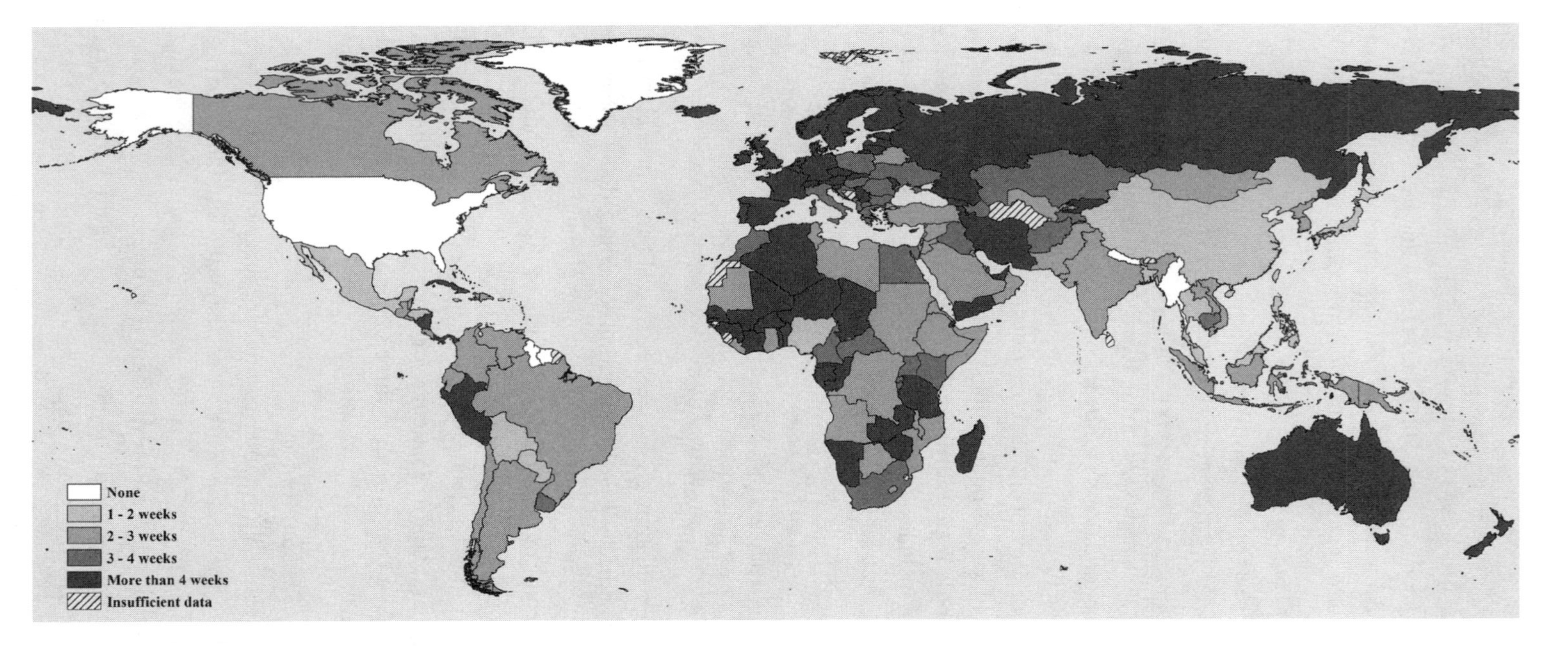

MAP 5.3 Global Availability of Paid Annual Leave

exacerbated health problems.[16] The availability of paid leave reduces both the spread of disease and the cost of obtaining proper medical treatment when necessary.[17] Furthermore, it affects people's performance because people cannot be as productive at work when they are sick as when they are healthy.

Most countries guarantee job protection and income for employees who become ill (see Map 5.4). The United States and the Republic of Korea are the only industrialized nations that lack sick leave legislation.

Two key elements define sick leave protection: the amount of time allowed and when—or how soon—it can be used. Paid leave for personal health needs is provided by 163 nations. Of these, ninety-eight guarantee at least six months of paid leave to recover from a serious illness. Only two countries provide less than ten days. Both high- and low-income countries consistently guarantee paid sick leave. The primary difference across nations is that higher-income countries are more likely to be able to guarantee longer income support during serious illness.[18]

A majority of nations (120 out of 163) have legislation to ensure that employees are covered on the very first day of any illness requiring absence from work (see Map 5.5). An additional ten countries provide coverage on day one only for "serious illnesses."[19]

Guarantee of Paid Leave for Mothers

The benefits of ensuring that mothers have time off around the birth or adoption of a child are numerous, varied, and well known. They include improving the health and development of the infant as well as the health and economic outcomes of the mother.

The importance of ensuring paid maternity leave was stipulated in the UN Convention on the Elimination of All Forms of Discrimination against Women (CEDAW), which has been accepted by 185 countries.[20] CEDAW specifies:

> In order to prevent discrimination against women on the grounds of marriage or maternity and to ensure their effective right to work, state parties shall take appropriate measures: (a) to prohibit, subject to the imposition of sanctions, dismissal on the grounds of pregnancy or of maternity leave and discrimination in dismissals on the basis of marital status; (b) to introduce maternity leave with pay or with comparable social benefits without loss of former employment, seniority, or social imbalances.[21]

Paid leave for new mothers is also protected under the International Covenant on Economic, Social and Cultural Rights: "Special protection should be

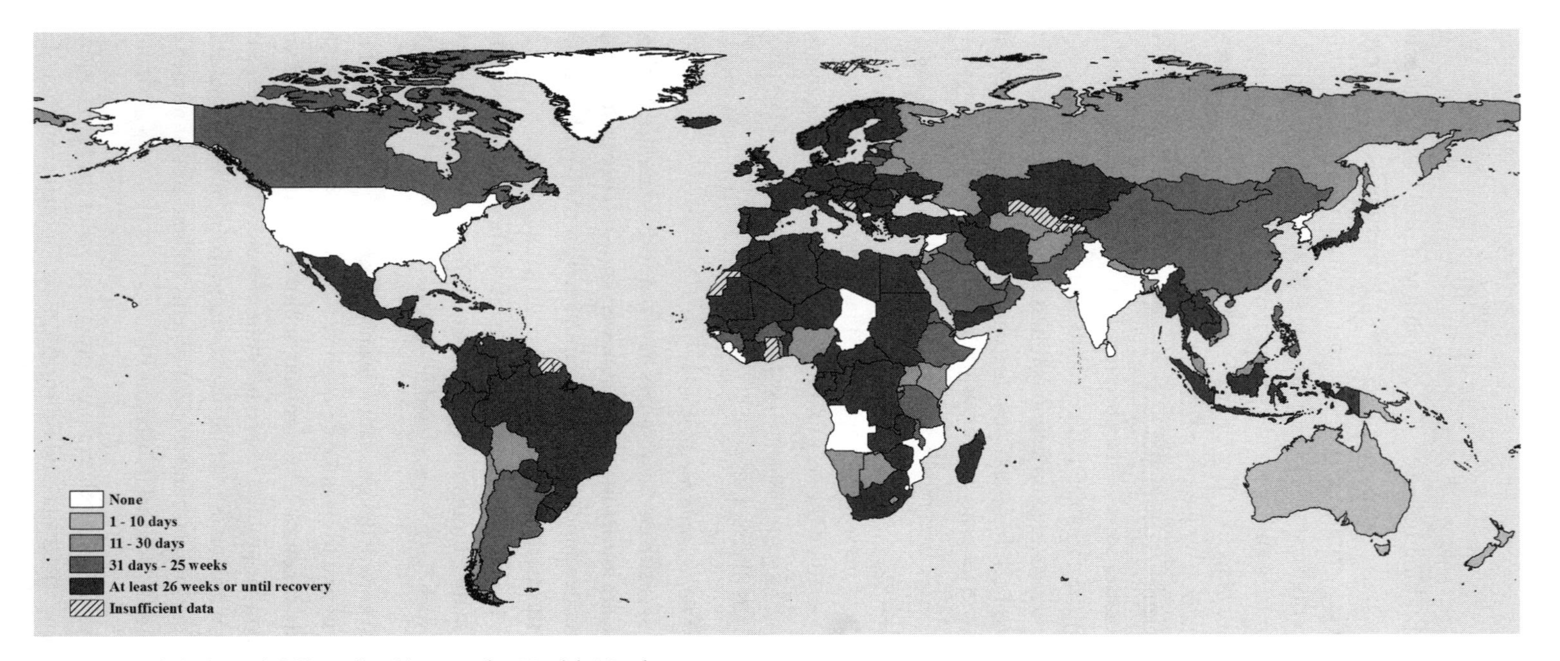

MAP 5.4 Global Availability of Paid Leave for Health Needs

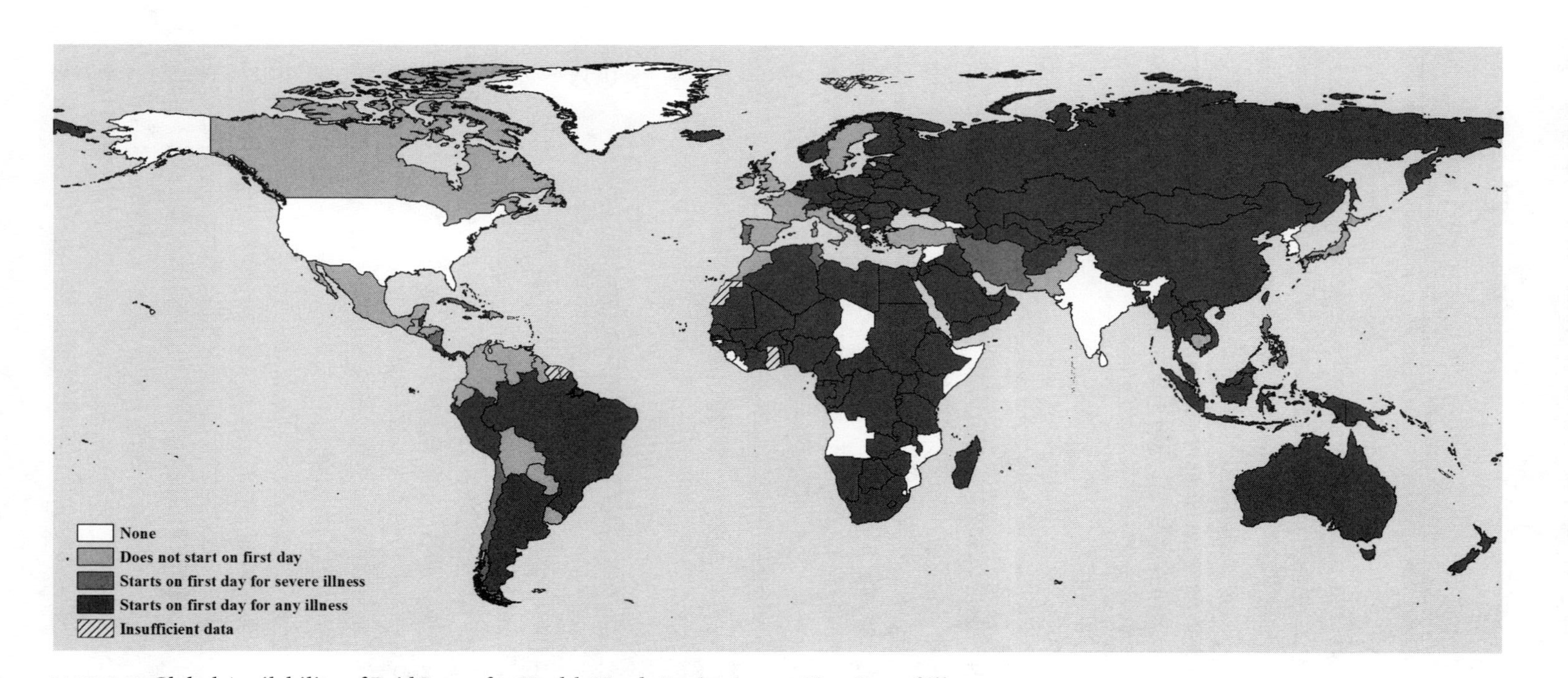

MAP 5.5 Global Availability of Paid Leave for Health Needs Beginning on First Day of Illness

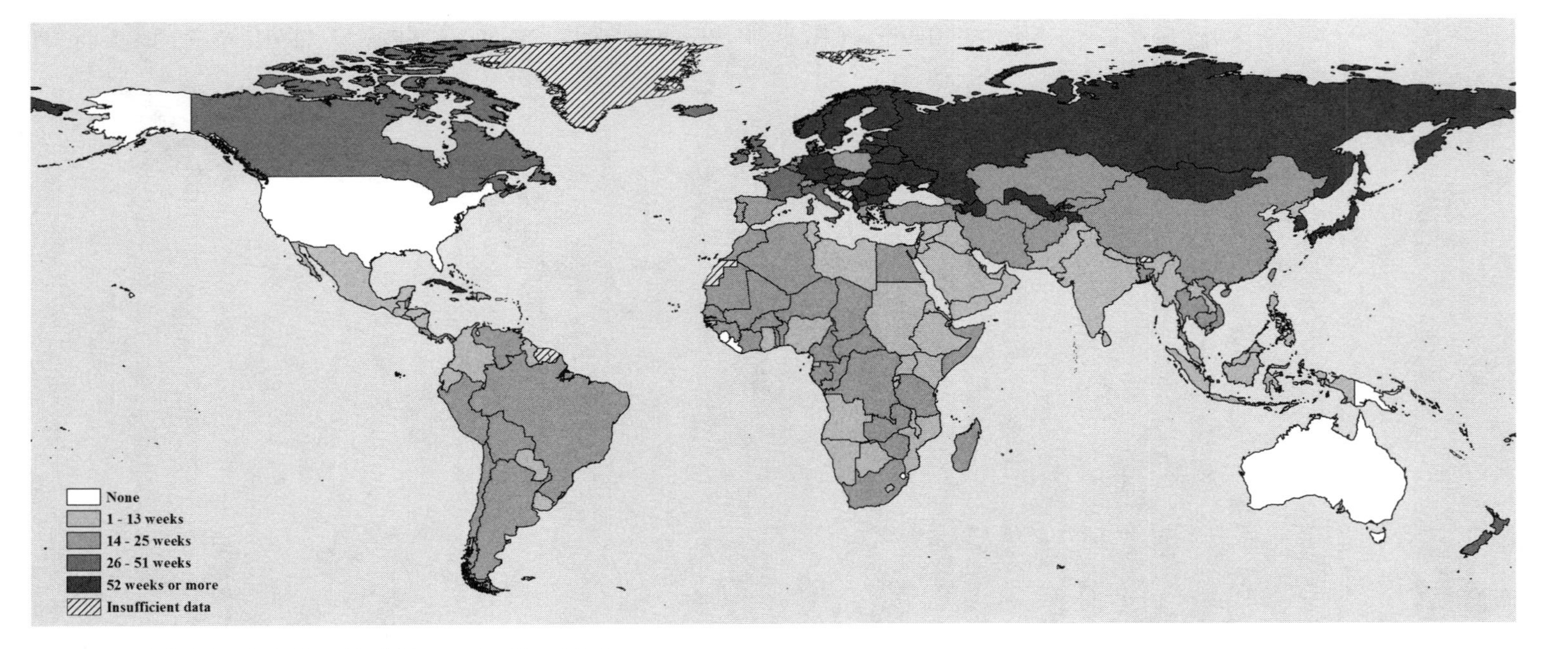

MAP 5.6 Global Availability of Paid Leave for New Mothers

accorded to mothers during a reasonable period before and after childbirth. During such period, working mothers should be accorded paid leave, or leave with adequate social security benefits."[22]

Paid leave for mothers is guaranteed in the national legislations of 177 nations, including nations from all levels of income and economic development and from all parts of the world (see Map 5.6). No other policy has achieved greater global consensus. One hundred and one countries for which we had sufficient data offer fourteen weeks or more of paid leave for new mothers, as is suggested by the ILO. Twenty-nine nations, mostly from Europe and Central Asia, guarantee one year or more.

Guaranteeing paid maternal leave is the norm across nations with different income levels. The only variation by income is in the duration of leave provided. The lower-income nations are somewhat more likely to provide relatively short leave (less than fourteen weeks), and the likelihood of being entitled to a period of long leave (six months or more) generally increases with country income. Six percent of low-income nations guarantee twenty-six weeks or more, while 16 percent of lower-middle-income nations, 24 percent of upper-middle-income nations, and 44 percent of high-income nations do so.[23]

Ensuring sufficient income for new mothers, as well as duration of leave, is something many countries have also put into legislation. For example, Croatia and Serbia offer at least one year of paid leave and guarantee full wages for the duration; Peru, Argentina, and Chile offer at least fifteen weeks with full wages; Bolivia guarantees three months of paid leave at 95 percent of regular wages; and Mongolia offers four months of paid maternity and up to three years of childcare leave at 70 percent of usual wages. Some nations also ensure that the lowest income mothers have adequate resources during their leave by guaranteeing a minimum level of benefits.

The exceptions we found to the near universality of providing paid leave include four countries—two poor and two quite affluent—that provide unpaid leave.[24] Swaziland provides twelve weeks of unpaid maternal leave while Papua New Guinea provides six weeks. In spite of its affluence, the United States also provides only twelve weeks of unpaid leave for mothers and fathers, while Australia provides one year of unpaid leave and a means-tested "baby bonus" benefit. If Australia begins paid parental leave in 2011 as planned, the United States will be left alone among affluent nations.

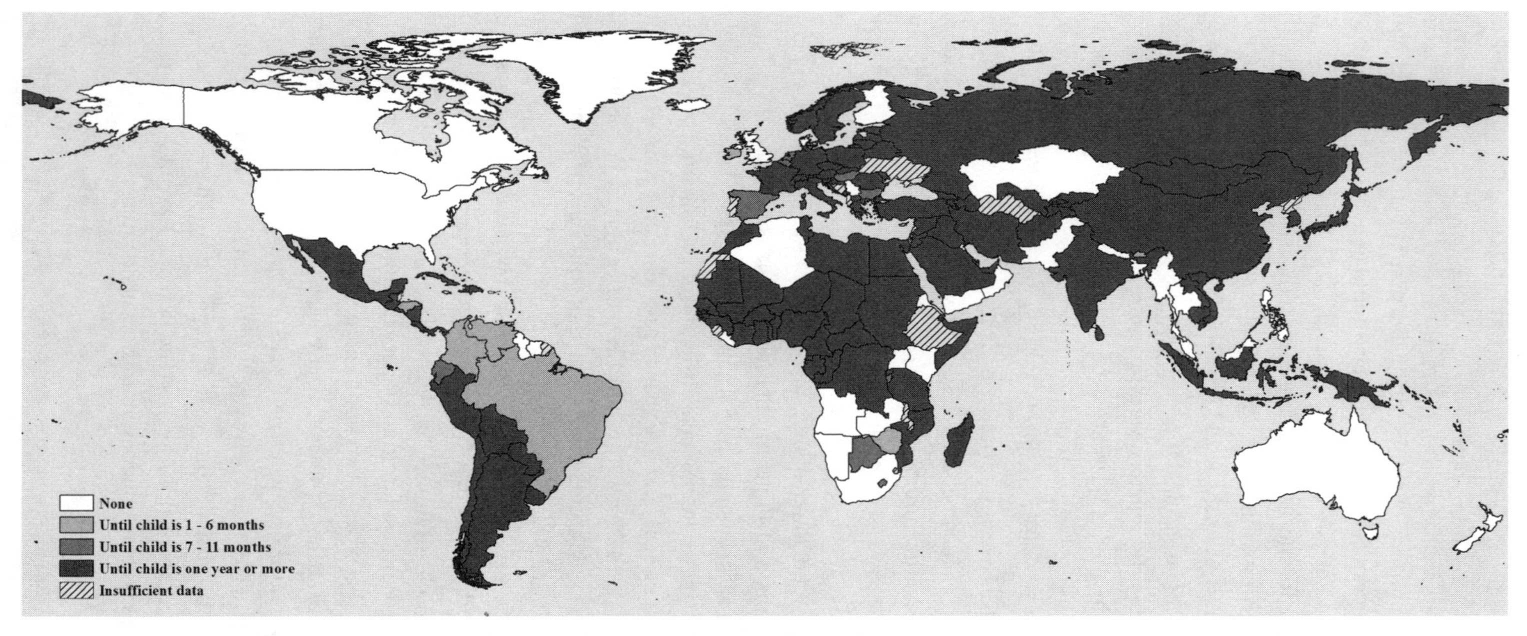

MAP 5.7 Global Availability and Duration of Breastfeeding Breaks at Work

Guarantee of Breastfeeding Breaks

Breastfeeding has been demonstrated to markedly reduce the risk of infections in infancy and early childhood, including diarrheal disease,[25] respiratory tract infections,[26] otitis media,[27] meningitis,[28] and other infections.[29] Studies have repeatedly shown that, as a result, breastfeeding leads to lower mortality rates.[30] It has demonstrable benefits to children's cognitive development[31] and to maternal health.[32]

UN conventions have recognized the importance to both mother and child of guaranteeing women the right to breastfeed without facing discrimination and of ensuring infants the right to the higher levels of health that breastfeeding provides. The Convention on the Rights of the Child (1989), signed by 193 countries, affirms "the right of the child to the enjoyment of the highest attainable standard of health" and calls for "appropriate measures to reduce infant and young child mortality." Specific reference is made to the "advantages of breastfeeding."[33] CEDAW, which as mentioned above has been ratified by 185 nations, states that women should have appropriate services in connection with pregnancy and lactation.[34] In 2000, working women's right to breastfeed was included in the International Labour Organization Conference's new Maternity Protection Convention (Convention 183). Among other rights, it calls for paid breastfeeding breaks and protection against discrimination on the basis of breastfeeding.[35] It is, however, still too early to know how many nations will ultimately approve this convention.

While the benefits of breastfeeding are well established, it can be difficult to continue breastfeeding while working away from one's infant if breaks are not granted to nursing mothers to go to breastfeed their child, if childcare facilities are not onsite or nearby, and if there are no facilities for using a breast pump and storing milk.[36] Have national policy makers passed legislation to reduce these difficulties, and have they ensured that mothers can breastfeed their infants for the six-month duration recommended by the World Health Organization?[37]

Breastfeeding breaks are provided in 132 nations (see Map 5.7), and 104 countries guarantee breastfeeding breaks until the child is at least one year old or for the duration of breastfeeding.

The majority of countries guarantee the right to breastfeed—with the greater protections among lower-income countries. Breastfeeding breaks are guaranteed by 78 percent of low-income nations, 77 percent of lower-middle-income nations, 69 percent of upper-middle-income nations, and 62 percent of high-income countries. While the absolute benefits to breastfeeding are greater in poor countries because of the frequently inadequate water supply and higher rates of infectious diseases among all children, the marked improvements in relative risk of morbidity and mortality attributable to breastfeeding hold in high-income countries as well.[38]

The high-income countries without protection for breastfeeding among working mothers include, among others, Australia, Denmark, Iceland, New Zealand, the United Kingdom, and the United States. In comparison, many low-income countries manage to provide breastfeeding breaks for one year or more, including Benin, Burkina Faso, Cambodia, Chad, Haiti, Laos, Mali, Papua New Guinea, Rwanda, Somalia, and Togo.

Where Do Countries Diverge? The Gaps in the Maps

In summary, the facts refute the claims that cultural differences are too great, that national income levels determine the nature of all labor policies, and that the global community could never reach a consensus on the components of a floor of decent working conditions. Over 150 nations have signed a series of major conventions reflecting their agreement on several key issues.

More compelling evidence than the signing of agreements—public acts that nations sometimes perform under pressure and without intentions of following up—is that over 150 countries have passed their own national legislation guaranteeing many of these basic protections.

The policies about which there is global consensus pertain to issues that have been recognized since the industrial revolution. First in Europe and North America where it began, and then in cities in Asia, the Pacific, Latin America, and Africa as it spread, the industrial revolution transformed the nature of work in one country after another. As large numbers of women and men left homesteads and shops to work for wages in factories, control of their work schedules shifted over to their employers. With this revolution came the ability to mass produce goods at unprecedented levels, but also a renewed vulnerability of working men and women to exploitative conditions. The proposals for limits of work hours and for essential leave arose directly from the types of work abuses the industrial revolution brought forth. Great campaigns were launched to advocate annual leave, days of rest, and maximum work weeks, including initiatives in England such as the Sadler Committee regarding conditions in textile factories,[39] the Ashley Commission regarding conditions in the mines,[40] and Chadwick's report on sanitary problems.[41] The world has since made dramatic progress in these areas.

Peter Gaskell described work in factories in England in the mid-1800s where children were "Cooped up in a heated atmosphere, debarred the necessary exercise, remaining in one position."[42] Working hours were long during the industrial revolution, both in America and Europe. Toward its inception in the 1800s, sewers in factories worked ten-hour days. Children and women working from home worked even longer shifts. Men working in iron production put in twelve-hour shifts. By the mid-1800s, twelve-hour shifts were common in workplaces such as brickyards and tanneries, regardless of age and gender.[43] Only legislation decreased these hours:

> Here, then, is the "curse" of our factory-system; as improvements in machinery have gone on, the "avarice of masters" has prompted many to exact more labor from their hands than they were fitted by nature to perform, and those who have wished for the hours of labor to be less for all ages than the legislature would even yet sanction, have had no alternative but to conform more or less to the prevailing practice, or abandon the trade altogether. This has been the case with regard to myself and my partners. We have never worked more than seventy-one hours a week before Sir John Hobhouse's Act was passed. We then came down to sixty-nine; and since Lord Althorp's Act was passed, in 1833, we have reduced the time of adults to sixty-seven and a half hours a week, and that of children under thirteen years of age to forty-eight hours in the week.[44]

The descriptions of working conditions in nineteenth-century English factories bear a remarkable resemblance to those of conditions in twentieth-century sweatshops half a world away. There was little or no protection against firing, and workers who lost their jobs faced a totally different level of economic vulnerability than when they had been growing their own crops and making their own clothes. Working hours had always been long in farming, crafts, and trades, but individuals also used to control their own schedules. They decided whether to take leave when they got sick or cut back their hours in off-seasons when planting and harvesting were not needed or when their trades were not in particularly high demand.

Many of the guarantees of humane labor conditions that are embodied in the laws discussed in this chapter are an expression of the global response to these risks brought forth by industrialization as it spread around the world. None of these protections came about rapidly; rather, they developed slowly over the course of more than a century—from the earliest enactment of paid maternity leave in 1883 in Germany to its recent passage in Lesotho in 2005.

While the maps in this chapter show that there is now an overwhelming global consensus regarding workers' rights to a weekly day of rest, paid annual leave, paid sick leave, and paid leave for new mothers, as well as large consensus on the right to breastfeeding breaks, there are some glaring geographical omissions—namely, the United States. The United States appears in white on nearly every map in this chapter because it has none of these policies in place. The United States does not require employers to provide annual leave or a mandatory day of rest each week, nor does it limit the duration of the workweek or mandatory overtime. Only unpaid leave for serious illnesses is provided through the Family and Medical Leave Act, legislation that covers only half of all workers in the country (only employees who have worked at least 1,250 hours for a firm employing over fifty people).

Why is the United States lagging so far behind? Some American administrations have said that the country simply could not compete in the global economy while providing these protections, an argument we already addressed at length and refuted in Chapter 3. Other administrations have said that putting these protections into policy is not necessary because companies provide them voluntarily. Unfortunately, the reality is that the majority of Americans do not consistently receive paid annual leave,[45] sick leave,[46] or breastfeeding breaks,[47] and only a very small fraction receives paid maternity leave.[48] The maps demonstrate that most countries in the world are playing by a different set of rules, or are at least aspiring to do so. Few would argue that the failure of the United States to abide by these rules is due to cultural differences or to Americans' not valuing sick leave or workers' ability to care for their children and aging parents.

Many of the issues surrounding excessive work hours and sweatshop conditions that were prevalent in nineteenth-century England remain a concern in parts of the world at the beginning of the twenty-first century, but new problems have emerged as well. The nature of work and of workers themselves changed dramatically in the twentieth century and continues to evolve today. Has labor policy kept in step with these changes? The maps in this chapter reveal widespread global consensus regarding many basic rights; however, are there some labor standards on which there has been less consensus and slower progress? What do we still need to work on?

ANSWERS TO COMPARISONS—PART 1

(1) Botswana
(2) Mexico
(3) Botswana
(4) United States
(5) United States
(6) Mexico
(7) Botswana
(8) Mexico
(9) Mexico
(10) Vietnam
(11) Russia

ANSWERS TO COMPARISONS—PART 2

Paid Annual Leave[49]

1.	Azerbaijan	d)	At least 21 days of leave
2.	Benin	j)	2 days of leave for each month of work
3.	China	g)	5 days of leave after 1 to 9 years of service, 10 days after 10 to 19 years, and 15 days after 20 years or more of service
4.	India	c)	1 day of leave for every 20 days worked during the previous year
5.	Mexico	b)	6 days of leave after 1 year of service, increasing annually to a maximum of 12 days
6.	Pakistan	a)	14 days of leave after one year of service
7.	Paraguay	h)	12 consecutive days of leave after up to 5 years of service, 18 consecutive days after 5 to 10 years, and 30 consecutive days after 10 years or more of service
8.	Russia	e)	28 days of leave
9.	Switzerland	f)	At least 4 weeks of leave for those aged 21 and over, and at least 5 weeks for those under 21
10.	United States	i)	None

Leave for New Mothers[50]

1.	Brazil	h)	120 days of leave paid at 100 percent of earnings
2.	Canada	d)	15 weeks of leave at 55 percent of earnings for childbirth, and 37 weeks of childcare leave
3.	Cuba	a)	18 weeks of leave at 100 percent of earnings, and 40 weeks of childcare leave paid at 60 percent of earnings
4.	Finland	f)	17.5 weeks of leave paid at 25 to 90 percent of earnings (with higher percentages paid to lower-wage earners) for childbirth, 26 weeks of paid parental leave, and paid "childcare leave" until the child is 3 years old
5.	India	c)	12 weeks of leave at 100 percent of earnings
6.	Malawi	e)	At least 8 weeks of leave at 100 percent of earnings every 3 years
7.	Mexico	g)	6 weeks of leave before childbirth and 6 weeks after childbirth, paid at 100 percent of earnings
8.	Mongolia	b)	22 weeks of leave at 70 percent of earnings, and unpaid "baby care" leave until the child turns 3
9.	United Kingdom	j)	6 weeks of leave paid at 90 percent of earnings, and 33 weeks paid at a flat rate or at 90 percent of earnings, whichever is lower
10.	United States	i)	12 weeks of unpaid leave

Sick Leave[51]

1.	Eritrea	e)	6 months; paid at 100 percent of earnings for the first month, 50 percent for the next 2 months, and unpaid thereafter
2.	Guatemala	d)	26 weeks paid at 66.6 percent of earnings, payable after a 3-day waiting period
3.	Iceland	h)	52 weeks in a 24-month period, paid at 100 percent of earnings for the first 14 days and at a flat rate thereafter

4.	Italy	a)	Up to 180 days; paid at 50 percent of earnings for the first 20 days and at 66.6 percent thereafter, payable after a 3-day waiting period
5.	Mexico	f)	52 weeks paid at 60 percent of earnings, payable after a 3-day waiting period
6.	Seychelles	g)	190 days; paid at 100 percent of earnings for the first 60 days and at a flat monthly rate thereafter
7.	Spain	j)	12 months; paid at 60 percent of earnings for days 4 to 20 and 75 percent thereafter, with a possible extension to 18 or 30 months for special cases
8.	Sweden	c)	Until recovery; paid at 80 percent of full earnings from days 2 to 14 with a ceiling on payments after day 15
9.	Tanzania	i)	126 days; paid at 100 percent of earnings for the first 63 days and 50 percent thereafter
10.	United States	b)	12 weeks of unpaid leave for a serious health condition

Breastfeeding Breaks[52]

			Mothers can take:
1.	Belarus	d)	One half-hour break every 3 hours in the child's first 3 years; women with two or more children under 3 years of age are entitled to one-hour breaks
2.	Dominican Republic	h)	Three 20-minute breaks per day in the child's first year
3.	India	e)	Two breaks per day in the child's first 15 months
4.	Italy	b)	Two one-hour breaks per day in the child's first year
5.	Jordan	g)	One hour per day in the child's first year
6.	Mexico	c)	Two half-hour breaks per day

7.	Norway	a)	Two half-hour breaks per day or reduce work hours by one hour per day
8.	Spain	i)	One hour of absence from work per day in the child's first 9 months, which can be divided into two breaks, or a half-hour reduction of the workday
9.	Syria	j)	One hour per day in the child's first year
10.	United States	f)	No breastfeeding breaks

6 Addressing Where the World Lags Behind

When we interviewed Pham Dieu Hien in Vietnam, the thirty-three-year-old seemed aged beyond her years. Hien grew up in the shadow of what Americans call the Vietnam War and Vietnamese call the American War—a war that claimed her father's life. This left Hien—at eight years old the oldest child in her family—to take total charge of caring for her younger siblings while attending school.

As she grew into adulthood and the Vietnamese government implemented Doi Moi—an initiative shifting the centrally planned Vietnamese regime to an increasingly open-market economy—the influx of foreign companies and the transition to private ownership made new types of work available. Hien took a job as a seamstress in an athletic shoe factory and got married soon thereafter. She continued to work while she was pregnant with her son Liep, even though her long hours and days were strenuous. In an effort to save most of her maternity leave to use after her child's birth, Hien worked even when she did not feel well, trying to rest at the factory and then return to work. Liep appeared healthy at birth, but it soon became obvious that he was not. His little body was violently rocked by convulsions. He was cared for by his grandparents, despite their own fragile health, and he was ultimately diagnosed with developmental delays as well as epilepsy.

Hien and her family were not alone in caring for a child with chronic conditions. Between 165 and 220 million children around the world are born with or will acquire a physical, behavioral, or learning disability during childhood,[1] and children living in developing countries, such as Vietnam, are at greater risk of being disabled.[2]

Poverty and chronic health and developmental problems limited Liep's life chances, and the deleterious working conditions his parents faced aggravated the situation further. Liep's father had a job playing a wind instrument at funerals, getting paid only per event. This meant that on days when he did not play, he had no income. His mother endured worse conditions at work, as she explained:

> Each time when I took time off—I was working for a Taiwanese athletic shoes employer—the schedule was very demanding. If I took off one day, then three days' salary would be taken off . . . When I had my son, I couldn't continue to work there because I couldn't take time off. If I took time off, the days off would be subtracted from my salary and I would end up not having any income.

This three-day wage penalty—the cost of each day spent caring for her ill son—made Hien's "job" look more and more like unpaid labor, eventually forcing her to look for other work. Hien's husband was able to help with their son's care to some extent while she worked, but he also had to divide his time between caring for his own father, who had hepatitis B, and for his mother, who had severe arthritis.

Vietnam had laws to guarantee that workers were paid sick leave for their own illnesses, but none to care for a sick child or ailing parent. The country also had legislation addressing workplace protections considered essential by most of the global community since the time of the industrial revolution, including overtime pay, a day of rest each week, and annual leave. However, Vietnam's public policies gave little recognition of the transformation that was beginning to occur in men's roles at home and that had already substantially occurred in women's roles at work. No paid leave was provided for new fathers, nor was there sufficient recognition of the fact that the majority of children were now being raised in households where all of the adults worked. In Vietnam, no leave of any kind was guaranteed to workers to care for children past infancy.

> The experience of Erlend Hansen, a machine operator at a Norwegian roofing product company called Isola, could hardly have been more different from Hien's. Erlend had previously worked at a gas company, but his night schedule left him exhausted and placed a strain on his family. This ultimately motivated his move to Isola, where he could work a variety of shifts and enjoyed more flexibility. Erlend's wife Freya had a job at a doctor's office, and together they

had three children, ages six, eleven, and fourteen. Their kids inevitably got sick from time to time, but because in Norway both working parents had a right to take paid days off when their children were sick, Erlend and Freya had no trouble alternating taking leave from their jobs to care for their sick children.

Erlend was hardly alone. Bergitta Olsen was a production worker and machine operator who also worked at Isola. She had initially planned to be there for only a short time, but she ended up staying on for twenty-one years. In describing what it was like to take time off to care for her own children, ages seven and fourteen, she said, "It's never a problem if I need to leave to do something for the kids. Two days ago I had to go meet with my children's teachers. I was on afternoon shift, so I left at 5 P.M. and then came back."

The Norwegians we spoke with knew that the ease with which they could balance working and caring for their families was thanks to the Norwegian government, as well as to their specific workplaces:

Lars Nilsen had worked for offshore oil companies, including Haliburton, before coming to Isola. He wanted to work closer to his parents, who helped to care for his three-year-old son. Like the other fathers, Lars took leave whenever he needed to attend to his child. He clearly recognized the role men were now playing in their children's lives: "Now fathers take as much responsibility as mothers . . . I've had to leave quickly to pick up my son a few times and have had no trouble."

Like Vietnam, Norway provides the basic level of protections that came into force when adults first began entering the industrial workforce. It guarantees overtime pay, a weekly day of rest, and sick leave for those who work. Unlike Vietnam, however, Norway has also made progress in addressing the second wave of changes in work that swept the world—the transformations that left most children and aging family members living in households where all adults work outside the home. Norway mandates that all employers provide ten days of leave for children's health issues and twenty days of compassionate care leave to provide care to a terminally ill family member, whether it be a child or an adult.

Twentieth-Century Transformations

To improve the conditions faced by working adults in today's environment requires knowing not only whether nations have addressed issues that first arose in the nineteenth century, but also whether nations are addressing the dilemmas that accompanied the dramatic demographic and labor force transformations in the last half of the twentieth century. This chapter will look at each of these transformations and their implications for labor policies, and will present data to assess how many countries have caught up and how many lag behind in their response.

Women's Roles and Women's Lives

A truly remarkable transformation in women's roles and lives has taken place over the course of the past century. Gains in equality across spheres—from education to work, from private life to participation in civic and political life—have occurred in nearly every region in the world. While these have not been unaccompanied by reversals and backlash, a girl born into the twenty-first century encounters markedly different chances than one born in the twentieth century. These changes have profound implications for the labor force.

Women's education rose rapidly in the second half of the twentieth century. One way to measure whether this rise led to equity is to look at whether the participation of girls and young women in educational institutions became the same as men's (equal to 100 percent), or if it is less or greater. Data from the World Bank's World Development Indicators, one of the largest global sources on trends in educational enrollment, show that the relative percentage of girls' secondary school enrollment (compared to boys') worldwide rose from 57 percent in 1960 to 94 percent in 2005.[3] Data for university enrollment are available from UNESCO—the other main repository for educational trend data—only as far back as 1990, but even over this shorter time frame significant gains for women occurred. The relative percentage of women's university enrollment (compared to men's) rose from 69 percent in 1990 to 86 percent in 2004 globally.[4]

While the extent of the increase varies, girls' and women's enrollment is increasing in both rich and poor countries. In many cases, women now exceed men in enrollment in high school and university. Higher-income nations saw a rise in the relative percentage of women's enrollment in university education (compared to men's) from 100 percent in 1990 to 124 percent in 2004.[5] In lower-income nations, the growth of girls' educational equality is at the primary and secondary school levels. In low-income nations, the relative percentage of girls' secondary enrollment (compared to boys') rose from 31 percent in 1960 to 80 percent in 2005, and in lower-middle-income nations from 53 percent to 100 percent.[6] The relative percentage of girls' enrollment in primary education (compared to boys') in low-income nations rose from 47 percent in 1960 to 91 percent in 2005, and in lower-middle-income nations from 73 percent to 99 percent. In higher-income nations where primary school enrollment rates were nearly as high among both girls and boys as far back as 1960, there was little room for growth. The relative percentage of girls' enrollment in primary education (compared to boys') rose from 92 percent in 1960 to 98 percent in 2005 in upper-middle-income nations and from 98 percent to 99 percent in high-income nations.[7]

In short, the trend has been toward greater gender equality in education and consequently in preparedness for more high-skilled jobs. Nearly every region in the world demonstrated important gains.[8] As girls' and women's education has risen, so too have their opportunities in the workplace.

The best available long-term data on the transformation in women's labor force participation are from the World Bank. In measuring equality in the workforce, the World Bank uses a different type of indicator than that used by the United Nations for education. It looks at the fraction of the labor force that is made up of women: when the fraction is fifty percent there are equal numbers of men and women in the labor force, when it is less than fifty percent there are fewer women than men, and when it is greater than fifty percent, there are more women than men.

Higher-income nations have seen a greater increase in women's role in the workforce than lower-income nations. In the high-income nations, the percentage of the labor force made up of women increased from 32 percent to 44 percent between 1960 and 2006. In upper-middle-income nations, the increase was from 29 percent to 42 percent, and only the lower-income countries experienced little change.[9]

Over the past half century in the United States, as in the North American region as a whole, the share of the labor force that is made up of women has climbed steadily. While only 32 percent of the labor force was female in 1960, by 2006 that figure had risen to 46 percent. The heightened labor force activity by women helped fuel national economic growth, kept family incomes from falling, and increased gender equity. In Canada, the rise over the same period was even more marked, with women constituting 25 percent of the labor force in 1960 and 47 percent in 2006. Western Europe saw similar growth in female labor force participation (35 percent to 46 percent).[10]

In most places around the world at the subregional level, women's participation in the labor force over the second half of the twentieth century saw increases similar to those in Western Europe and North America. The regions experiencing a marked rise in the percentage of the paid labor force that was comprised of women from 1960 to 2006 include the Caribbean (26 percent to 39 percent), Central America (16 percent to 36 percent), South America (21 percent to 43 percent), Oceania (27 percent to 46 percent), Northern Europe (33 percent to 47 percent), and Southern Europe (25 percent to 42 percent). Increases also occurred in Southern Africa, where women's share of the labor force rose from 31 percent in 1960 to 38 percent in 2006; in Central Asia, where the percentage rose from 42 percent to 46 percent; and in South East Asia, where the percentage rose from 35 percent to 42 percent.

A second pattern can be seen in Eastern, Mid- and Western Africa, where women worked at high rates historically, and where rates have stayed high. This is also the case in Eastern Europe, where the female share of the labor force stayed virtually the same (from 47 percent to 48 percent). Only in West and South Asia was there a slight decline in the female share of the workforce. Between 1960 and 2006, the fraction of the labor force comprised of women went from 31 percent to 28 percent in West Asia and from 31 percent to 30 percent in South Asia. A stalled trend also occurred in Northern Africa, where the increase was only from 24 percent, the lowest rate in Africa, to 25 percent.[11] These regions include some of the nations where women do not have equal opportunities to work due to religious law.

Caregiving for Children

For many centuries the majority of men and women worked to sustain themselves in agriculture and in crafts based out of the home and the farm. During this time, men and women commonly worked alongside children they cared for and children who were being apprenticed to learn—both formally and informally—the skills they would need to survive economically. When the industrial revolution came, and with it large-scale public education, the world in which adults worked and children learned was divided. For a historically brief period, men in the formal labor force far outnumbered women and tasks were largely split. Such gendered divisions of work are not unique in history, but what was truly distinct at that time was the *scale* of the separation of work and caregiving.

Global data on the extent to which people are engaged in paid labor outside of their homes only date back to 1960. Yet in much of North America and Europe as well as in parts of Asia and Latin America, women and men began to leave working at home and on the farm to join the industrial labor force long before that point. Data on labor have been collected in the United States for more than two centuries and illustrate the kind of transformation that likely occurred throughout North America, in much of Europe, as well as in parts of Asia and Latin America. In the United States in 1830, 70 percent of children were being brought up in families operating farms, while only 15 percent had a father working for wages elsewhere.[12] A century later, a clear majority of children were being raised in families in which fathers earned wages or salaries outside the home or farm,[13] and the proportion of children growing up on family-run farms had shrunk to 30 percent.[14] Women's entry into the wage and salary labor force transpired in nearly as large numbers, but it occurred twice as fast as that of men during the second half of the twentieth century. With the majority of women participating in the industrial and postindustrial labor force, the ways in which families met their caregiving needs were completely transformed. With increasing wage work, more and more parents were earning a living away from their homes and the children and adult family members they cared for. Workers maintained less control over their hours and conditions of work, as labor conditions were increasingly prescribed by supervisors and managers.

A relative silence exists when it comes to data about caregiving roles on a global basis. Contributing to the silence may have been that caregiving was undervalued as a role borne by women who were not in positions of power; that caregiving was noticed less because the labor was unpaid; or that the gender imbalance in global statistical agencies and leading academic institutions meant that less attention was paid to this field. Whatever the reason, few historical statistics on caregiving were gathered, and even present-day globally comparative statistics are scarce. We do not know how many hours men and women spend caring for children, elderly parents, and disabled or other family members in most countries around the world today. We know even less about how many hours children and adults spent on these essential tasks two decades ago, five decades ago, or in the last century.

Yet some relevant trends can be observed and some crucial changes inferred. When women have access to education, they have on average fewer children and their children are likely to survive longer. Similarly, when women are in the workforce, they also have on average fewer children. The transformation in both men and women's work means that more children than in recent history are currently being raised in households in which all adults work at a distance from their caregiving. In some of the few countries for which data exist, men are now carrying more of the caregiving responsibilities than in the past, but the sharing across genders more often than not remains far from equal.

How many children globally are being brought up in households where all adults earn a living outside the home? A conservative estimate places this figure at 340 million children under the age of six worldwide.[15] We examined diverse countries using detailed surveys of families' living conditions. In Mexico many children are reared in extended-family households; nevertheless, in 30 percent of households with children under five years old, all adult members work for pay outside of the home. The case is similar for children growing up in Botswana, where in 29 percent of households with children under five, all household adults are in the paid labor force. Children in other countries are even more likely to live in households where all adults are active in the labor force: 41 percent in Brazil, 50 percent in Russia, and 68 percent in Vietnam.

The chances of growing up in a home where all adults work for pay are even greater for school-age children. In Botswana, 31 percent of school-age children live in such households, and the proportions increase elsewhere: 34 percent in Mexico, 49 percent in Brazil, 63 percent in Russia, and 78 percent in Vietnam. We estimate that across the globe at least 590 million children between the ages of six and fourteen live in households where all parents and adult extended family members in the household are working.[16]

Aging of the Population and Care of the Elderly

The need for working adults to care for aging family members is a rapidly growing phenomenon driven both by the exploding size of the aging population and by the rising paid labor force participation of women, who traditionally cared for older family members.

In 2005 there were 672 million people worldwide aged sixty and older. (While the age at which health problems and care needs most commonly increase varies by country, sixty and older is frequently reported by UN bodies.) This number is expected to triple, reaching two billion by 2050. Advances in medicine have resulted in higher survival rates for disabled and elderly adults. The global population aged eighty or over—the age group likely to require the most care—is projected to grow even more rapidly, increasing almost fivefold (from 88 million in 2005 to 402 million in 2050).[17]

While low-income nations often have smaller proportions of elderly populations than higher-income nations, it is in the low-income countries where this age group is growing most rapidly. In these nations the population of people aged sixty or older is expected to quadruple from 155 million in 2005 to 656 million in 2050, and the population of those over eighty is expected to increase sixfold from fourteen million in 2005 to eighty-eight million by 2050. The impact of this marked demographic transformation on low-income countries is likely to be substantial given the already strained resources and existing challenges in these countries. In high-income nations, the population of those aged eighty and older is expected to grow threefold from 38 million in 2005 to 111 million in 2050.[18]

As the aging population increases, the population of full-time caregivers is declining in many places around the globe. While women continue to perform the bulk of caregiving for elderly and disabled family members in developing and industrialized nations alike, the traditional base of available full-time caregivers is shrinking as more women worldwide take up full-time work.[19]

Yet family members remain a major source of social support for the elderly throughout the world. Research from Asian countries, including China,[20] India,[21] Republic of Korea,[22] Malaysia,[23] Nepal,[24] and Taiwan,[25] reveals that the vast majority of elderly people count on their children for care when they are sick; similar evidence is available from regions and countries as divergent as the Caribbean,[26] Saudi Arabia,[27] Turkey,[28] and Botswana.[29] The elderly in the United States and Europe are no different in relying on extended family and friends for unpaid care. In fact, more than half of the elderly inhabitants of OECD countries who are in need of care receive assistance from their children or grandchildren.[30] These demands have significant implications for workplace policies. In the United States alone, over forty-four million adults provide unpaid care to an elderly family member or other adults in need of care.[31]

24/7 Economy and Globalization

The "24/7 economy" is a commonplace term indicating the never-closing economy that exists today. In this environment, people are increasingly working evenings, nights, and weekends. "Bankers' hours," the notion that a well-paid, highly skilled worker would be done with work by 5 P.M., is now as antiquated as the term "ice box," dating from when ice was used for refrigeration. At the high end of the pay scale, financial consultants in the West work round-the-clock in order to be available when stock markets are open around the world. At the low end of the pay scale, low-wage workers are filling factories and call centers that operate twenty-four hours a day. At both ends of the spectrum, technologic advances have enabled employees in one part of the world to work with clients and companies thirteen thousand miles and twelve time zones away. The pressures for evening, night, and weekend work have thus risen further.

The European Foundation for the Improvement of Living and Working Conditions surveyed company managers in twenty-one European Union member states about work schedules at their establishments in 2005.[32] They measured the amount of evening, night, and weekend work by counting the number of respondents who reported that a significant proportion (at least one in five) of their employees was required to work during a nonweekday shift. Using this measure, 25 percent of European managers surveyed required a significant proportion of their workforce to work regularly on Saturdays, 15 percent required a significant proportion to work on Sundays, and 9 percent required employees to work a night shift or some hours between 10 P.M. and 6 A.M. Some nations substantially exceeded these averages. In the United Kingdom, for example, 38 percent of firms required a significant proportion of their employees to work on Saturdays.

The picture is little better in the United States, where certain sectors have been deeply affected by shift work. In the hospitality industry, 38 percent of workers do not work a regular daytime shift and 15 percent work evening shifts; in food services, those proportions are 43 percent and 18 percent, respectively, with the remainder working night shifts, rotating or split shifts, or other irregular schedules. The transportation industry has also been hit hard, with over 29 percent of the workforce working irregular schedules or evening and night hours.[33] Harriet Presser, a U.S. expert on shift work, accurately notes that much of the evening and night work in the United States is low paying and addresses the needs of local rather than global markets, providing services such as twenty-four-hour nursing attendance and food and recreational services.[34]

Implications for Labor Policy

Important implications for needed labor protections arise from the marked increase in the number of workers who are simultaneously engaged in paid work and unpaid caregiving for children, the elderly, or disabled family members, and in the gradually increasing extent to which men and women are more equitably sharing both unpaid and paid work. Just as paid sick leave was crucial for the health of the individual employee when most families had only one adult involved in paid work, today, leave to care for family members is essential for the health of families when all adults in the household work for pay. Similarly, just as paid maternity leave was essential to decent working conditions in a world where women were expected to be the sole providers for infants and children, paid paternity leave is equally essential in order to achieve gender equity.

How far have we come? What do we know about what is still needed? Although the set of demographic transformations that left most children and elderly being cared for by adult family members who had jobs outside of the home occupied the majority of the twentieth century, the passage of guarantees for a floor of decent working conditions is ongoing and still catching up. Perhaps this is not surprising, given that transformations in labor conditions and public- and private-sector policies often lag decades behind social changes, but the cost of delay is high.

Leave for Children's Health Needs

Luis Marquez and Pham Dieu Hien are far from being the only parents whose working conditions markedly affect their ability to care for their children's health. The single best predictor of whether parents take care of their sick children themselves are their working conditions.[35]

Over forty years of research has demonstrated that parents play a critical role in the speed and quality of children's recovery from serious illnesses and injuries, even when doctors, nurses, and other healthcare professionals are available.[36] Parents' irreplaceable roles in assisting children's recovery has been documented both for outpatient procedures[37] and for hospitalization.[38] When parents have to be absent, their sick children suffer.[39] When parents care for their own sick children, children show a more rapid rate of recovery, whether this is measured by vital signs or by earlier hospital discharge. Evidence supporting the importance of parents' availability to help with children's health is clear across a wide range of chronic and acute diseases.[40] Research has demonstrated the tremendous benefits of parental care for children with epilepsy,[41] asthma,[42] and diabetes.[43] Parental involvement is often crucial for children with chronic conditions, in assisting with daily medical routines such as monitoring diet and blood glucose levels and administering medications.

Moreover, children's anxiety typically decreases with greater parental care,[44] and their psychological adjustment to having a serious disease improves.[45] Parental emotional support and involvement are important to children suffering physical ailments;[46] it is equally critical for children facing mental health problems.[47] Because of the importance of parental care, pediatricians have increasingly offered parents the chance to become involved in different aspects of the care of their children's health.[48]

Finally, parents can contribute to the prevention of many of the leading causes of mortality in children worldwide, including vaccine-preventable diseases, diarrhea, respiratory infections, and perinatal problems.[49] However, the extent to which parents can help prevent these deaths is frequently determined by their working conditions. For example, parents are critical to the success of immunizations. In many parts of the world, parents or other adult care providers must take time off work to take their children to clinics or physicians' offices for immunizations or must be home during the day when immunization campaigns occur.[50] Without flexibility or leave from work for children's health needs, parents often forgo crucial disease prevention. In a U.S. study, researchers found that when employees of a large firm reported barriers to leaving work, their children were significantly more likely to be underimmunized.[51] The importance of working conditions was confirmed when researchers directly asked parents about the factors that affected their ability to vaccinate their children. Studies in Haiti,[52] Indonesia,[53] and the United States[54] have found that parents report work schedule conflicts as a significant barrier to getting their children immunized. As noted earlier, similar barriers are encountered when it comes to breastfeeding, which is known to be one of the most important ways to decrease diarrheal disease and respiratory infections.

While children may suffer if parents and caregivers do not have guarantees of paid leave for children's health needs, society pays a price as well. Children sent to daycare while sick with contagious diseases exacerbate the higher rate of observed infections in daycare centers,[55] including higher rates of respiratory infections,[56] otitis media,[57] and gastrointestinal infections.[58] Children left home alone may be unable to consult physicians for diagnoses, medications, or emergency help if their conditions worsen.

Working conditions can determine whether parents are able to care for their children's health. In the United States—a country where the availability of paid sick leave is limited—parents who have paid sick days are more than five times as likely to be able to care for their sick children themselves as parents who do not have paid sick days.[59] Without paid leave to care for children's health needs, working families are placed at risk economically, experiencing wage and job loss when they take time off to care for family members.[60] A comprehensive longitudinal study of working poor families and job loss in the United States found that the ability of working poor mothers to keep their jobs was dramatically affected by their health and the health of their children, even taking into account the mother's years of education, her skills, and the local environment in which she was working. Having a health problem led to a 53 percent increase in job loss among low-wage mothers, and having a child with health problems led to a 36 percent increase in job loss.[61]

The need for and benefits of paid leave for children's health needs may be clear, but how many nations have actually acted on these findings? Of the sixty-five countries with policies enabling working parents to take time off to care for sick children, seventeen provide unpaid leave. Forty-eight countries have policies guaranteeing employees paid leave specifically to care for their children when they are ill (see Map 6.1). Regionally, this type of leave is guaranteed by 68 percent of nations in Europe and Central Asia, 16 percent of nations in East Asia and the Pacific, 9 percent in the Americas, and 11 percent in Sub-Saharan Africa. Only one country in each of the regions of the Middle East and North Africa and South Asia ensures paid leave to care for sick children.

The global provision of paid leave for children's health needs reflects a clear gradient in country income. While only 10 percent of low-income nations provide paid leave to care for ill children, it is guaranteed in 20 percent of lower-middle-income nations, 27 percent of upper-middle-income nations, and 53 percent of high-income nations. Yet the decision reflects political will as well as income, as the regional data illustrate. In the Americas region, of the six nations providing leave for children's health, the three providing only unpaid leave include one very wealthy nation, the United States, and one nation that is among the wealthiest in the Caribbean, the Bahamas, as well as the lower-income Dominican Republic. Canada, an economically successful, industrialized nation with far better protections generally than those in the United States, ensures that leave is paid, while two far poorer nations, Nicaragua and El Salvador, have also passed laws to provide paid leave.

Of the forty-five countries for which data were available to determine the duration of leave granted, just under half mandate that employers guarantee one to ten days of paid leave, while just over half guarantee eleven days or more of paid leave for children's health needs. Fifteen countries guarantee paid leave of thirty-one days or more.[62]

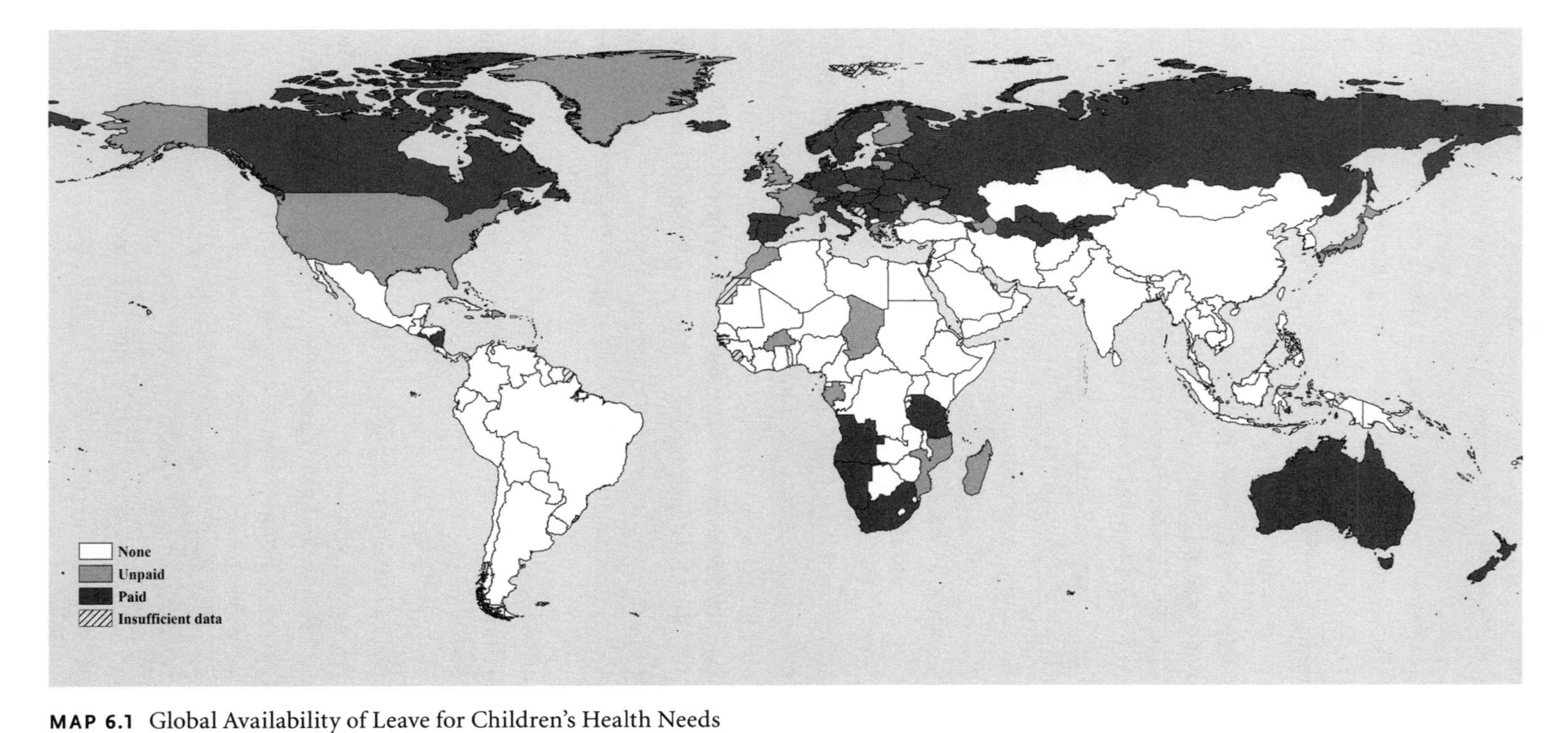

MAP 6.1 Global Availability of Leave for Children's Health Needs

NOTE: Among those countries that provide leave, some only provide it in case of serious illness, hospitalization, or urgent health needs.

Leave to Care for the Health of Elderly and Disabled Family Members

Beyond the importance to the health of children, working conditions also profoundly affect the health of elderly, disabled, and other adults who receive care from employed family members. Research has consistently indicated that adults with more social supports from friends and family live longer.[63] Obtaining higher levels of social support is linked with greater quality of life and chances of survival from postmyocardial infarction,[64] advances in the functional status of stroke victims over time,[65] and better treatment outcomes for mental illness, among other conditions.[66]

Working adults who provide care for other adult members of their families can face formidable obstacles to balancing their multiple responsibilities. Without workplace supports that enable them to fulfill their caregiving responsibilities, both the health and income of working caregivers are often jeopardized. Exacerbated when demands are high, supports low, and working conditions poor, these caregivers have higher rates of heart disease and depression, among other physical and mental health conditions.[67] Furthermore, in the absence of flexibility and paid leave, caring for adult family members can result in wage and job loss.[68]

Flexible scheduling, part-time parity,[69] and leave policies are currently the main workplace resources that are available to those managing employment and adult caregiving responsibilities. Without adequate paid leave and flexibility, it can be difficult for workers to meet their families' health needs.[70] Given the simultaneous global trends of population aging and changes in the labor force makeup, along with the importance of family caregiving to adult health outcomes, how many nations have enacted legislation to ensure that working adults can provide this vital support for their elderly family members?

Workplace policies have been slow to reflect the fact that many working adults are caring for adults as well as children. Only thirty-three countries provide workers with paid leave to care for adult family members: twenty-three from Europe and Central Asia; three from the Americas (Canada, El Salvador, and Nicaragua); three from East Asia and the Pacific (Japan, Australia and New Zealand); one from South Asia (Maldives); three from Sub-Saharan Africa (Angola, Namibia, and Burkina Faso); and none from the Middle East or North Africa (see Map 6.2). Higher-income nations are more likely to guarantee this paid leave: 35 percent of high-income nations provide

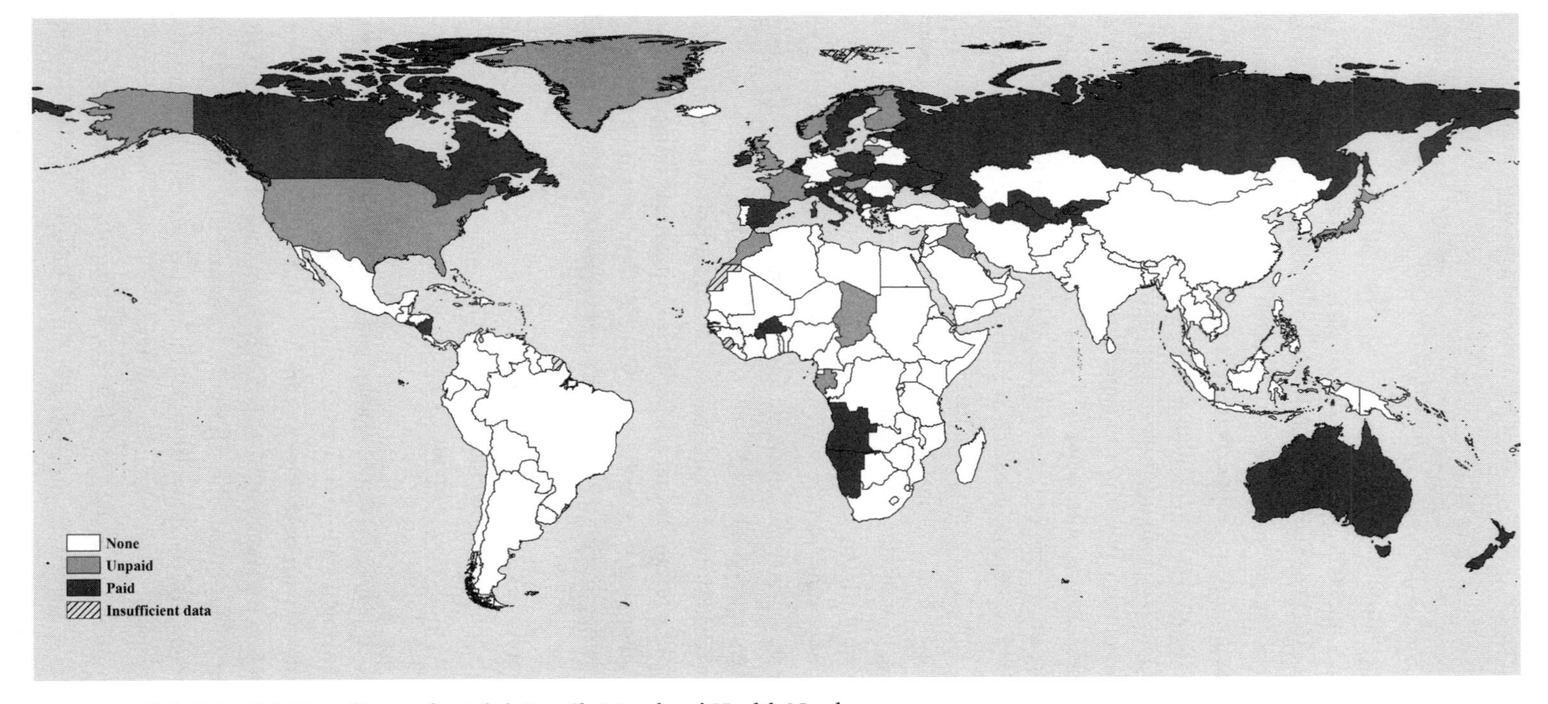

MAP 6.2 Global Availability of Leave for Adult Family Members' Health Needs

NOTE: Among those countries that provide leave, some only provide it in case of serious illness, hospitalization, or urgent health needs.

it, while only 16 percent of upper-middle- and lower-middle-income countries and 8 percent of low-income nations do so.[71]

Sixteen countries provide unpaid leave, yet the laws providing this leave often have significant limitations. Countries sometimes specify that employees are eligible to take leave to care for family members only in certain family relationships, limit leave to cases where family members are seriously or terminally ill, or require a waiting period before payment of benefits begins. For example, through the Family and Medical Leave Act, the United States provides workers with twelve weeks of unpaid leave to care for adult family members; however, only half of workers are covered under the FMLA. In order to be covered, a worker must have been employed by the employer for at least twelve months and have worked at least 1,250 hours in the previous year. The firm must also employ at least fifty employees within a seventy-five-mile radius. Furthermore, the FMLA provides leave only to care for an immediate family member (spouse, child, or parent) who has "a serious health condition." In Morocco, employees are entitled to two days of leave, but only when a child or a spouse is having surgery. In Nicaragua the leave is only for the "grave illness" of a family member, and in Hungary, the unpaid leave covers only close relatives requiring "long-term nursing or care at home." This is a policy area where much progress is needed even in the nations where policies exist. Each of these policies leaves substantial gaps in the ability to provide preventive care, address acute illnesses and injuries, and care for a full range of chronic conditions.

Leave for Children's Educational Needs

The story of Luis Marquez, highlighted in Chapter 2, exemplifies what the brief review of research below demonstrates: working conditions affect the degree to which parents can be involved in their children's education, and children's educational outcomes are markedly influenced by their parents' involvement.[72] A range of studies from North America, Europe, Asia, and the Pacific demonstrate the clear impacts. Studies from both the United States and Britain found that young, school-age children in first and second grades whose parents are actively involved in their education perform better on both reading and math tests as well as on tests of their emotional and social development.[73] In junior high school[74] and high school,[75] children's academic achievement is significantly improved with greater parental engagement. When parents are more engaged, children score better in language and mathematics, exhibit fewer behavioral problems, and sustain greater academic persistence and lower dropout rates.[76] Parental involvement also contributes to the quality of the education of all children within a school.[77] Studies from Australia have similarly shown that parental involvement strongly influences educational outcomes, but beyond that have documented that it is crucial for successful transitions after school.[78]

While most individual studies have been conducted in single countries, on the whole the evidence is clear that the importance of parental participation in children's education is a global phenomenon, affecting children and parents in both industrialized and developing nations.[79] Importantly, as gender equity is growing both at home and at work, fathers' roles are increasingly essential in children's school performance.[80]

A fair amount is also known about how parents can support children who are at risk educationally, including those living in poverty and those with learning disabilities. Low-income children fare better in their education when their parents are involved in their schools.[81] Improvements also occur when parents are involved in helping children learn skills during after-school hours. Time spent together bolsters children's educational chances regardless of whether or not parents have received any specific training.[82] When parents are provided with training, international studies have established that the educational returns on this extracurricular time with children increase.[83] Instructing parents on the best ways to read to their children improves receptive language capacities in particular.[84] Similarly, the oral-reading scores of low-income children significantly improve when their parents are coached in the techniques for allowing children sufficient time to attempt words, correcting after hesitations, and prompting children to repeat words.[85]

Educational outcomes for children with learning disabilities are likewise much improved by parental involvement in their education, both at school and helping at home with homework and reading or math.[86] Children with learning difficulties whose parents are trained and spend time working with them at home fare better on standardized reading tests than children with similar challenges who receive support only at school.[87] While most of the research has concentrated on reading because language-based learning disabilities are the most frequently diagnosed type of disability, there is also strong evidence that parental involvement is important for success in math.[88] Support for homework is critical in helping children with learning disabilities reach their full potential.[89] The structured environments that parents can foster for their children's learning, including rewarding efforts, form the foundation.[90]

Active parental involvement in children's education can occur only when work schedules afford parents the time to be with their children in out-of-school hours as well as the flexibility to meet with teachers or consult with specialists during work days. The negative impact of work-related barriers to parental involvement can be marked. In our U.S. studies, children were 17 percent more likely to score in the bottom quartile of math tests for every hour their parents worked regularly in the evening.[91] Worse yet, when parents had to work at night, their children were nearly three times as likely to be suspended from school.[92]

Low-income children, whose parents face far more work-related obstacles to participating in their education, are at an even greater educational disadvantage. When compared to middle-income parents, low-income parents less frequently have access to paid leave and flexibility at work—policies that parents often need to draw upon in attending to their children's educational, developmental, and health needs during working hours.[93] Data from Britain show that while teachers find that parents who are professionals show greater interest in their children's education, this is largely due to the greater time constraints faced by other working parents.[94] Our research on working families in the United States revealed that two out of five low-income parents confront difficulties in taking part in school meetings, trips, or events. Apart from these organized activities, nearly one in five low-income parents we interviewed had little or no time with their children during the work week because of their work schedules.[95]

It is clear from the evidence that parental involvement is crucial for the positive educational development of children. When parents cannot be adequately available due to restrictive working conditions, long hours, and poor schedules, their children's futures are at risk.[96] Given the importance of parental involvement to children's educational outcomes, how many nations have enacted legislation to make this feasible?

Guarantees of paid leave that can be used for children's educational needs are less common than other forms of leave (see Map 6.3). To our knowledge, only Greece offers paid leave specifically for children's educational needs. Greece offers fully paid family leave for up to four days a year for a working parent to visit a child's school. Switzerland mandates that employers provide flexibility in scheduling for family needs, including the education of children

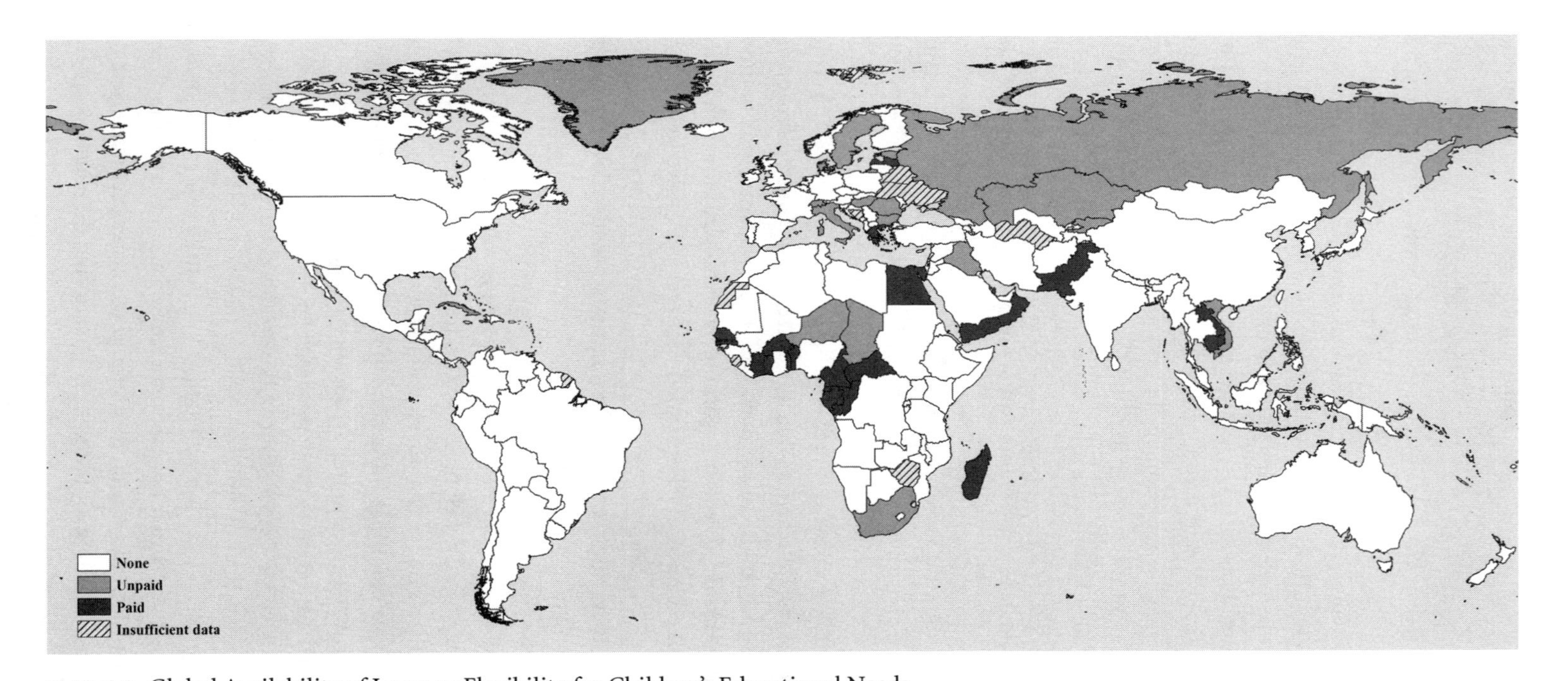

MAP 6.3 Global Availability of Leave or Flexibility for Children's Educational Needs

up to age fifteen. Without limiting it to education leave, forty-one other countries provide leave (twenty-three paid and eighteen unpaid) for children's or family needs that could be used for children's educational or school issues.

Leave for New Fathers

The transformations that have occurred in women's and men's work and family lives make it just as urgent for working men to receive adequate leave to care for family members as it is for women. If family care policies are not equally available to men and women, gender equity in the workplace is impossible to achieve. In the absence of such policies many women will carry double the workload of most men (when combining their paid and unpaid work), men will not have the same opportunities as women to develop relationships with their children and aging family members, and children will be unlikely to receive as much parental care as they would otherwise benefit from.

Paternity leave is one of the key policies for improving gender equity at home, and for contributing to the healthy development of newborns.[97] Moreover, paternity leave is central to the reduction of marital stress; fathers who have longer paternity leaves are more involved with their infants and families.[98] A study of dual-earner parents with at least one child aged three to five months found that in addition to enhancing infant development, fathers' supportive roles helped prevent maternal depression.[99]

The impact of paternity leave policies—when they are sufficiently long in duration and are paid at a meaningful level—on equity in the workplace can be as important as their impact on equity at home. In nearly every country, women are disadvantaged in promotions and pay because of childbearing. The expectation in the workplace is that women will bear the bulk of parental leave for infants as well as subsequent work interruptions to care for their children. Men taking paternity leave can encourage changes in attitudes at work as well as at home.[100]

Leave that is specifically reserved for fathers can provide important advantages over general parental leave, which can be taken by either parent. The OECD's *Babies and Bosses* studies observed that when weeks of paid parental leave were provided specifically for fathers and paid well enough not to impose a large financial penalty for taking them, use of this leave by men in Sweden and in Finland increased. In contrast, general parental leave policies, while gender neutral on paper, were often not so in practice. These Scandinavian countries became aware of the differential uptake of parental leave by mothers and fathers and responded by creating a portion of parental leave that

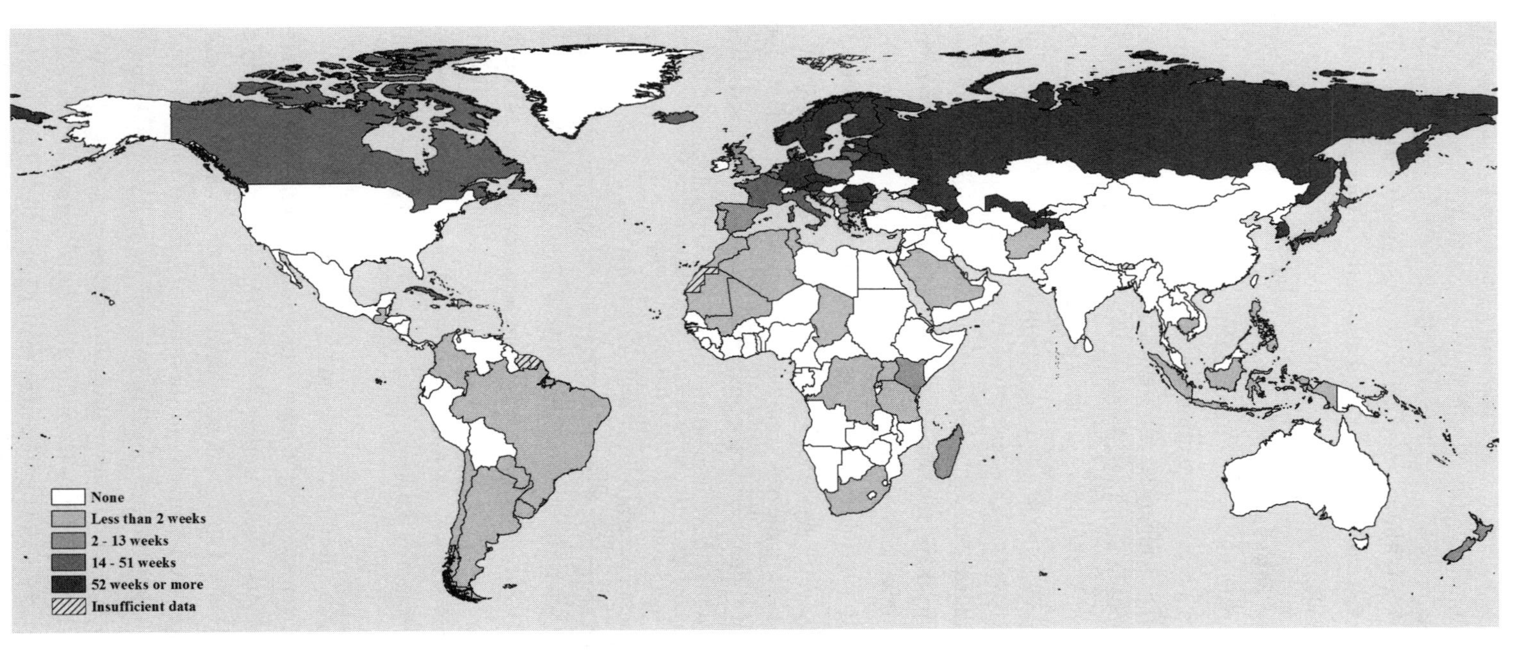

MAP 6.4 Global Availability of Paid Leave for New Fathers

was "use it or lose it" for dads only. The impact was marked, a signal both for employers who had been discouraging fathers from taking parental leave and for men who had deferred it themselves. Once men began to stay home with infants, the gender balance shifted in Swedish homes as fathers started taking greater responsibility for childcare and becoming more deeply involved in their children's lives over time.[101]

Clearly, while policies already in existence need to be more effective, getting paternity leave on the books in the many places where it is not is the first step. Given the importance of paternity leave to infants' development and the potential it offers for setting a precedent for gender equity at home and at work, how many countries actually have paid paternity leave policies?

Fifty-four countries in our global sample guarantee paid paternity leave. Within these countries, forty-one offer 100 percent of usual wages for at least some portion of the leave; however, the duration of the leave is miniscule compared to maternity leave. Only twenty-three countries offer one week or more of paid paternity leave, and only eleven guarantee two or more weeks.

When considering the paid leave available to new fathers in the form of either paternity or parental leave, the number of countries expands to seventy-four, but a handful are paid at an extremely low rate and the duration of the leaves in most cases still falls far short of the leave available to new mothers (see Map 6.4). Only thirty-one of these countries offer fourteen or more weeks of paid leave to fathers. Regionally, the variation is enormous: 71 percent of nations in Europe and Central Asia provide paid leave for men around childbirth, compared to only 29 percent in South Asia and 23 percent in Sub-Saharan Africa.

The guarantee in the United States of only twelve weeks of unpaid parental leave is stingy even by unpaid standards. When combining all forms of paid and unpaid leave available to new fathers, forty countries offer twenty weeks or more, and thirty-three of these offer one year or more. Among the other affluent nations that offer unpaid parental leave, Israel provides fifty-two weeks, as does Australia, which also provides a means-tested "baby care" check.[102] Perhaps the most significant omissions are the countries that have no paternal leave of any kind—either paid or unpaid—in spite of their ability to afford it. Among these are Switzerland, Kuwait, Brunei, Qatar, and the United Arab Emirates.

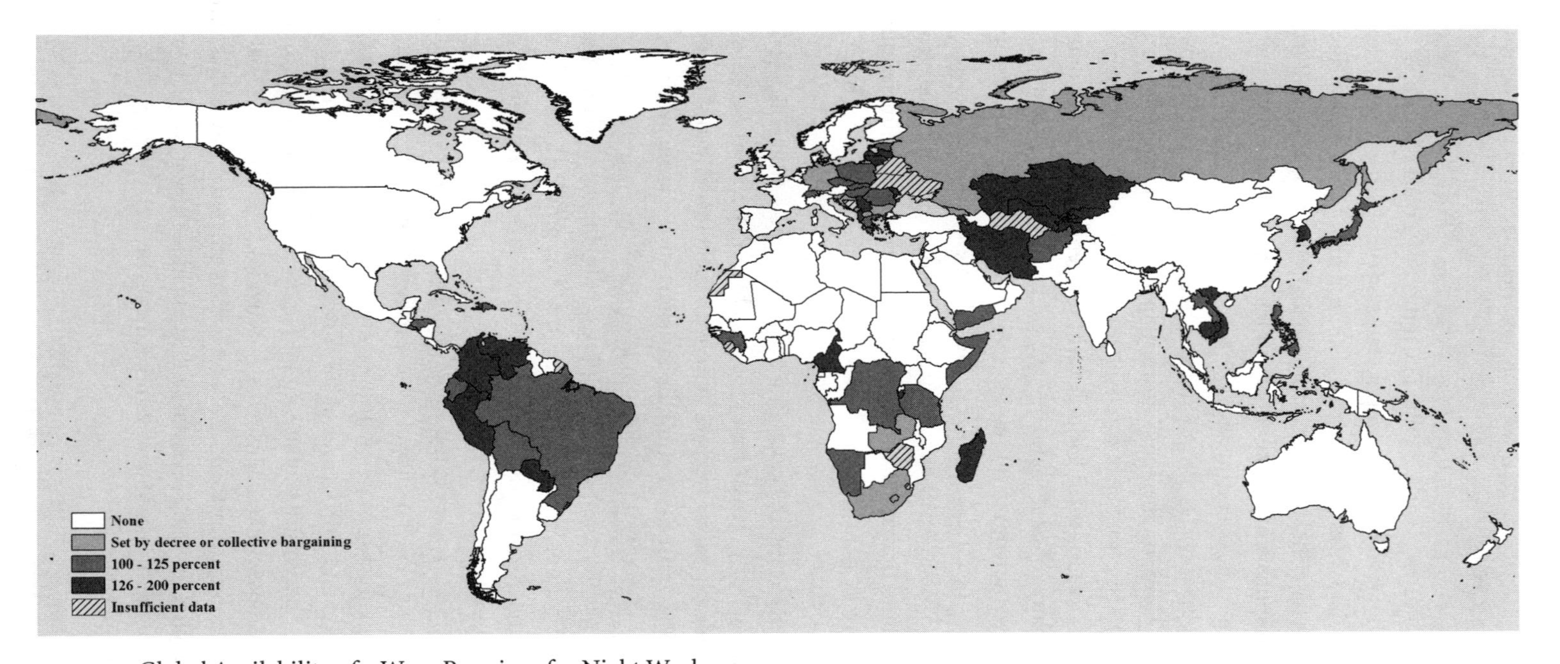

MAP 6.5 Global Availability of a Wage Premium for Night Work

Night Wage Premium and Restrictions on Night Work

While the notion of evening and night work is by no means new, the extent to which adults are working evenings and nights away from the people they are caring for has dramatically increased. Beyond the impact this has on the health and well-being of the employees themselves, it also has profound effects on their families. As reviewed earlier, marital disruption increases with shift work,[103] as do educational problems for children.

The negative effects of routine evening and night work can be reduced by decreasing the frequency of mandatory non-day shifts and by increasing the income or supports offered to those who work evenings and nights while caregiving. In the absence of supports, paid child and eldercare is often particularly difficult to find or unavailable in the evenings or during the night, and it is markedly more expensive.

A minority of nations globally have enacted legislation to address the issues associated with the around-the-clock shifts that derive from the 24/7 economy. Sixty-one nations guarantee a wage premium for night work, and twenty nations have mandated restrictions on work at night such as limiting frequency or number of hours, or providing supports such as transportation for all workers. One hundred and twenty-three nations have mandated bans or restrictions on night work for minors, and fifty-one have bans or restrictions on requiring pregnant or nursing mothers to work at night. Twenty-three nations require that employees pass a medical exam before employers ask them to work at night. Of the forty-nine nations for which the night work wage premium is set in legislation (versus by decree), just over half pay between 101 percent and 125 percent of usual hourly wages, and just under half provide premiums from 126 percent to 150 percent (see Map 6.5).

The highest-income countries are less likely than all other income brackets to guarantee night wage premiums: only 21 percent offer premiums, compared to 35 percent of low-income nations, 40 percent of lower-middle-income nations, and 42 percent of upper-middle-income nations. In fact, only seven high-income nations make this guarantee: Greece, Japan, Estonia, Czech Republic, Switzerland, Luxembourg, and the Republic of Korea. However, high-income nations—including many European nations—are more likely than low-income nations to place broad restrictions on night work for all workers (17 percent versus 7 percent).

Filling in the Gaps

We have shown in Chapters 2 and 3 that the most competitive nations around the world and those with low unemployment have been able to pass legislation that ensures that working men as well as women are able to care for newborn children, that parents can care for their children when they are sick, and that adult children can care for their own ailing parents. In fact, investing in families and equity through this kind of legislation actually contributes to making countries competitive.

Yet it is clear from the stark differences in the maps in this chapter and those in the previous chapter that we still have a long way to go. While the overwhelming majority of the nations studied have passed legislation guaranteeing all workers sick leave, paid annual leave, and a weekly day of rest and guaranteeing maternity leave to female workers, globally the process of passing legislation needed for the current generation has only just begun. Far fewer countries have policies for paid paternity leave or paid leave to care for sick children or aging family members.

Legislation is needed on a global scale in order to make certain that fathers can be just as involved as mothers at home and that women can be just as involved as men in the workforce, while also ensuring that working caregivers can provide their children and aging family members with the necessary support. Legislation is necessary in each of these areas but is not sufficient in and of itself. The ways in which laws are implemented are clearly crucial to the impact they may have.

7 Moving from Evidence to Action: Raising the Floor of Working Conditions and Equity

PAID SICK DAYS MAY NOT SEEM IMPORTANT—unless you are Pham Dieu Hien in Vietnam, who loses three days' wages for every day she misses work to care for her sick son; as a result, she can barely afford to feed her family. Paid leave may not seem worth fighting for—unless you are Agnes Charles in the United States, who could not afford to stay home to care for her daughter when her asthma began acting up; her daughter's asthma then spiraled out of control and landed her in the hospital. Paid maternity leave and breastfeeding breaks may seem like an extravagance—unless you are Leti Marta in Honduras, who had to go back to work and stop breastfeeding just six weeks after giving birth because her work did not provide parental leave or breastfeeding breaks; as a result, her daughter became severely malnourished. Restrictions on mandatory overtime may seem unnecessary—unless you are Gabriela Saavedra, also in Honduras, who runs the risk of being fired if she refuses to work fifteen to twenty-two hours a day in an apparel factory; consequently, she barely gets to see her daughter, whom she has to leave attended only by another child while she is at work due to the lack of caregiving options. Annual leave may seem like a luxury—unless you are Mpho Sithole in Botswana, who uses her leave to travel home once a year to visit family, or Le Thi Ha in Vietnam, who is able to see her parents and children only during these short breaks from work.

While raising the floor of global working conditions is particularly important to the poor and to the marginalized, setting a decent floor also matters to people of every race, class, gender, and nationality. Working conditions define the quality of the daily lives of over three billion adults around the world, and they determine the quality of the lives of those who depend on these workers, including children, siblings, elderly family members, and friends.

Importance of Protections to Individuals' and Families' Economic Survival

During the 1990s and periods of economic boom, economic vulnerability was particularly experienced by individuals and families who had fewer financial assets or who were less competitive in the job market. In 2009, the range of individuals profoundly affected is widening due to the financial crisis. A number of the basic protections for working adults and their families that are discussed in this book are essential to reduce the economic vulnerability of nations and individuals.

Sick leave is illustrative. Workers who lack paid sick leave are markedly more likely to lose wages and jobs when they become ill, which in turn increases their chances of dropping below the poverty line. The lack of sick leave has widespread and lasting economic implications for nations as well as individuals. In Australia, the number of bankruptcies rose sharply in the late 1990s, and the majority of these were personal bankruptcies to which illness was a key contributor.[1] Research also showed that medical crises were a primary cause of bankruptcy in the United States, accounting for 54.5 percent of bankruptcy cases. This implies that approximately two million Americans suffered medical bankruptcy, including those who filed for bankruptcy as well as their family members.[2] Limited paid sick leave in both countries increases the likelihood of bankruptcy by leading to illness-related income and job loss, which in the United States is compounded by mounting debt due to the lack of health insurance.

The lack of protections for working caregivers provides another critical example of how inadequate working conditions hurt individuals and economies. We examined job loss among low-income women across the United States over a fifteen-year period and found that one of the most frequent causes of job loss was the birth or illness of a child.[3] Studies in other industrialized nations similarly found that parenting puts women's employment and long-term earnings at risk. A study in Japan found that even when taking into account other factors that often influence employment, compared to women without children, the likelihood of employment was 31 percent lower for married women with infants, 19 percent lower for those with preschool children, and 3 percent lower for those with school-aged children.[4] Pay gaps are as notable as employment gaps. The penalty for women having two children compared to women without children ranged from 5 percent less pay in Canada to 24 percent in the United Kingdom.[5] Sweden, with progressive labor and family policy in place, was the only country that had no wage penalty, regardless of the number of children.

All countries can afford to guarantee job and income security for workers who become ill or who need to care for a newborn infant or a sick child. The costs associated with most of the protections discussed in this book are modest, even before taking into account the productivity gains to which they would contribute. Moreover, the costs of any paid leave are higher in high-income countries that can better afford it, and lower in low-income countries where wages—and thus the proportionate cost of leave—are lower.

Improving Working Conditions Is Feasible Even in Difficult Economic Periods

As we write this conclusion in early 2009, the world is in the midst of what many see as the worst economic crisis since the Great Depression of the 1930s. As a result, leaders will inevitably ask whether improving working conditions should be a priority at a time like this; shouldn't all of our energy be focused on economic survival, on holding on to existing jobs, and on finding jobs for the growing number of unemployed workers?

These are indeed critical questions, but they overlook how often adults lose jobs because of poor working conditions—when they are sick and cannot take leave, for example, or when they have a newborn and cannot return to a job. Inherent in questions surrounding whether job growth or improving working conditions should be a priority is the fallacy that the two objectives compete in a zero-sum game. Although this misconception is refuted by the evidence in Chapters 2 and 3, it underlies much of the ongoing reticence to address working conditions through improved labor legislation. Moreover, in bad economic times, the reluctance to improve social supports is fuelled by the assumption that new programs—whether they advocate childcare, parental leave, or long-term illness insurance—are simply unaffordable in the current budget environment.

Although the current economic downturn, combined with the enormous amount of debt accrued by countries such as the United States and the United

Kingdom during recent years, will influence the type of initiatives that governments take on, it is unrealistic to think that governments will completely refrain from spending. The real question is not *whether* large investments will be made, but rather *where* money should be invested. During the Great Depression of the 1930s, governments around the world passed major social and labor legislation in addition to making large investments in physical infrastructure, public works, and public employment. As part of the second New Deal, the U.S. Congress passed the Social Security Act of 1935, ensuring for the first time at the federal level a continued income for elderly and retired workers.[6] Acknowledging the need for such public reforms and marking the passage of this momentous law on August 14, 1935, President Roosevelt declared, "We can never insure one hundred percent of the population against one hundred percent of the hazards and vicissitudes of life, but we have tried to frame a law which will give some measure of protection to the average citizen and to his family against the loss of a job and against poverty-ridden old age."[7] Besides social insurance, the United States also passed the Fair Labor Standards Act of 1938 that established a forty-hour work week and guaranteed a federal minimum wage.[8]

Other countries passed major labor legislation to improve working conditions during the Great Depression of the 1930s. In 1933 Mexico passed a minimum wage law for all workers; Canada passed a similar law in 1935.[9] Argentina and Cuba guaranteed maternity benefits in 1934, Iceland and Peru in 1937, and Bolivia and Trinidad and Tobago in 1939.[10] Chile, Colombia, Mexico, and Panama passed laws for paid annual leave in 1931, Brazil and Uruguay in 1933, Cuba in 1935, and Venezuela and France in 1936.[11]

It is not surprising that economic crises often result in governments passing major new legislation. Gaps in existing policies and practices become most evident at times of increased economic insecurity. Individuals, families, and entire populations are more likely to encounter serious deprivation when their country lacks an adequate foundation of protections and when the economic systems themselves are hobbled.

This is clearly not to say that any and all changes should be passed in times of economic difficulty. Rather, the current economic crisis should focus our attention on the important steps that can be taken to improve the lives of individuals, families, and communities: providing them with a better safety net while safeguarding economic productivity.

Much of the legislation and the social supports passed during the Depression of the 1930s have stood the test of time. They have proven themselves valuable in times of economic growth as well as decline. We believe that many of the basic protections discussed in this book can markedly improve the lives of poor and middle-class individuals and families in affluent countries and in poor nations alike. Moreover, many of these protections are needed more urgently in times of economic vulnerability. This final chapter discusses the changes that individual countries and the global community as a whole can afford to make to ensure better working conditions for all while still encouraging economic progress.

Critical Roles for Public and Private Sectors

The evidence presented in this book clearly demonstrates that countries can set a floor of humane working conditions that do not impede companies from succeeding economically. Businesses can afford to provide their employees with short-term leave when they or their children are sick, with a day of rest each workweek, with annual leave, and with job-protected leave to meet other common and essential family responsibilities. They can also guarantee not to discriminate against employees on the basis of gender, race or ethnicity, religion, or any other characteristic that is irrelevant to their ability to do the job. Although countries can implement the labor protections described in the earlier chapters while succeeding in the global market, some labor protections can inhibit the competitiveness of individual countries. Excessive limitations on the ability of firms to lay off employees when economically necessary, for example, may reduce companies' willingness to hire in the first place in some countries. But the new global research presented in this book together with previous longitudinal empirical work demonstrate how social spending and labor protections including paid leave, limits on maximum hours, and similar workplace protections enhance economic growth and performance.[12]

While employers can and should play an important role in ensuring decent working conditions for their employees, government has an essential role in contributing to social insurance systems that pay for maternity and paternity leave and for long-term illness leave. Not only does providing these financial safety nets through a governmental system protect people from becoming destitute when they are seriously ill, when they have a newborn to care for, or when they face other major life events, but it also decreases the likelihood that current and future employees with family responsibilities or chronic conditions will face discrimination in the workplace. If these lengthy leave benefits are paid for by employers alone, the incentives are too strong not to hire people who are likely to become parents or who suffer from chronic health conditions. While always present, these discriminatory incentives become even greater in periods when companies feel economically threatened, due either to national economic conditions or to sectoral competition.

Certain fundamental aspects of a social safety net implicate both government *and* business. Companies should never be allowed to fire workers on a discriminatory basis, but as noted previously, they need to be able to lay off employees who are not adequately performing their jobs or when the business can no longer afford to pay them. Workers and their families need a financial safety net, but it need not necessarily be provided by the employer. Many countries have found it fiscally impossible to require employers to fund long-term unemployment coverage. This is where government can step in to ensure that employees receive income while they are retraining and looking for work. The joint shouldering of this responsibility between the private and the public spheres can significantly improve a country's ability to compete.

Our global research on 190 countries around the world and our in-depth studies of individual countries revealed an essential feature common to most successful nations: their ability to find solutions that benefit both employed adults and businesses. In writing about the best way for companies to compete, Michael Porter, a world-renowned Harvard Business School expert on competitiveness, discussed the importance of social investments to economic outcomes, and conversely, the importance of economic success to social conditions.[13] In order to succeed as individual countries or as a world economy, private-sector leaders need to publicly recognize the importance of social investments to the development of a healthy, well-educated workforce that forms the foundation of economic success. Likewise, those advocating for the welfare of individuals, families, and communities need to recognize that economically unviable solutions are helpful neither to companies nor to the populations they target.

Concrete Steps to Make It Happen

To improve working conditions sustainably and universally, action is needed by individual consumers, employees and employers, national governments, and global intergovernmental organizations. The changes that need to occur at each of these levels are equally important and interconnected.

Individual Actions

Many major social transformations—from the attainment of equal rights for women to the increased global availability of HIV/AIDS treatment and prevention—have originated in actions by small groups of individuals. The movement against the legal slave trade in the British Empire, which had become deeply politically and economically entrenched in society, began with rebellions by handfuls of slaves and free individuals, including the dozen men who met in a London print shop in 1787 to form the Society for Effecting the Abolition of the Slave Trade.[14] Free and enslaved, the abolitionist movement's members at times became discouraged and convinced that all was lost, but additional members joined their ranks. In the end, the movement succeeded: the Slave Trade Act was passed in 1807, followed by the Slavery Abolition Act of 1833, making slavery illegal throughout most of the British Empire.

Nearly two centuries later, anthropologist Margaret Mead penned her famous assertion: "Never doubt that a small group of thoughtful, committed citizens can change the world. Indeed, it is the only thing that ever has."[15] Mead could not have been more accurate in her assessment that most such movements start small, and in underscoring the importance and power of individual actions.

Other movements aimed at addressing extreme poverty have been equally small at their inception. In 1972, Ela Bhatt founded the Self Employed Women's Association and created a bank for some of the world's poorest women in India. Muhammad Yunus founded a parallel initiative, the Grameen Bank, in 1976 in Bangladesh to provide small loans to poor, rural adults—primarily women—who lacked access to traditional banking facilities that would enable them to start their own businesses and potentially work their way out of poverty. The Grameen Bank began when Yunus, an economist at the University of Chittagong, initiated a research project in a single nearby village, Jobra, to assess the feasibility of a system to provide credit to the poorest citizens. Groups of five people voluntarily combined their resources as collateral to back loans made to members of the group. Additional team members became eligible to apply for loans when the first few recipients had established good records of repayment. The Self Employed Women's Association and Grameen concepts of microcredit led to the development of similar banks in other countries, the totality of which now serve more than one hundred million people worldwide.[16]

The actions of committed citizens have often helped the world overcome obstacles or impasses that governments had previously found insurmountable.[17] Individuals can have a similarly substantial impact on the effect of working conditions on health, welfare, and equity in the following ways:

- In civil society: Contact Congressional leaders, members of Parliament, presidents, and prime ministers to ask what they are doing to ensure decent working conditions both nationally and globally. In countries that provide paid maternity leave but not paternity leave, explain how paternity leave promotes equity; if labor laws do not guarantee sick leave, describe the ways in which sick leave improves health and productivity. Elected representatives will pay attention when they begin receiving thousands of letters, e-mails, and calls.
- At work: Find out if all employees at their workplace are guaranteed decent working conditions. If professionals receive benefits such as paid annual leave and sick leave, inquire about the benefits the custodians receive. Raise awareness within companies by repeatedly bringing up the need for decent working conditions for all employees.
- In the marketplace: Use purchasing power to support companies and countries that have demonstrated their commitment to providing decent working conditions. Before buying a product that lacks information on its manufacturing conditions, ask the retailer about its origins. More retailers will recognize the importance of labor standards if customers repeatedly raise these issues. Visit corporate websites and send companies brief e-mails to inquire about their labor practices. The impact would be significant if thousands more people in each country did this even twice a year.

It will be difficult for historians to establish the date of inception of the movements to promote decent working conditions, and it will be nearly as challenging to accurately decipher the roles played by the numerous parties involved. Individuals and businesses have advocated for improved working conditions; consumers have banded together to fight sweatshops; sports leagues have boycotted equipment manufactured using child labor; unions have coordinated, moving from localized self-interest to a truly global commitment; and individual employers have stepped forward and made improvements to their own labor standards. Individual actions can and do play a critical role in improving social conditions—whether they be accomplished by the first or the thousandth actor.

National Strategies

As detailed in Chapters 2 and 3, countries are succeeding economically while guaranteeing decent working conditions. More than two-thirds of the countries ranked by the World Economic Forum as being the most competitive over the past ten years guarantee sick leave, paid annual leave, a weekly day of rest, paid leave for new mothers, paid leave for new fathers, and leave for children's health needs. Likewise, more than two-thirds of the OECD countries with the lowest unemployment rates over the past decade have been able to ensure all the same protections for working women, men, and their families, as well as to provide breastfeeding breaks to nursing women. A clear majority of the most competitive and lowest unemployment countries also provide pay premiums for or limits on mandatory overtime and leave to care for adult family members.

How do these countries guarantee decent working conditions for their populations while successfully competing economically? Their experiences serve as lessons to other nations seeking to improve the lives of all people living and working within their borders. Despite the diversity in their geographies and cultures, these countries' approaches revealed commonalities and lessons.

1. Countries cannot compete sustainably while a large proportion of their citizens live in desperate poverty. The most effective way to increase national competitiveness, while lifting the next generation out of poverty, is to simultaneously provide the education and training people need to earn higher wages and the job protections they need to succeed at work themselves. Specifically this requires:
    - Making higher education readily affordable and available to young adults before they enter the labor force
    - Making continuing education affordable and available to adults of all ages who need to retrain once they are in the labor force
    - Mandating job-protected leave for illness so that adults do not lose their jobs when they become sick
    - Prohibiting sweatshop hours and conditions and limiting mandatory night shifts so that working parents can contribute to the healthy development of their children

- Providing quality, affordable early childhood care and education so that children living in poverty have an equal start in education, and their parents have an equal chance at success in the work force

2. Countries cannot compete effectively in the global economy unless women and men have equal opportunities to be active in the labor force. Essential to achieving equal opportunities is removing the barriers for both women and men to succeed at work while caring for children and aging family members at home. Specifically this means:
   - Providing for paid leave and flexibility to care for children and aging and disabled family members
   - Providing paid leave for new fathers as well as new mothers, and incorporating mechanisms that provide incentives for equal uptake by men and women
   - Passing and enforcing labor legislation that prohibits discrimination on the basis of gender, marital status, pregnancy, and caregiving
   - Providing early education and care programs for school-age children that more closely match the workweek and annual work calendar
3. Unless countries provide a safety net for periods without wages, working men and women and their families remain vulnerable to serious economic deprivation. These periods include times when individuals are unable to work due to illness, due to caring for a newborn child or a seriously ill family member, and due to unemployment. Along with social insurance, countries need policies that facilitate the return of women and men to work in each of these cases.

Global Initiatives

Individual countries can successfully improve their own working conditions and social supports when governments are motivated. In many countries, popular movements have successfully placed pressure on public leaders to improve the quality of life at work. A number of nations have recognized the long-term economic rewards of investing in such decent working conditions as adequate sick leave and parental leave as well as the workplace policies that facilitate parents and people with health conditions to return to work. For nations lagging behind in these and other foundational labor policies, international pressure has the potential to play an important role in improving working conditions.

ILO Report Cards A powerful first step in transforming the incentives for nations to improve their working conditions would be for the ILO to post an online "report card" showing which countries have passed laws to provide decent working conditions, in accordance with international agreements and conventions they have signed. Countries that have neither signed basic international agreements nor passed any laws guaranteeing decent work would stand out from those who have demonstrated their commitments to humane working conditions. This process would begin introducing transparency to labor conditions, just as other initiatives in both the public and private sectors have sought to bring more transparency to other issues of global governance.

A second step is to monitor the enforcement of existing labor laws. For nearly a century, the ILO has made enormous progress in achieving international agreements that provide a foundation of labor standards on paper. It has, however, done far too little to enforce these agreements. The world of work could truly be transformed, and with it the lives of working adults and of the children and elderly family members they care for, if countries were held accountable for carrying out their pledges. In 2009, ninety years after the passage of the first ILO agreement on working conditions in 1919, the ILO still lacks an objective system for tracking countries' passage and implementation of national legislation to uphold and apply the labor standard agreements they have signed. The only information available from the ILO regarding the implementation of labor standards is far from transparent. Countries write reports describing their own achievements, and NGOs then submit their critiques, but the degree and comprehensiveness of their reviews vary substantially among countries. The resulting documentation is often thousands of pages long, difficult to sift through, and short on conclusions.

The report card should include information gathered in each country about the legislated guarantees of every person's basic rights at work and about the implementation of those rights. Most countries carry out some form of routine national surveys. A set of core questions about working conditions could be embedded in these surveys in order to obtain a representative response regarding individuals' experiences at work.[18] The survey responses would provide information both to the countries themselves as they seek to improve the quality of workplaces and to the international community. Survey data should be supplemented by unannounced worksite visits by independent teams of reviewers from other nations. These teams would examine companies' working conditions and conduct in-person, private interviews of employees at all different levels.[19] In addition, they would speak to employers and representatives of government and civil society in a variety of sectors.

While in the past there have been occasional boycotts of individual brands associated with profiting from sweatshop labor, and while a small number of brands have gained market share from their reputation for good labor practices, in general the average consumer has little information about the conditions under which the commodities they want to buy were produced. This lack of informed purchasing could change dramatically if national labor report cards were readily available. A majority of consumer goods bear labels indicating country of origin. If consumers could simply look online to find out which countries guarantee and implement decent working conditions, they could make educated choices about which countries to support with their purchases. This would give a whole new meaning to the term "purchasing power." The information provided in these ILO report cards would empower consumers in their decision making and would reward countries that have good working conditions.

Similarly, companies could take labor conditions into account when deciding where to base their manufacturing, knowing that they could profit from gains in both productivity and public relations by establishing their factories in countries with decent working conditions. They would also be aware of the potential penalties consumers might exact for operating in countries with poor labor conditions. At present, wholesalers, retailers, and manufacturers who seek to source their goods and services from subcontractors with good reputations have to investigate each subcontractor individually. This due diligence is a formidable task for large wholesalers and retailers that may be purchasing four thousand to forty thousand different goods. Manufacturers may have to deal with hundreds of subcontractors of components or parts of the parent company's product. In both cases, corporations' ability to make a commitment that all of their employees, as well as those working for their subcontractors, face humane working conditions would be greatly enhanced if companies could simply refer to an online report card to identify labor standards in the countries where they operate rather than having to investigate individual firms one by one.

Ensuring Countries Are Transparent Having failed to concretely address the ongoing concerns of tens of millions of people around the world that increased free trade has come at the cost of good jobs, decent working conditions, and a healthy environment, the World Trade Organization (WTO) has been facing a barrage of demonstrations against globalization. Protests have been directed both at the WTO's trade agreement efforts and at the national governments that support the organization.

The WTO's insistence that it cannot consider labor standards in the negotiation of trade agreements has been based on the contention that the essential components of good working conditions and beliefs regarding their importance are inherently and profoundly different around the world. The many examples put forth in Chapter 5 show that there is in fact a tremendous amount of global consensus regarding many of the basic labor protections that are needed worldwide.

A valuable first step for the WTO would be to acknowledge this consensus, and to ensure that global trade agreements begin to hold all countries accountable for implementing their own labor laws. To date, only a handful of trade agreements have included measures to ensure enforcement of a subset of domestic labor laws, including those related to the labor principles and rights enumerated in the 1998 ILO Declaration on the Fundamental Principles and Rights at Work.[20] While a step in the right direction, these trade agreements suffer from a series of critical limitations. First, the agreements have no real power to apply trade sanctions as a remedy for the failure to enforce labor legislation that guarantees the ILO's Fundamental Principles.[21] Second, while the core principles are absolutely essential, they are not sufficient to ensure an adequate standard of decent working conditions. The research cited in the earlier chapters demonstrates that working conditions such as reasonable hours, paid time off to care for one's own and family members' needs are critical both to workers' health and well-being and to that of their families. Third, the standards have been incorporated in bilateral and multilateral, not global, agreements. Although bilateral or multilateral trade agreements that effectively ensure essential labor protections would offer significant progress toward improving global working conditions, interventions to encompass workers globally are also needed.

To protect more working men and women, the WTO should include a floor of humane labor standards in global agreements. There is no factual foundation to the rhetoric that claims that cultural differences between countries are too great to allow for agreements regarding the improvement of working conditions. The governments of over 150 countries have passed legislation to guarantee paid sick leave, annual leave, a weekly day of rest, and paid leave for new mothers; over 130 nations additionally guarantee overtime wage premiums or compensation and breastfeeding breaks. At a minimum, countries should be required to abide by their existing labor laws and the international agreements they have signed. In imposing these requirements, the WTO would provide the kind of transparency to working conditions that it has demanded in other areas, such as unfair awarding of contracts, conflicts of interest, and corruption. A wide range of enforcement mechanisms could be considered. Countries that fail to abide by their own labor laws could be required to pay tariffs, and the earnings from those tariffs could be used to promote better working conditions. Conversely, countries that have demonstrated the greatest improvement in their working conditions could be provided with trade preferences, as discussed in the Cambodia case in Chapter 4.

Redefining the Notion of Community

While the mechanisms for ensuring the global enforcement of a foundation of decent working conditions require planning, cooperation, and courage, they are no more complex and demanding than other global challenges the world has undertaken. The principal arguments against change in this area have been that decent working conditions are unaffordable and that the world could never reach consensus on the needed changes. Yet our findings refute both of these contentions. There is no evidence that countries cannot compete while having strong labor standards or that they cannot create and keep jobs while ensuring that those jobs are good jobs. The belief that individuals should have decent working conditions and that work should support the health and welfare of individuals and their families is held across the full range of economies, political systems, and geographies. Moreover, citizens across countries and cultures have expressed their widespread support of governments taking an active role in improving the living conditions of each country's poorest children, adults, and families.[22]

The world could move toward either of two equilibria: the global erosion of basic labor protections, or the establishment of decent working conditions worldwide. Achieving the latter requires recognizing that all people—regardless of where they live or the type of labor they are engaged in—have a right to humane conditions at work. Just as important, it requires understanding that the barriers to addressing poverty, disadvantage, and inequality are insurmountable without creating a floor of decent working conditions for all.

REFERENCE MATTER

Appendix

Creation of a Global Labor Policy Database

We set out to examine a series of working conditions that affect workers' ability to meet health and welfare needs, and that could be analyzed in a comparable way across countries. We focused on the daily lives of working men and women, their ability to continue to earn a living when special needs arose, and their ability to care for their families on a routine basis. While it was not possible to obtain globally comparative data on anywhere near all of the conditions that matter, the policies we examined include those that have achieved: (1) widespread recognition based on the weight of the research evidence, or (2) consensus in international agreements, treaties, covenants, and other legal documents as being important to the health and well-being of working women, men, and their families.

We realize that many crucial labor protections extend beyond the scope of this book. One in particular is worth noting. The right to decent wages is critical to workers' ability to support their own health and security and that of their families. Improved working conditions are necessary to ensure health and economic security, but they are not sufficient without decent wages to fundamentally alter income and gender disparities. At the time of this research, adequate comparable data on minimum wages were not available, including adjustments for purchasing power differences and indications of whether countries' minimum wages are "living" wages, meaning that they are sufficiently high to enable a full-time worker to exit poverty. This information is urgently needed. At the same time, adequate minimum wages without an accompanying floor of decent working conditions are not sufficient to ensure health and economic security.

We sought data on all 192 United Nations member nations. We succeeded in gathering policy data on 190 countries representing the full range of political, social, and economic systems.[1] For the sake of comparability and because countries can vary in their approaches to common policy goals, we selected the essential, core features of a given policy and then systematically analyzed and categorized the approach taken by each country.

We sought to examine the conditions facing the majority of working adults in each country. While policies that are targeted at the lowest-income workers are critically important, we did not incorporate them here because our goal was to report on policies that are universal or nearly universal at least in their coverage of the formal sector. Similarly, when policies provide additional benefits for a specific sector of the workforce, for example, the public sector, again, we did not include these because our focus was on policies that are broadly applied across a country's population.

Policies and Their Dimensions

We examined the working conditions that affect employees themselves. In order to balance the full range of demands on their lives, the basic needs of women and men include having a reasonable number of hours of work and some time off during the week. They also include being able to take leave when they are sick and having flexibility when urgent needs arise. We also analyzed the working conditions that affect the families of working men and women, such as the ability of working adults to care for newborn and newly adopted children, to care for the health of older children, to meet children's educational needs, and to care for adult family members' health. We examined policies that were specifically designed to meet these needs, such as parental leave, breastfeeding breaks, and leave or flexibility for family illness, as well as policies regarding the impact of the workday on employees' ability to spend time with their families, such as policies surrounding evening and night work.

For each of these policies, we examined a range of dimensions. In the case of policies regarding leave and flexibility, these included the duration of leave that was provided; the timing of the leave (whether it was effective immediately or subject to a delay, or whether its use was subject to stipulations, etc.); how much salary or wage income was provided during the leave; whether this leave was funded by employers or a social insurance system; and whether certain criteria had to be met in order to receive the leave (for example, whether the leave was only for a given severity of illness).

Range of Approaches

Differences in the characteristics of policies can reflect different conceptions or assumptions. For example, some countries have waiting periods before covering sick leave. Frequently this is because the sick leave is designed primarily for coverage during serious illnesses and hospitalization. In contrast, other nations begin sick leave on the first day to ensure that it is available for common illnesses, acute infectious diseases, and preventive healthcare. In the case of maternity leave, some nations stipulate that a certain amount be reserved for use prior to childbirth in order to provide incentives to employees and employers alike for women to begin maternity leave during the final weeks of pregnancy. This approach is also used to distinguish the amount of leave needed by birth mothers and adoptive mothers. Other nations let women decide the timing of maternity leave and the proportions used before and after the arrival of a newborn. In providing for leave to care for a young child, many nations stipulate that the majority of this leave should be taken during infancy or immediately following maternity leave in order to care for infants when quality, nonparental care is least likely to be available. Other countries provide the same duration of leave but allow all parents to take this leave at their own discretion any time during a three-year or longer period. This approach leaves it to parents to determine when is best for their relationship building and for meeting childcare needs.

Policies regarding overtime and night work took two forms: those that required employers to pay a premium to employees for working extended hours or nonday hours, and those that placed limitations or restrictions on the practice. The former reflected a compensatory model—providing disincentives to employers and compensations for higher costs to employees—and the latter reflected a protective model.

Data Sources

National Labor Codes and Legislation

Our primary source of data was original legislation. We analyzed labor codes and other labor-related legislation. Our multilingual research team is fluent in five of the six official UN languages—English, French, Spanish, Chinese, and Arabic—as well as five additional languages.

The vast majority of the legislation used in our analyses is from NATLEX, a global database of legislation pertaining to labor, social security, and human rights from 189 countries (as well as additional territories).[2] It is maintained by the International Labour Organization. Information in the NATLEX database is continuously updated upon receipt of official country publications of enacted laws. We carefully reviewed every labor code and piece of available legislation related to the policies we were examining. Our final review of legislation from or linked through the NATLEX database was completed in August 2008.[3] We searched comprehensively through the websites for which NATLEX provided links in order to locate the full texts of legislation listed but not available in the NATLEX database. Additional sources of legislation include country websites, the law libraries of Harvard and McGill Universities and of the International Labour Organization in Geneva.

Government websites often contain access to primary sources that are not available elsewhere. Searches for both legislation and policy reviews on government websites were completed in August 2008.

When no link to full-text legislation was provided in NATLEX, we searched through the following databases of laws: the World Bank's Doing Business Law Library,[4] the Lexadin World Law Guide,[5] and the World Legal Information Institute's (WorldLII) databases.[6]

Global Databases that Compile Legislation and Policy Information

We examined the Social Security Programs Throughout the World (SSPTW) database, the most comprehensive source of global data on social security policies including Old Age, Disability, and Survivors; Sickness and Maternity; Work Injury; Unemployment; and Family Allowances.[7] SSPTW contains data on 164 of the 190 countries in our database. The SSPTW supplemented the paid leave data we obtained from labor codes for countries where such policies are mandated by social security laws, and provided details about paid leave policies, such as wage-replacement information, which is not always included in labor codes.[8]

The information in the SSPTW report is based on data collected in the Annual Survey on Developments and Trends conducted by the International Social Security Association (ISSA), as well as other supplemental sources.

Findings from both legislation and SSPTW were also checked against a series of other reliable, global sources, including the ILO Working Time Database (which has data on only 108 countries but occasionally presented information more clearly than the legislation and served as a useful cross-check for our database),[9] the ILO Maternity Protection Database,[10] and the World Alliance for Breastfeeding Action's Status of Maternity Protection by Country (which provided useful confirmatory details on the duration of maternity leave).[11]

Regional and Country-Specific Sources

Between June 2003 and August 2008, we reviewed the following sources for regional data: European Industrial Relations Observatory Online;[12] the International Network on Leave Policies and Research;[13] the OECD Directorate for Family, Labor and Social Affairs, Social Policy Division;[14] the Center for Economic and Policy Research;[15] and the Clearinghouse on International Developments in Child, Youth and Family Policies.[16] We also reviewed country reports when data on individual nations were missing.[17]

Comparability

In order to map policies around the world, to statistically compare the frequency of approaches in high- and low-income nations, and to analyze the relationship between policies and employment and competitiveness, we codified the policies into a comparable format. A detailed description of how this was done will be available online with an accessible database. The coding is illustrated here for the cases of leave duration and wage replacement.

When duration of benefits varied by tenure, we conservatively used the amount available to the worker with the shortest tenure (and retained the tenure requirements in the database). When duration varied by routine and special circumstances, we included the amount available to all workers under usual circumstances, not just in exceptional cases. For example, if the law guaranteed two days of leave in the event of a child's illness, but four days if the child is hospitalized, we coded two days' leave. Other variations in how the duration was specified in different countries' legislation included illness leave for oneself or a family member with no specified time limit. For example, the legislation might stipulate that the leave lasted "as long as the doctor determines," "for the duration of illness," or "until recovery." We kept all details and exact original language but coded duration as equivalent to the highest category of days available.

In some countries, reimbursement is based on a flat rate to be paid to those taking the leave, while in others, workers are granted a fixed percentage of their normal wage, either for the full duration of the leave or for part of the leave, and another fixed percentage during the remainder. Still other policies grant workers a percentage of their normal wages that varies depending on their tenure, occupation, location, and type of disease, or is given simply as a range, such as 70 percent to 100 percent of wages (without stipulating what determines where in the range a worker falls). We therefore captured wage-replacement type and the minimum rate (universally offered) and maximum rate (offered to certain categories of workers or under certain conditions) guaranteed.

Data Checking and Verification

Throughout the data collection process, we continuously updated our data sources to include any new legislation and releases of the global databases. Our process of building the database included reviewing and coding all legislation by multiple research team members, as well as thoroughly cross-checking our findings with other reliable, global sources (described above). In many instances, the sources were complementary in nature, such as a database with consistent but less complete data than the legislation but in no way conflicting with it. In others, we investigated and tried to reconcile any discrepancies between sources that were identified. We gave precedence to original legislation over other sources, as the former is the primary source. As in any data pursuit of this magnitude, some legislation may be missing. We welcome readers who are aware of any corrections to contact the authors through the Institute for Health and Social Policy. Updates will be incorporated and made available along with the full appendix online.

Analyses Conducted

Unemployment Rates

We examined the relationship between labor protections and unemployment rates. Global unemployment rate data from the World Bank's World Development Indicators were used in the first set of analyses.[18] In the second set of analyses, we examined Standardised Unemployment rates (SURs) for all thirty OECD nations.[19] These OECD data are based on household surveys, which are generally accepted as the best sources for labor market statistics. These unemployment data represent a more comparable labor market series across OECD countries than unemployment data from administrative sources because the surveys are all gathered using the same collection instrument and with the same methods.

Competitiveness

We examined data from the Global Competitiveness Report published by the business-led World Economic Forum to see whether nations with guarantees of decent working conditions have been able to maintain high levels of global economic competitiveness. Competitiveness rankings of nations worldwide were generated from the Growth Competitiveness Index (used from 1987 to 2005), which was renamed the Global Competitiveness Index in the Report's 2006/2007 issue. The Index is intended to measure an economy's capacity to achieve sustained economic growth. The report includes a ranking of the economic competitiveness of nations worldwide. Each nation's ranking is based on its scores on a series of indicators deemed to be the key drivers of economic growth and competitiveness.[20]

Income and Geographic Indicators

Variation in trends across the different regions and income levels were analyzed using income categories and regional classifications from the World Bank.[21]

Acknowledgments

A RESEARCH INITIATIVE OF THIS SIZE owes an immeasurable debt to scores of people. The project blossomed completely when Jody moved to McGill in 2005 to found the Institute for Health and Social Policy. The academic leadership at McGill had a remarkable level of commitment to the development of research that could impact policy, and an exceptional ability to bridge disciplines. In particular, Jody is indebted to Heather Munroe-Blum, Anthony Masi, Denis Thérien, Richard Levin, and Chris Manfredi for their support in launching this research. The intellectual support for this project from faculty across the university—from medicine to arts to science, and from law to management to education—was invaluable. The Canadian government has shown remarkable skill at developing mechanisms that allow researchers across disciplines to take on innovative subjects. Both this initiative and Jody were incredibly fortunate to benefit from two of these mechanisms, including funding from the Canadian Foundation for Innovation and from the Canada Research Chairs programs.

The project would never have gotten off the ground nearly a decade ago had Harvard University not provided us with an invaluable home. Leaders at the university, including Harvey Fineberg as Dean and Provost and Barry Bloom as Dean, were willing to let us take the gamble that it was worthwhile and supported our efforts intellectually and practically. Lisa Berkman and our colleagues in the Department of Society, Human Development and Health provided first Jody and then Alison and our team with a rich home. Early critical funding came from the Ford Foundation and the Canadian Institute for Advanced Research.

At its core, this project was a deep collaboration that involved both the daily and long-term commitment of an extensive team of researchers to examine the policies of countries around the world. Gathering and analyzing labor legislation for 190 countries is simply a massive undertaking. Ensuring that the information included in the database was as accurate as possible—that each detail was questioned, examined, checked, and verified and that none was omitted—was feasible only with the unfailing and tireless efforts and attention to detail of a group of staff and students that started small and grew in numbers.

The beginning of the policy analysis required time and energy in the development of the conceptual framework and the components of the database, and the initial collection and review of legislation and social policy. Our team at the Harvard School of Public Health shaped these early efforts. The dedicated efforts of Stephanie Breslow, Aron Fischer, Francisco Flores, Lola Kassim, April Kuehnhoff, and Stephanie Simmons resulted in the first global report on labor in 2004.

This global rights initiative grew at McGill to address a far wider range of social and economic rights that impact the health, well-being, development, and lives of adults and children alike. The efforts involved in carefully reading and analyzing tens of thousands of pages of policy documents, legislation, and constitutions from around the world grew with the project. This undertaking would never have been possible without the immense intellectual engagement, patient effort, and deep commitment of the WoRLD team at McGill. Jeff Hayes developed the electronic databases templates, trained team members in their use, worked through countless individual country policy questions with us, conducted the statistical analyses, and brought a deep understanding both of social inequalities and of data challenges to the project. Giulia El-Dardiry and Anna Shea coordinated the massive team efforts. Diving rapidly into the data and providing immensely talented analyses were Magdalena Barrera, David Baumann, Adele Cassola, Stephanie Coen, Carrie Dickenson, Amy Raub, Erin Rogers, Ceyda Turan, and Ilona Vincent. A particularly careful legal eye was provided by Gabriella Kranz. Anke Schliwen brought expertise and focus on paid sick leave policies and social insurance. Researchers who focused on in-depth studies of policies in individual nations provided critical details; for these contributions we are indebted to

Marian Baird, Martine Chaussard, Lisa Dancaster, Megan Gerecke, Chunbao Liu, Baijayanta Mukhopadhyay, and Damian Oliver. The final stage of mapping was transformed by the thoughtful contribution of David Baumann.

Any endeavor this large could only have been successful with the highest level of management skills. We have been remarkably lucky to have Angel Elechiguerra leading in this capacity.

An enormous amount of research went into examining the background evidence on the impact of labor conditions on health and well-being, and the relationship between labor protections and economic outcomes. Bringing breadth and depth to this work through their thorough, thoughtful, and analytical reviews of the literature were Elisheva Bouskila, Martine Chaussard, Sara Coen, Zoë Costa-von Aesch, Ian Cummins, Megan Gerecke, Susanne Greisbach, Kristen McNeill, Danielle Rodin, Ronen Shnidman, Parama Sigurdsen, Izabela Steflja, Elina Suzuki, and Sara Thiam.

The immense level of detail involved in reporting on working conditions in 190 countries had enormous implications for writing the book, as well as for conducting the research. We are deeply grateful to those who spent time with us daily trying to make the findings accessible. The entire manuscript could not have been put together without the immensely careful and insightful input at many stages of Parama Sigurdsen. Stephanie Coen went through all the details in the first draft with care. New to the field of labor and social policy, Melanie Benard edited the full manuscript when we rewrote it and brought to her work an exceptional attention to detail, fresh questions to ensure that every section was accessible to those with and without special expertise, and an exceptional editorial ability to make complex issues more readable. During the last stages of the book, Kristen McNeill managed countless critical details with extraordinary poise and professionalism, proofread the entire book, raised essential points on consistency and language, and coordinated the daunting but vital task of ensuring accurate referencing and formatting of the manuscript to meet with the publisher's requirements.

It is because of the incalculable contributions of the research team that the book is dedicated to them. Once written, we were incredibly fortunate to have found at Stanford University Press an exceptional editorial team to shepherd the book. Stacy Wagner brought a deep understanding of why the book mattered and why it mattered for the findings to be rapidly made public. Jessica Walsh made sure that no loose ends got lost. Mariana Raykov managed the process of bringing the book to press extraordinarily well, while Mary

Barbosa brought a careful and inquisitive eye to copyediting the manuscript. We cannot close without thanking our families who made this possible from beginning to end.

In the Earle/Barnard household it is often joked that Alison likes to live her work. In the final stretch of writing a book on working conditions, she worked long hours, worked at night, and travelled away from her family. Her husband, Steve, and daughters Emily and Lindsey know that in truth it is a deep commitment to improving the working conditions of many adults around the world with far fewer supports and resources than she has that keeps her up at night. Alison is deeply grateful for Steve's support and encouragement, and for all his extra help at home as she worked on the book. Alison's other greatest debt goes to her two daughters. She is grateful for their patience and cooperation, and mostly for the inspiration they gave her to try to make it possible for all working adults to be available for their family members on a routine basis and at critical times without fear of being penalized at work. As this book goes off to press, Alison hopes the girls have developed a greater understanding of their place in what is an enormous yet interdependent world, and that Steve is inspired to travel to the places she has talked so much about. To her friends, her daughters' afterschool babysitter Alex Hoey, her brother Randy, her sister Cynthia, and her parents and in-laws, Alison owes a huge "thank you" for the many hours of help with the girls and for providing places to work, places to print, and places to rest. Their kindness and support have been critical to making this book possible.

Close friends and family sustained Jody's sense of humor and sense of what mattered throughout this project. Being entangled in global conditions has a long history in Jody's family. She is thankful for the start her family gave her and hopeful for the future places her children are likely to carry this engagement. Jody's great-grandfather emigrated from Eastern Europe to the United States in search of better working conditions. To save on bus fares, he found himself walking from town to town, selling goods from a backpack. Her parents and her brother had spent stretches of time abroad before her to study in Europe, then she followed suit to study in the Middle East and Africa and then to work. When Jody took her first job after attending university, it was in a small village in Tanzania. Her half dismayed, half bemused grandfather remarked, "backpack to backpack in four generations" but then, at her grandmother's urging, supported her venturing off. Her sense that books might be able to touch people undoubtedly came from her earliest memories of her mother sharing books on daily life in Africa with her. Her belief that laws can grant crucial rights to citizens across countries has indelibly been influenced by her father's work in this area, even as he repeatedly reminded her as this book was being written that having laws on the books is not enough. Jody is deeply grateful to them all and to her husband, Tim, who after a honeymoon working at the Albert Schweitzer Hospital in Gabon, decided on a life's work in global health. Somehow, still, he found time to help with this book in more ways than can be counted—from debating to editing, and from supporting some of the chaotically full weeks to sharing the inevitable ups and downs of a project this large. At sixteen and twenty, Jody's sons, Ben and Jeremy, have each studied or worked on three continents—showing how increasingly global each generation is becoming and bringing her life repeated surprises and joy.

Notes

Abbreviations

CEDAW	Convention on the Elimination of All Forms of Discrimination against Women
EC	European Commission
EU	European Union
FDI	foreign direct investment
FMLA	Family and Medical Leave Act
GCI	Global Competitiveness Index
HDR	Human Development Report
ICESCR	International Covenant on Economic, Social and Cultural Rights
ILO	International Labour Organization
IMSS	Instituto Mexicano del Seguro Social (Mexican Social Security Institute)
ISSA	International Social Security Association
ISSSTE	Instituto de Seguridad y Servicios Sociales de los Trabajadores del Estado (State Employees' Social Security and Social Services Institute)
LFS	Labor Force Survey
NAFTA	North American Free Trade Agreement
NGOs	non-governmental organizations
OECD	Organisation for Economic Co-operation and Development
SSPTW	Social Security Programs Throughout the World
SURs	Standardised Unemployment rates
UN	United Nations
WEF	World Economic Forum
WorldLII	World Legal Information Institute
WTO	World Trade Organization

Chapter 1

1. Analysis of the Bureau of Labor Statistics' National Compensation Survey (March 2008) with adjustment for workers who have less than the average minimum tenure requirement, as reported in J. Heymann, H. J. Rho, J. Schmitt, and A. Earle, *Contagion Nation: A Comparison of Paid Sick Day Policies in 22 Countries* (Washington, DC: Center for Economic Policy Research, 2009), http://www.cepr.net/documents/publications/paid-sick-days-2009-05.pdf (accessed June 9, 2009).

2. V. Lovell, *No Time to Be Sick: Why Everyone Suffers When Workers Don't Have Paid Sick Leave* (Washington, DC: Institute for Women's Policy Research, 2004), http://www.iwpr.org/pdf/B242.pdf (accessed March 4, 2009).

3. International Labour Organization, "C29 Forced Labour Convention 1930," http://www.ilo.org/ilolex/cgi-lex/convde.pl?C029 (accessed March 3, 2009).

4. International Labour Office, *A Global Alliance Against Forced Labor: Global Report under the Follow-up to the ILO Declaration on Fundamental Principles and Rights at Work* (Geneva: International Labour Organization, 2005), http://www.ilo.org/public/english/standards/relm/ilc/ilc93/pdf/rep-i-b.pdf (accessed October 16, 2008).

5. V. Lovell, *No Time to Be Sick: Why Everyone Suffers When Workers Don't Have Paid Sick Leave* (Washington, DC: Institute for Women's Policy Research, 2004), http://www.iwpr.org/pdf/B242.pdf (accessed March 4, 2009).

6. In contrast to the Western press, the press in India and China has highlighted the greater job opportunities that were created in low- and middle-income countries and the declines in poverty attributed to job acquisition.

7. K. Heiler, "The 'Petty Pilfering of Minutes' or What Has Happened to the Working Day in Australia?" *International Journal of Manpower* 19, no. 4 (1998): 266; I. Kawachi, "Globalization and Workers' Health," *Industrial Health* 46 (2008): 421–23; A. S. Ostry and J. M. Spiegel, "Labor Markets and Employment Insecurity: Impacts of Globalization on Service and Healthcare-Sector Workforces," *International Journal of Occupational and Environmental Health* 10, no. 4 (2004): 368–74; H. Bielenski, "New Patterns of Employment in Europe," in *Labour Market Changes and Job Insecurity: A Challenge for Social Welfare and Health Promotion*, ed. J. E. Ferrie, M. G. Marmot, J. Griffiths, and E. Ziglio, European Series no. 81 (Geneva: WHO Regional Publications, 1999).

8. A. De Ruyter and J. Burgess, "Part-time Employment in Australia: Evidence for Globalization?" *International Journal of Manpower* 21, no. 6 (2000): 452–63; R. Locke, T. Kochan, and M. Piore, "Reconceptualizing Comparative Industrial Relations: Lessons from International Research," *International Labour Review* 134, no. 2 (1995): 139–61; A. Goudswaard and F. Andries, *Employment Status and Working Conditions* (Luxembourg: European Foundation for the Improvement of Living and Working Conditions, Office for Official Publications of the European Communities, 2002); I. Kawachi, "Globalization and Workers' Health," *Industrial Health* 46 (2008): 421–23; G. Standing, "Globalization, Labour Flexibility and Insecurity: The Era of Market Regulation," *European Journal of Industrial Relations* 3 (1997): 7–37; R. M. D'Souza, L. Strazdins, L. L.-Y. Lim, D. H. Broom, and B. Rodgers, "Work and Health in a Con-

temporary Society: Demands, Control, and Insecurity," *Journal of Epidemiology and Community Health* 57 (2003): 849–54.

9. A. S. Ostry and J. M. Spiegel, "Labor Markets and Employment Insecurity: Impacts of Globalization on Service and Healthcare-Sector Workforces," *International Journal of Occupational and Environmental Health* 10, no. 4 (2004): 369–70.

10. Bureau of Labor Statistics, U.S. Department of Labor, "Number of Jobs Held, Labor Market Activity, and Earnings Growth Among the Youngest Baby Boomers: Results from a Longitudinal Survey" (June 27, 2008), http://www.bls.gov/news.release/pdf/nlsy.pdf (accessed October 15, 2008).

11. For examples of the global response to the AIDS pandemic, see The Global Fund to Fight AIDS, Tuberculosis and Malaria website, http://www.theglobalfund.org/EN/; Friends of the Global Fund to Fight AIDS, Tuberculosis and Malaria website, http://www.theglobalfight.org/; Global AIDS Alliance website, http://www.globalaidsalliance.org (all accessed February 26, 2009).

12. ILO, "Global Trends in Employment: Productivity and Poverty Reduction" (January 2008), http://www.ilo.org/wcmsp5/groups/public/—-dgreports/—-dcomm/documents/publication/wcms_090106.pdf (accessed February 24, 2009).

13. While the amount of data varies by country, 190 is the number of UN nations on which our primary sources, NATLEX (the ILO's database of national labor and related legislation) and Social Security Programs Throughout the World (SSPTW), had collected at least some data. NATLEX provided data on 189 countries, and SSPTW provided data on 164.

14. S. J. Heymann, A. Earle, and A. Hanchate, "Bringing a Global Perspective to Community, Work and Family: An Examination of Extended Work Hours in Families in Four Countries," *Community, Work and Family* 7, no. 2 (2004): 247–72.

15. A. Earle and S. J. Heymann, "Work, Family, and Social Class," in *How Healthy Are We? A National Study of Well-Being at Midlife,* ed. O. G. Brimm, C. Ryff, and R. Kessler (Chicago: University of Chicago Press, 2004).

16. S. J. Heymann, *The Widening Gap: Why American Families Are in Jeopardy and What Can Be Done About It* (New York: Basic Books, 2000).

17. In the 1998 General Social Survey, men were more likely than women to report having flexible work hours that allow them to vary or make changes in their start and end times. The gender difference in scheduling flexibility increased with age. See L. Golden, "Flexible Work Schedules: Which Workers Get Them?" *American Behavioral Scientist* 44, no. 7 (2001): 1157–78.

18. S. J. Heymann, *The Widening Gap: Why American Families Are in Jeopardy and What Can Be Done About It* (New York: Basic Books, 2000).

19. E. Fodor and D. Redai, "Differences Between Men and Women in Work Quality," in *Quality of Life in a Changing Europe*, European Commission (Utrecht: Utrecht University, 2008).

20. S. J. Heymann, *Forgotten Families: Ending the Growing Crisis Confronting Children and Working Parents in the Global Economy* (New York: Oxford University Press, 2006).

21. In the Global Working Families study, a family was classified as living in poverty if the parent interviewed was earning less than the equivalent of US$10 per day. (Local currency was adjusted for both exchange rates and purchasing power parity across nations to be equivalent to what can be bought on US$10 per day.) For full description of findings, see S. J. Heymann, *Forgotten Families: Ending the Growing Crisis Confronting Children and Working Parents in the Global Economy* (New York: Oxford University Press, 2006).

22. S. J. Heymann, ed. *Global Inequalities at Work* (New York: Oxford University Press, 2003).

23. S. J. Heymann, *Forgotten Families: Ending the Growing Crisis Confronting Children and Working Parents in the Global Economy* (New York: Oxford University Press, 2006); S. J. Heymann and C. Beem, eds., *Unfinished Work: Building Equality and Democracy in an Era of Working Families* (New York: New Press, 2005); S. J. Heymann, ed., *Global Inequalities at Work* (New York: Oxford University Press, 2003); S. J. Heymann, *The Widening Gap: Why America's Working Families Are in Jeopardy and What Can Be Done About It* (New York: Basic Books, 2000); S. J. Heymann, F. Flores-Macias, J. Hayes, M. Kennedy, A. Earle, and C. Lahaie, "The Impact of Migration on the Well-Being of Transnational Families: New Data from Sending Communities in Mexico," *Community, Work and Family* 12, no. 1 (2009): 91–103; D. Rajaraman, A. Earle, and S. J. Heymann, "Working HIV Caregivers in Botswana: Spill-over Effects on Work and Family Well-Being," *Community, Work and Family* 11, no. 1 (2008): 1–17; P. H. Vo, K. Penrose, and S. J. Heymann, "Working to Exit Poverty While Caring for Children's Health and Development in Vietnam," *Community, Work and Family* 10, no. 2 (2007): 197–99; S. J. Heymann, A. Earle, D. Rajaraman, C. Miller, and K. Bogen, "Extended Family Caring for Children Orphaned by AIDS: Balancing Essential Work and Caregiving in High HIV Prevalence Nations," *AIDS Care* 19, no. 3 (2007): 337–45; A. Earle and S. J. Heymann, "A Comparative Analysis of Paid Leave for the Health Needs of Workers and Their Families Around the World," *Journal of Comparative Policy Analysis* 8, no. 3 (2006): 241–57; A. Earle, J. Z. Ayanian, and S. J. Heymann, "What Predicts Women's Ability to Return to Work After Newly Diagnosed Coronary Heart Disease: Findings on the Importance of Paid Leave," *Journal of Women's Health* 15, no. 4 (2006): 430–41; C. Miller, S. Gruskin, D. Rajaraman, V. D. Subramanian, and S. J. Heymann, "The Orphan Crisis in Botswana's Working Households: Growing Caregiving Responsibilities in the Absence of Adequate Support," *American Journal of Public Health* 96, no. 8 (2006): 1429–36; S. J. Heymann, K. Penrose, and A. Earle, "Meeting Children's Needs: How Does the U.S. Measure Up?" *Merrill-Palmer Quarterly* 52, no. 2 (2006): 189–216; C. A. Bergstrom and S. J. Heymann, "Impact of Gender Disparities in Family Carework on Women's Life Chances in Chiapas, Mexico," *Journal of Comparative Family Studies* 36, no. 2 (2005): 267–88; S. J. Heymann, A. Earle, and A. Hanchate, "Bringing a Global Perspective to Community, Work and Family: An Examination of Extended Work Hours in Families in Four Countries," *Community, Work and Family* 7, no. 2 (2004): 247–72; S. J. Heymann, P. H. Vo, and C. A. Bergstrom, "Child Care Providers' Experiences Caring for Sick Children: Implications for Public Policy," *Early Child Development and Care* 172, no. 1 (2002): 1–8; A. Earle and S. J. Heymann,

"What Causes Job Loss Among Former Welfare Recipients? The Role of Family Health Problems," *Journal of the American Medical Women's Association* 57 (2002): 5–10; S. J. Heymann and A. Earle, "The Impact of Parental Working Conditions on School-Age Children: The Case of Evening Work," *Community, Work and Family* 4, no. 3 (2001): 305–25; S. J. Heymann and A. Earle, "Low-income Parents: How Do Working Conditions Affect Their Opportunity to Help School-Age Children at Risk?" *American Educational Research Journal* 37, no. 2 (2000): 833–48; S. J. Heymann, "What Happens During and After School: Conditions Faced by Working Parents Living in Poverty and Their School-Age Children," *Journal of Children and Poverty* 6, no. 1 (2000): 5–20; S. J. Heymann, S. Toomey, and F. Furstenberg, "Working Parents: What Factors Are Involved in Their Ability to Take Time off from Work When Their Children Are Sick?" *Archives of Pediatrics and Adolescent Medicine* 153, no. 8 (1999): 870–74; S. J. Heymann and A. Earle, "The Impact of Welfare Reform on Parents' Ability to Care for Their Children's Health," *American Journal of Public Health* 89, no. 4 (1999): 502–5; S. J. Heymann, A. Earle, and B. Egleston, "Parental Availability for the Care of Sick Children," *Pediatrics* 98, no. 2, part 1 (1996): 226–30; M. Chaussard, M. Gerecke, and S. J. Heymann, *The WECanada Work Equity Index: Where the Provinces Stand* (Montreal: Institute for Health and Social Policy, McGill University, 2008); S. J. Heymann and M. Barrera, "Addressing Poverty in a Globalised Economy" (Policy Network Progressive Governance Paper, April 3, 2008); S. J. Heymann, A. Earle, and J. Hayes, *Work, Family, and Equity Index: How Does the U.S. Measure Up?* Project on Global Working Families (Cambridge, MA: Harvard School of Public Health and Institute for Health and Social Policy, McGill University, 2007); S. J. Heymann, *How Are Workers with Family Responsibilities Faring in the Workplace?* (Geneva: ILO, 2004); S. J. Heymann, UNESCO Policy Briefs: "The Impact of AIDS on Early Childhood Care and Education" (June 2003), "The Role of Early Childhood Care and Education in Ensuring Equal Opportunity" (November–December 2003), "School Children in Families with Young Children: Educational Opportunities at Risk" (February 2003),"Social Transformations and Their Implications for the Global Demand for ECCE" (November–December 2002).

24. This effort was greatly facilitated by the ILO's efforts to collect the world's labor codes and legislation, and the U.S. Social Security Administration's efforts to collect and describe the world's social security systems. While neither initiative had created a quantitatively analyzable or publicly available database of information that compared elements of countries' policies, their global work laid invaluable foundations. More information can be found at the ILO's NATLEX website, http://www.ilo.org/dyn/natlex/natlex_browse.home and at Social Security Programs Throughout the World (SSPTW), Research, Statistics, & Policy Analysis Data, Social Security Online, http://www.ssa.gov/policy/docs/progdesc/ssptw/ (both accessed February 26, 2009).

25. P. Krugman, "Toyota, Moving Northward," *New York Times*, July 25, 2005.

26. Full title of the U.S.–Cambodia Trade Agreement: Agreement Relating to Trade in Cotton, Wool, Man-made Fiber, Non-Cotton Vegetable Fiber and Silk Blend Textiles and Textile Products Between the Government of the United States of America and the Royal Government of Cambodia.

Chapter 2

1. Using the conversion rate of the time period of the interviews, Summer 2007, 1 Polish Zloty = 0.36755 US Dollar.

2. Using the conversion rate of the time period of the interviews, Summer 2007, 1 Iceland Krona = 0.01670 US Dollar.

3. See, for example, D. Fuller and D. Geide-Stevenson, "Consensus Among Economists: Revisited," *Journal of Economic Review* 34, no. 4 (2003): 367–87; Y. Ghellab, "Minimum Wages and Youth Unemployment" (ILO Employment and Training Papers 26, 1998), http://www.ilo.org/public/english/employment/strat/download/etp26.pdf (accessed February 27, 2009); C. Brown, C. Gilroy, and A. Kohen, "The Effect of the Minimum Wage on Employment and Unemployment," *Journal of Economic Literature* 20, no. 2 (1982): 487–528 and "Time-Series Evidence of the Effect of the Minimum Wage on Youth Employment and Unemployment," *Journal of Human Resources* 18, no. 1 (1983): 3–31; A. J. Wellington, "Effects of the Minimum Wage on the Employment Status of Youths: An Update," *Journal of Human Resources* 26, no. 1 (1991): 27–46.

4. D. Neumark and W. Wascher, "Minimum Wages and Employment: A Review of Evidence from the New Minimum Wage Research" (National Bureau of Economic Research Working Paper no. W12663, November 2006); T. Yuen, "The Effect of Minimum Wages on Youth Employment in Canada: A Panel Study," *Journal of Human Resources* 38 (Summer 2003): 647–72; M. Campolieti, M. Gunderson, and C. Riddell, "Minimum Wage Impacts from a Prespecified Research Design: Canada 1981–1997," *Industrial Relations: A Journal of Economy and Society* 45, no. 2 (2006): 195–216.

5. Among those who find that increasing the minimum wage does have an impact, it is most commonly argued that this impact is first and foremost on teenage employment and secondarily on the youngest adults in the labor force. For example, see R. Saunders, *Lifting the Boats: Policies to Make Work Pay* (Vulnerable Worker Series, Canadian Policy Research Networks, June 2005); D. Neumark and W. Wascher, "Minimum Wages and Employment: A Review of Evidence from the New Minimum Wage Research" (National Bureau of Economic Research Working Paper no. W12663, November 2006); D. Deere, K. M. Murphy, and F. Welch, "Employment and the 1990–1991 Minimum-Wage Hike," *American Economic Review* 85, no. 2 (1995): 232–37.

6. M. D. Turner, "The Low-Wage Labor Market: Does the Minimum Wage Help or Hurt Low-Wage Workers?" U.S. Department of Health and Human Services, Assistant Secretary for Planning and Evaluation (ASPE), http://aspe.hhs.gov/hsp/lwlm99/turner.htm (accessed May 28, 2009); D. Card and A. B. Krueger, "Minimum Wages and Employment: A Case Study of the Fast-Food Industry in New Jersey and Pennsylvania," *American Economic Review* 84, no. 4 (1994): 772–92; D. Card and A. B. Krueger, "Minimum Wages and Employment: A Case Study of the Fast-Food Industry in New Jersey and Pennsylvania: Reply," *American Economic Review* 90 (2000): 1397–420.

7. The World Bank's World Development Indicators (WDI) database defines unemployment as: "the share of the labor force that is without work but available for and seeking employment. Definitions of labor force and unemployment differ by country." Some countries, such as those in the OECD, include the informal economy in

these calculations. To our knowledge, however, there is no global source of data on the number or fraction of adults who are too discouraged to seek work. We used the average of the years of WDI data available between 2003 and 2006. World Bank, "World Development Indicators Online" (WDI Online), http://web.worldbank.org/WBSITE/EXTERNAL/DATASTATISTICS/0,,contentMDK:20398986menuPK:64133163pagePK:64133150piPK:64133175theSitePK:239419,00.html (accessed June 10, 2009).

8. We began with an interest in examining evening and night work separately. However, most of the legislation refers only to night work or combines these concepts. The legislative definitions used for "night" work vary, with the earliest considering that this begins at 6 P.M. and the latest at midnight. The overwhelming majority consider night work to begin between 9 P.M. and 11 P.M.

9. The OECD describes its mandate as "bring[ing] together the governments of countries committed to democracy and the market economy from around the world to: support sustainable economic growth; boost employment; raise living standards; maintain financial stability; assist other countries' economic development; contribute to growth in world trade." See OECD, "About OECD," http://www.oecd.org/pages/0,3417,en_36734052_36734103_1_1_1_1_1,00.html (accessed February 27, 2009).

10. Unemployment data from all thirty OECD nations uses the following definition of unemployed persons: "persons of working age who . . . are without work and are both available for and are actively seeking work." The unemployment rate is defined as "the number of unemployed persons as a percentage of civilian labor force [which consists of] civilian employees, the self-employed, unpaid family workers, and the unemployed." For further information on the development of this unemployment definition, see OECD, "Sources and Definitions," http://stats.oecd.org/mei/default.asp?lang=e&subject=10 (accessed July 31, 2009).

11. "Leave for new mothers," "maternal leave," and "leave for mothers around the birth or adoption of a new baby" are all defined as the sum total of leave available to women through maternity leave and parental leave.

12. "Leave for new fathers," "paternal leave," and "leave for fathers around the birth or adoption of a new baby" are all defined as the sum total of leave available to men through paternity leave and parental leave.

13. Employees with at least two years of tenure are provided with up to 720 days of sick leave.

14. "Bangladesh Sets US$25 Minimum Wage for Garment Workers After Months of Street Protests," *International Herald Tribune*, October 5, 2006.

15. World Bank, "World Development Indicators Online" (WDI Online), http://web.worldbank.org/WBSITE/EXTERNAL/DATASTATISTICS/0,,contentMDK:20398986menuPK:64133163pagePK:64133150piPK:64133175theSitePK:239419,00.html (accessed June 10, 2009); International Energy Agency, "Natural Gas by Country/Region," http://www.iea.org/Textbase/stats/prodresult.asp?PRODUCT=Natural%20Gas (accessed June 12, 2009); Organization of the Petroleum Exporting Countries, "Annual Statistical Bulletin 2007," http://www.opec.org/library/Annual%20 Statistical%20 Bulletin/pdf/ASB2007.pdf (accessed June 12, 2009); Norwegian Ministry of Petroleum

and Energy, "Norway's Oil and Gas Resources" (November 21, 2007), http://www.regjeringen.no/en/dep/oed/Subject/Oil-and-Gas/Norways-oil-and-gas -resources.html?id=443528 (accessed February 27, 2009).

16. International Institute for Labor Studies, *World of Work Report 2008: Income Inequalities in the Age of Financial Globalization* (Washington, DC: International Labour Organisation, 2008), http://www.ilo.org/public/english/bureau/inst/download/world08.pdf (accessed November 17, 2008).

17. In Norway, most of the bargaining is carried out on a sectoral level and is coordinated by the Norwegian Confederation of Trade Unions (Landsorganisasjonen) and the Confederation of Norwegian Enterprises (Nœringslivets Hovedorganisasjon). See A. Vamvakidis, "Regional Wage Differentiation and Wage Bargaining Systems in the EU" (IMF Working Paper WP/08/43, 2008); L. Kensworthy, "Wage-Setting Measures: A Survey and Assessment," *World Politics* 54 (October 2001): 57–98.

18. Statistics Norway, "Main Economic Indicators 1998–2010, Accounts and Forecasts" (2007), http://www.ssb.no/kt_en/arkiv/ttab-2007-09-06-01-en.html (accessed November 17, 2008).

19. Z. Tzannatos, "Women and Labor Market Changes in the Global Economy: Growth Helps, Inequalities Hurt and Public Policy Matters," *World Development* 27, no. 3 (1999): 551–69.

20. Norwegian Ministry for Education and Research, "Educational Support," http://www.regjeringen.no/en/dep/kd/Selected-topics/study-financing-.html?id=1422 (accessed November 17, 2008).

21. Norwegian Ministry for Education and Research, "Education—From Kindergarten to Adult Education" (2007), http://www.utdanningsdirektoratet.no/upload/Brosjyrer/Education_in_Norway.pdf (accessed November 17, 2008).

22. In 1991, over one in four adults in Norway between the ages of twenty-five and sixty-four had completed a postsecondary education, and by 2006 this had increased to 33 percent. See OECD, Norwegian Directorate for Education, Education at a Glance 2003: OECD indicators, "Table A2.4: Trends in educational attainment at tertiary level (1991–2001)," http://lysander.sourceoecd.org/vl=893695/cl=20/nw=1/rpsv/cgi-bin/fulltextew.pl?prpsv=/ij/oecdthemes/99980029/v2003n8/s1/p1l.idx and "Table A1.3a: Population that has attained tertiary education (2006)," http://www.oecd.org/dataoecd/23/46/41284038.pdf (both accessed November 17, 2008).

23. OECD Statistics Directorate, StatExtracts, "Harmonised Unemployment Rates and Levels (HURs)," http://stats.oecd.org/wbos/Index.aspx?QueryName=251&QueryType=View (accessed February 27, 2009).

24. Higher education was defined as tertiary education of a range of types. For detailed descriptions, see OECD, Education at a Glance 2008: OECD indicators, http://www.oecd.org/dataoecd/10/7/41274044.pdf (accessed November 17, 2008).

25. OECD, Education at a Glance 2008, OECD Indicators, "Table A8.5a: Trends in unemployment rates by educational attainment (1997–2006)," http://www.oecd.org/dataoecd/23/46/41284038.pdf (accessed November 17, 2008).

26. OECD, Norwegian Directorate for Education and Training, "Improving

School Leadership: Country Background Report for Norway" (2007), http://nslf.no.a2n.no/images/Marketing/Aktuelt/OECD-rapport_om_skoleledelse_2007.pdf (accessed November 17, 2008).

27. The other countries that do not charge tuition are the Nordic nations (Denmark, Finland, Sweden, and Iceland) as well as the Czech Republic, Ireland, and Poland. See OECD, Education at a Glance 2008: OECD Indicators, http://www.oecd.org/dataoecd/23/46/41284038.pdf (accessed November 17, 2008).

28. OECD, Education at a Glance 2008: OECD Indicators, page 265, http://www.oecd.org/dataoecd/23/46/41284038.pdf (accessed November 17, 2008).

29. OECD, Education at a Glance 2008: OECD Indicators, "Table A1.3a. Population that has attained tertiary education (2006)," http://www.oecd.org/dataoecd/23/46/41284038.pdf (accessed November 17, 2008). While providing affordable access to advanced education, Norway has also focused on improving the quality of education and its relevance to the labor market. The country has worked to conform to the European Commission's recommendations from the Bologna Process, the aims of which included improving the uniformity and recognition of education across the continent. See OECD, Norwegian Ministry for Education and Research, "Thematic Review of Tertiary Education: Country Background Report for Norway" (January 2005), http://www.oecd.org/dataoecd/22/55/35585126.pdf (accessed November 17, 2008).

30. Using summer 2004 conversion rate of 1 Norwegian Kroner = 0.14565 US Dollar. Norwegian Ministry for Education and Research, "Early Childhood Education and Care Policy," http://www.regjeringen.no/en/dep/kd/Selected-topics/kindergarden/early-childhood-education-and-care-polic.html?id=491283 (accessed November 17, 2008).

31. Norwegian Ministry of Labour and Social Inclusion, "The Norwegian Social Insurance Scheme 2008," A-0008 E, http://www.regjeringen.no/en/dep/aid/doc/veiledninger_brosjyrer/2008/the-norwegian-social-insurance-scheme-20.html?id=507092&epslanguage=EN-GB (accessed November 17, 2008). Recognizing the greater difficulty of rearing children for single parents, the latter are eligible for an additional cash benefit equivalent to the amount paid for having an additional child. See Norwegian Labour and Welfare Administration, "Child Benefit," http://www.nav.no/805368051.cms (accessed November 17, 2008).

32. Norwegian Ministry for Education and Research, "Early Childhood Education and Care Policy," http://www.regjeringen.no/en/dep/kd/Selected-topics/kindergarden/early-childhood-education-and-care-polic.html?id=491283 (accessed November 17, 2008).

33. J. Currie and T. Duncan, "Does Head Start Make a Difference?" *American Economic Review* 85, no. 3 (1995): 341–64.

34. R. McKay, L. Condell, and H. Ganson, *The Impact of Head Start on Children, Families and Communities: Final Report of the Head Start Evaluation, Synthesis, and Utilization Project* (Washington, DC: CSR, 1985).

35. S. Andrews, J. Blumenthal, D. Johnson, et al., "The Skills of Mothering: A

Study of Parent Child Development Centers," *Monographs of the Society for Research in Child Development* 46, no. 6 (1982), Serial no. 198; W. Barnett, "Long-Term Effects of Early Childhood Programs on Cognitive and School Outcomes," *The Future of Children* 5, no. 3 (1995): 25–50; F. Campbell and C. Ramey, "Effects of Early Intervention on Intellectual and Academic Achievement: A Follow-up Study of Children from Low-Income Families," *Child Development* 65 (1994): 684–98; D. Johnson and T. Walker, "A Follow-up Evaluation of the Houston Parent Child Development Center: School Performance," *Journal of Early Intervention* 15, no. 3 (1991): 226–36.

36. Norwegian Ministry for Education and Research, "Early Childhood Education and Care Policy," http://www.regjeringen.no/en/dep/kd/Selected-topics/kinder garden/early-childhood-education-and-care-polic.html?id=491283 (accessed November 17, 2008).

37. Norwegian Ministry for Education and Research, "Education—From Kindergarten to Adult Education" (2007), http://www.utdanningsdirektoratet.no/upload /Brosjyrer/Education_in_Norway.pdf and "The Norwegian Education System," http://www.regjeringen.no/en/dep/kd/Selected-topics/compulsory-education/The-Norwegian-Education-System.html?id=445118 (both accessed November 17, 2008).

38. A. Skevik, "Family Policies in Norway," third report for the Welfare Policy and Employment in the Context of Family Change project, Norwegian Social Research (NOVA) (June 5–6, 2003; revised July 2003), http://www.york.ac.uk/inst/spru/ research/nordic/norwpoli.PDF (accessed February 27, 2009).

39. Utdanningsdirektoratet (Norwegian Directorate for Education and Training), Grunnskolens Informasjonssystem (GSI) (Elementary school database), http://www .wis.no/gsi/tallene/ (accessed November 17, 2008).

40. When an employee is going to be terminated because the company is downsizing, closing, or for other reasons reducing staff, he or she receives a warning in advance. This warning period must be at least two months if the employee had been continuously employed in the company for five years, three months if the employment period was ten years, four months if the employee is aged fifty or older, five months if aged fifty-five or older, and six months if aged sixty or over. In cases of layoff, the employer must pay the regular wage for the first two to three weeks of the layoff period. See Act No. 62 of 2005, respecting working environment, working hours, and employment protection, etc. Working Environment Act, as subsequently amended by Act of 23 February 2007, Chapter 15, Termination of Employment Relationship, http://www .arbeidstilsynet.no/binfil/download.php?tid=42156 (accessed June 9, 2009).

41. Norwegian Ministry of Labour and Social Inclusion, "The Norwegian Social Insurance Scheme 2008," A-0008 E, http://www.regjeringen.no/en/dep/aid/ doc/veiledninger_brosjyrer/2008/the-norwegian-social-insurance-scheme-20 .html?id=507092&epslanguage=EN-GB (accessed November 17, 2008).

42. This section on economic strategy builds on the insights of T. Qvale (interview by S. J. Heymann and S. Simmons, August 8, 2007), Work Research Institute, Oslo, Norway.

43. UNDP, *Human Development Report 2007/08*, http://hdr.undp.org/en/media/HDR_20072008_EN_Complete.pdf (accessed November 17, 2008).

44. UNDP, *Human Development Reports*, http://hdr.undp.org/en/reports/ (accessed November 17, 2008).

45. UNDP, *Human Development Report 2007/08*, http://hdr.undp.org/en/media/HDR_20072008_EN_Complete.pdf (accessed November 17, 2008).

46. Norwegian Directorate of Immigration (UDI), "A Guide for Residents of Asylum Reception Centres," http://www.nyinorge.no/modules/module_123/proxy.asp?c=29&d=1 (accessed February 27, 2009).

47. The government has set targets for reducing disparities in income, health and education outcomes, and labor force participation between immigrants and citizens as well as for increasing the number of immigrants working in the public sector. See Norwegian Ministry of Labour and Social Inclusion, "Targets for Social Inclusion of the Immigrant Population," http://www.regjeringen.no/en/dep/aid/Topics/Integration-and-diversity/midtspalte/targets-for-social-inclusion-of-the-immi.html?id=504173 (accessed November 17, 2008).

48. UNDP, "Table 1. Human Development Index," *Human Development Report 2007/08*, http://hdr.undp.org/en/media/HDR_20072008_EN_Complete.pdf (accessed April 15, 2008).

49. World Bank, "World Development Indicators Online" (WDI Online), http://web.worldbank.org/WBSITE/EXTERNAL/DATASTATISTICS/0,,contentMDK:20398986menuPK:64133163pagePK:64133150piPK:64133175theSitePK:239419,00.html (accessed June 10, 2009).

50. For 1970 data, see World Bank, "World Development Indicators 2002" (CD-ROM, 2002); for 2005 data, see World Bank, World Development Indicators Online" (WDI Online), http://web.worldbank.org/WBSITE/EXTERNAL/DATASTATISTICS/0,,contentMDK:20398986menuPK:64133163pagePK:64133150piPK:64133175theSitePK:239419,00.html (accessed February 26, 2009).

51. World Bank, World Development Indicators Online (WDI Online), http://web.worldbank.org/WBSITE/EXTERNAL/DATASTATISTICS/0,,contentMDK:20398986menuPK:64133163pagePK:64133150piPK:64133175theSitePK:239419,00.html (accessed February 26, 2009).

52. D. Boamah, "The Effect of Human Capital on Economic Growth in the Caribbean" (Central Bank of Barbados, Working Papers, ii, 1997).

53. OECD Statistics Directorate, StatExtracts, "Survey Based Unemployment Rates and Levels," OECD Main Economic Indicators (MEI), http://www.oecd.org/document/15/0,3343,en_2649_33715_1873295_1_1_1_1,00.html#unemployment_statistics (accessed November 17, 2008); ILO, "Global Employment Trends: January 2008," http://www.ilo.org/public/english/employment/strat/download/get08.pdf (accessed November 17, 2008).

54. R. Freeman and R. Oostendorp, "Occupational Wages around the World (OWW) Database," http://www.nber.org/oww/ (accessed May 28, 2009).

55. Bangladesh Bureau of Statistics, "Key Findings of Labor Force Survey 2005–

2006," http://www.bbs.gov.bd/dataindex/labour_%20force05-06.pdf (accessed February 27, 2009).

56. Norwegian Ministry of Labour and Social Inclusion, "Regulation 29 June 2005 on general application of wage agreements for construction sites in the Oslo Fjord Region" (June 25, 2005), http://www.regjeringen.no/en/dep/aid/doc/lover_regler/forskrifter/2005/Regulation-29-June-2005-on-general-appli.html?id=450481 (accessed February 27, 2009).

57. UNDP, *Human Development Report 2007/08*, http://hdr.undp.org/en/media/HDR_20072008_EN_Complete.pdf (accessed February 27, 2009).

Chapter 3

1. Australian Chamber of Commerce and Industry, "No Jobs But More Union Power in Labor Industrial Relations Policy," Media Release, April 28, 2007.

2. "Labor Law Revision Benefits All," *Jakarta Post*, April 9, 2006.

3. "Tussle Ahead over Labor Law," *Jakarta Post*, March 29, 2006.

4. "Indonesian Workers Protest Proposed Labor Law Changes," *Dow Jones International News*, May 2, 2006.

5. "Call for Labor Law Compromise," *Jakarta Post*, May 3, 2008; "Minister Pledges to Resolve Labor Regulation Problems," *Jakarta Post*, March 24, 2008: Business section.

6. "Apindo Vows to Intensify Cooperation with Workers," *Jakarta Post*, March 29, 2008; "Taiwanese Firms to Invest in Labor-Intensive Sectors," *Jakarta Post*, March 19, 2008.

7. E. Azly, "Thousands of Workers Hit the Streets in Jakarta to Celebrate May Day," *Nationwide International* (Antara, Indonesia), May 1, 2008: News section.

8. "European Union Chamber of Commerce in China welcomes the promulgation of the Labour Contract Law," European Union Chamber of Commerce in China (July 1, 2007), http://www.europeanchamber.com.cn/view/media/fullview?cid=1126#content.

9. US-China Business Council, Comments on the Draft Labor Contract Law of the People's Republic of China (April 19, 2006).

10. "China Due to Enact New Labor Law After Heated Debate," *Associated Press*, June 27, 2007. The objection to the new labor law expressed by U.S. and other business groups was reported to have been based on a fear that the regulations would be enforced differentially, with non-Chinese firms being subject to far stricter monitoring and higher standards of compliance. See "Foreign Corporations' Opposition to the New Chinese Labor Contract Law and Their Impact" (September 2007), National Labor Committee, http://www.nlcnet.org/article.php?id=473 (accessed May 28, 2009) and The American Chamber of Commerce in Shanghai, "Comments on Draft Two of the PRC Labor Contract Law," translated from Chinese, http://www.amcham-shanghai.org/AmChamPortal/MCMS/Presentation/Template/Content.aspx?Type=31&Guid=%7B67A59D61-0FAF-4391-9F00-5B2F529C6704%7D (accessed May 28, 2009).

11. "China Passes a Sweeping Labor Law," *New York Times*, June 30, 2007.

12. "China's Legislature Approves New Labor Law," *Associated Press*, June 29, 2007.

13. U.S. Senate Committee on Health, Education, Labor, and Pensions, *The Healthy Families Act: Safeguarding Americans' Livelihood, Families and Health with Paid Sick Days* (February 13, 2007), http://help.senate.gov/Hearings/2007_02_13/2007_02_13.html (accessed February 26, 2009).

14. "Employers Oppose Proposed Healthy Families Act," *Northeast Pennsylvania Business Journal*, June 1, 2007.

15. Ibid.

16. U.S. Senate Committee on Health, Education, Labor, and Pensions, Roundtable Discussion: The Family Medical Leave Act: A Dozen Years of Experience (June 23, 2005), http://help.senate.gov/Hearings/2005_06_23/2005_06_23.html (accessed February 27, 2009).

17. European Commission, "A Stronger Union for a Better World" (June 29, 2007), http://ec.europa.eu/commission_barroso/president/focus/eu2007pt/index_en.htm (accessed February 4, 2008).

18. Commission of the European Communities, "Modernising Labour Law to Meet the Challenges of the 21st Century" (Green Paper, November 22, 2006), http://ec.europa.ue/employment_social/labor_law/docs/2006/green_paper_en.pdf (accessed February 27, 2009).

19. Select Committee on European Union Minutes of Evidence, "Examination of Witnesses (Questions 40–60)" (March 29, 2007), page 83, http://www.publications.parliament.uk/pa/ld200607/ldselect/ldeucom/120/7032907.htm (accessed February 26, 2009).

20. J. Bhagwati, "Trade Liberalization and 'Fair Trade' Demands: Addressing the Environmental and Labour Standards Issues," *World Economy* 18, no. 6 (1995): 745–59; J. Heintz, "Global Labor Standards: Their Impact and Implementation" (Working Paper no. 46, Series of the Political Economy Research Institute, University of Massachusetts, Amherst 2002).

21. S. S. Golub, "International Labor Standards and International Trade" (Working Paper of the International Monetary Fund WP/97/37, 1997); R. N. Block, K. Roberts, C. Ozeki, and M. J. Roomkin, "Models of International Labor Standards," *Industrial Relations* 40, no. 2 (2001): 258–92; T. N. Srinivasan, "International Trade and Labour Standards from an Economic Perspective," in *Challenges to the New World Organization*, ed. P. Van Dijck and G. Faber (Boston: Kluwer Law International, 1996), 219–43; W. M. Corden and N. Vousden, "Paved with Good Intentions: Social Dumping and Raising Labour Standards in Developing Countries," in *Globalization Under Threat: The Stability of Trade Policy and Multilateral Agreements*, ed. Z. Drabek (Cheltenham, UK: Edward Elgar, 2001), 124–43; D. Brown, A. V. Deardorff, and R. M. Stern, "Trade and Labor Standards" (Discussion Paper no. 394, School of Public Policy, University of Michigan, March 14, 1997).

22. T. Palley, E. Drake, and T. Lee, "The Case for Core Labor Standards in the International Economy: Theory, Evidence, and a Blueprint for Implementation"

(AFL-CIO Economic Policy Papers, no. E041, 1999); R. Buchele and J. Christensen, "Productivity, Real Wages, and Workers' Rights: A Crossnational Comparison," *Labour* 9, no. 3 (1995): 405–22.

23. R. N. Block, K. Roberts, C. Ozeki, and M. J. Roomkin, "Models of International Labor Standards," *Industrial Relations* 40, no. 2 (2001): 258–92.

24. R. Blank and R. B. Freeman, "Evaluating the Connection Between Social Protection and Economic Flexibility," in *Social Protection and Economic Flexibility: Is There a Trade-Off?* ed. R. Blank (Chicago: University of Chicago Press, 1994).

25. S. Braun, "Core Labor Standards and FDI: Friends or Foes? The Case of Child Labor," *Review of World Economics* 142, no. 4 (2006): 765–91; M. Busse and S. Braun, "Trade and Investment Effects of Forced Labor: An Empirical Assessment," *International Labor Review* 142, no. 1 (2003): 49–71; D. Kucera, "Core Labor Standards and Foreign Direct Investment," *International Labor Review* 141, no. 1–2 (2002): 31–69.

26. M. Busse, "Foreign Direct Investment and Fundamental Workers' Rights," *Journal of International Relations & Development* 5, no. 2 (2002): 143–55; E. Neumayer and I. De Soysa, "Globalization and the Right to Free Association and Collective Bargaining: An Empirical Analysis," *World Development* 34, no. 1 (2006): 31–49.

27. M. Busse, "Comparative Advantage, Trade and Labor Standards," *Economics Bulletin* 6, no. 2 (2002): 1–8. Also see M. Busse, "Foreign Direct Investment and Fundamental Workers' Rights," *Journal of International Relations & Development* 5, no. 2 (2002): 143–55; M. Busse, "Do Labor Standards Affect Comparative Advantage in Developing Countries?" *World Development* 30, no. 11 (2002): 1921–32.

28. E. Neumayer and I. De Soysa, "Globalization and the Right to Free Association and Collective Bargaining: An Empirical Analysis," *World Development* 34, no. 1 (2006): 31–49; D. Kucera, "Core Labor Standards and Foreign Direct Investment," *International Labor Review* 141, no. 1–2 (2002): 31–69; D. Kucera and R. Sarna, "How Do Trade Union Rights Affect Competitiveness?" (Working Paper no. 39, Policy Integration Department, Statistical Development and Analysis Group, International Labor Office, 2004).

29. V. H. Dehejia and Y. Samy, "Trade and Labor Standards: Theory and New Empirical Evidence," *Journal of International Trade and Economic Development* 13, no. 2 (2004): 179–98; V. Dehejia and Y. Samy, "Labor Standards and Economic Integration in the European Union: An Empirical Analysis" (CESifo Working Paper no. 1746, CESifo GmbH, CESifo Working Paper Series, 2006); C. Van Beers, "Labor Standards and Trade Flows of OECD Countries," *World Economy* 21, no. 1 (1998): 57–73; T. Aidt and Z. Tzannatos, *Unions and Collective Bargaining: Economic Effects in a Global Environment* (Washington, DC: World Bank, 2002).

30. OECD, *Trade, Employment and Labor Standards: A Study of Core Workers' Rights and International Trade* (Paris: OECD, 1996).

31. For more information on Core Labor Standards, see International Labour Organization, "International Labour Standards," http://www.ilo.org/global/What_we_do/InternationalLabourStandards/lang—en/index.htm (accessed March 3, 2009); ILO, "Fundamental Rights at Work and International Labour Standards"

(2003), http://www.ilo.org/wcmsp5/groups/public/—-ed_norm/—-normes/documents/publication/wcms_087424.pdf (accessed February 26, 2009).

32. The World Economic Forum (WEF) is an international organization made up primarily of business leaders, as well as government officials and academic researchers. Much of the data used in the Competitiveness Reports are obtained through a global network of 104 research institutions and academics that partner and collaborate with WEF, as well as from a survey of eleven thousand business leaders from 131 nations. The categories are weighted in order to more accurately account for levels of development in measuring each indicator's impact on competitiveness. From 1987 to 2005, the Index was named the "Growth Competitiveness Index"; its name then changed to the "Global Competitiveness Index" in the 2006/7 issue of the Report. See World Economic Forum, "Our Organization," http://www.weforum.org/en/about/Our%20Organization/index.htm (accessed February 26, 2009).

33. Of the remaining four, Switzerland guarantees three weeks of paid sick leave, Singapore offers paid leave for more than two weeks, and New Zealand offers five days per year, although in New Zealand unused sick leave can be carried over to subsequent years and can accumulate up to twenty days. Again, the United States provides no paid leave.

34. Using a February 2009 conversion rate of 1 Australian Dollar = 0.65068 US Dollar, AUS$5,000 = US$3,253.

35. Average weekly earnings: $898. See Australian Bureau of Statistics, "6302.0—Average Weekly Earnings, Australia" (August 2008), http://www.abs.gov.au/ausstats/abs@.nsf/mf/6302.0/ (accessed February 9, 2009).

36. Using a February 2009 conversion rate of 1 Australian Dollar = 0.65068 US Dollar, AUS$75,000 = US$48,800.

37. Rankings are from The World Economic Forum's 2008–2009 Global Competitiveness Report. See K. Schwab and M. E. Porter, "The Global Competitiveness Report 2008–2009," World Economic Forum (2008), http://www.weforum.org/pdf/GCR08/GCR08.pdf (accessed March 3, 2009).

38. Y. C. Ng, P. Jacobs, and J. A. Johnson, "Productivity Losses Associated with Diabetes in the US," *Diabetes Care* 24 (2001): 257–61; J. Crystal-Peters, W. H. Crown, R. Z. Goetzel, and D. C. Schutt, "The Cost of Productivity Losses Associated with Allergic Rhinitis," *American Journal of Managed Care* 6 (2000): 373–78; T. D. Szucs, "Influenza: The Role of Burden-of-Illness Research," *Pharmacoeconomics* 16, Suppl. 1 (1999): 27–32; J. L. Severens, R. J. Laheij, J. B. Jansen, E. H. Van der Lisdonk, and A. L. Verbeek, "Estimating the Cost of Lost Productivity in Dyspepsia," *Alimentary Pharmacology Therapy*, 12 (1998): 919–23; J. P. Leigh, W. Seavey, and B. Leistikow, "Estimating the Costs of Job Related Arthritis," *Journal of Rheumatology* 28 (2001): 1647–54.

39. X. H. Hu, L. E. Markson, R. B. Lipton, W. F. Stewart, and M. L. Berger, "Burden of Migraine in the United States: Disability and Economic Costs," *Archives of Internal Medicine* 159 (1999): 813–18; W. F. Stewart, J. A. Ricci, E. Chee, S. R. Hahn, and D. Morganstein, "Cost of Lost Productive Work Time Among US Workers With Depression," *Journal of the American Medical Association* 289, no. 23 (2003): 3135–44;

R. N. Kumar, S. L. Hass, J. Z. Li, D. J. Nickens, C. L. Daenzer, and L. K. Wathen, "Validation of the Health-Related Productivity Questionnaire Diary (HRPQ-D) on a Sample of Patients with Infectious Mononucleosis: Results from a Phase 1 Multicenter Clinical Trial," *Journal of Occupational and Environmental Medicine* 45, no. 8 (2003): 899–907.

40. R. Z. Goetzel, et al., "Health, Absence, Disability, and Presenteeism Cost Estimates of Certain Physical and Mental Health Conditions Affecting U.S. Employers," *Journal of Occupational and Environmental Medicine* 46, no. 4 (2004): 398–412; R. C. Kessler, P. E. Greenberg, K. D. Mickelson, et al., "The Effect of Chronic Medical Conditions on Work Loss and Work Cutback," *Journal of Occupational and Environmental Medicine* 43, no. 3 (2001): 218–25; R. C. Kessler, C. Barber, A. Beck, et al., "The World Health Organization Health and Work Performance Questionnaire," *Journal of Occupational and Environmental Medicine* 45, no. 2 (2003): 156–174; W. N. Burton, D. J. Conti, C. Y. Chen, et al., "The role of health risk factors and disease on worker productivity," *Journal of Occupational and Environmental Medicine* 41, no. 10 (1999): 863–877.

41. M. Chatterji and C. J. Tilley, "Sickness, Absenteeism, Presenteeism, and Sick Pay," *Oxford Economic Papers* 54 (2002): 669–87.

42. D. B. Gilleski, "A Dynamic Stochastic Model of Medical Care Use and Work Absence," *Econometrica* 66 (1998): 1–45; G. Aronsson, K. Gustafsson, and M. Dallner, "Sick But Yet at Work: An Empirical Study of Sickness Presenteeism," *Journal of Epidemiology and Community Health* 54 (2000): 502–9; A. Grinyer and V. Singleton, "Sickness Absence as Risk-Taking Behaviour: A Study of Organizational and Cultural Factors in the Public Sector," *Health, Risk, & Society* 2 (2000): 7–21; G. Johannsson, "Work-Life Balance: The Case of Sweden in the 1990s," *Social Science Information* 41 (2002): 303–17.

43. V. Lovell, *No Time to Be Sick: Why Everyone Suffers When Workers Don't Have Paid Sick Leave* (Washington, DC: Institute for Women's Policy Research), 2004, http://www.iwpr.org/pdf/B242.pdf (accessed February 26, 2009); J. D. Skatun, "Take Some Days Off, Why Don't You? Endogenous Sick Leave and Pay," *Journal of Health Economics* 22, no. 3 (2003): 379–402.

44. A. Spurgeon, J. M. Harrington, and C. L. Cooper, "Health and Safety Problems Associated with Long Working Hours: A Review of the Current Position," *Occupational and Environmental Medicine* 54 (1997): 367–75.

45. E. Shepard and T. Clifton, "Are Longer Hours Reducing Productivity in Manufacturing?" *International Journal of Manpower* 21 (2000): 540–52.

46. Researchers studying productivity in the construction business in the United States found a 10 to 15 percent loss of productivity on average among workers whose hours exceeded forty hours per week. See H. R. Thomas and K. A. Raynar, "Scheduled Overtime and Labor Productivity: Quantitative Analysis," *Journal of Construction Engineering and Management* 123, no. 2 (1997): 181–88. For Canadian studies on overtime and productivity, see A. S. Hanna and D. G. Heale, "Factors Affecting Construction Productivity: Newfoundland versus Rest of Canada," *Canadian Journal of*

Civil Engineering 21 (1994): 663–73; R. Sonmez, "Impact of Occasional Overtime on Construction Labor Productivity: Quantitative Analysis," *Canadian Journal of Civil Engineering* 34 (2007): 803–8.

47. T. Shimizu, S. Horie, S. Nagata, and E. Marui, "Relationship Between Self-Reported Low Productivity and Overtime Working," *Occupational Medicine* 54 (2004): 52–54.

48. A. C. Macedo and I. L. Silva, "Analysis of Occupational Accidents in Portugal between 1992 and 2001," *Safety Science* 43 (2005): 269–86; O. A. Ergor, Y. Demiral, and Y. B. Piyal, "A Significant Outcome of Work Life: Occupational Accidents in a Developing Country, Turkey," *Journal of Occupational Health* 45 (2003): 74–80; A. E. Dembe, J. B. Erickson, R. G. Delbos, and S. M. Banks, "The Impact of Overtime and Long Work Hours on Occupational Injuries and Illnesses: New Evidence from the United States," *Occupational and Environmental Medicine* 62 (2005): 588–97; A. Baker, K. Heiler, and S. A. Ferguson, "The Impact of Roster Changes on Absenteeism and Incident Frequency in an Australian Coal Mine," *Occupational and Environmental Medicine* 60 (2003): 43–49; K. Hänecke, S. Tiedemann, F. Nachreiner, and H. Grzech-Sukalo, "Accident Risk as a Function of Hours at Work and Time of Day as Determined from Accident Data and Exposure Models for the German Working Population," *Scandinavian Journal of Work, Environment & Health* 24, Suppl. 3 (1998): 43–48; "More OT, Higher Absenteeism Marked Work Practices in 2004," *Occupational Health & Safety* 74, no. 3 (2005): 12.

49. S. Folkard and D. A. Lombardi, "Modeling the Impact of the Components of Long Work Hours on Injuries and 'Accidents.'" *American Journal of Industrial Medicine* 49 (2006): 953–63.

50. M. Shields, "Long Working Hours and Health," *Perspectives on Labour and Income* 12, no. 1 (2000): 49–56; A. Spurgeon, *Working Time: Its Impact on Health and Safety* (Geneva: International Labour Organization, 2003), http://www.ilo.org/public/English/protection/condtrav/publ/wtwo-as-03.htm (accessed February 4, 2009); L. Nylén, M. Voss, and B. Floderus, "Mortality Among Women and Men Relative to Unemployment, Part Time Work, Overtime Work, and Extra Work: A Study Based on Data from the Swedish Twin Registry," *Occupational and Environmental Medicine* 58 (2001): 52–57.

51. P. Knauth, "Extended Work Periods," *Industrial Health* 45 (2007): 125–36; "More OT, Higher Absenteeism Marked Work Practices in 2004," *Occupational Health & Safety* 74, no. 3 (2005): 12; A. Baker, K. Heiler, and S. A. Ferguson, "The Impact of Roster Changes on Absenteeism and Incident Frequency in an Australian Coal Mine," *Occupational and Environmental Medicine* 60 (2003): 43–49.

52. R. N. Block, K. Roberts, C. Ozeki, and M. J. Roomkin, "Models of International Labor Standards," *Industrial Relations* 40, no. 2 (2001): 258–92.

53. J. Waldfogel, Y. Higuchi, and M. Abe, "Family Leave Policies and Women's Retention After Childbirth: Evidence from the United States, Britain, and Japan," *Journal of Population Economics* 12, no. 4 (1999): 523–45; S. Macran, P. Dex, and H. Joshi, "Employment after Childbearing: A Survival Analysis," *Work, Employment, and Society* 10,

no. 2 (1996): 273–96; Y. Higuchi, "Effects of Job Training and Productivity Growth on the Retention of Male and Female Workers in Japan," in *Labour Market and Economic Performance: Europe, Japan, and the USA,* ed. T. Tachibanaki (London: Macmillan, 1994); Y. Higuchi, "Child Care Leave in Japan: Marriage, Childbirth, and Job Retention for Women," in *Frontiers of Japanese Human Resource Practices,* ed. Y. Sano (Tokyo: Japanese Institute of Labour, 1997); S. McRae, *Maternity Rights in Britain* (London: Policy Studies Institute, 1991); S. McRae, "Returning to Work After Childbirth: Opportunities and Inequalities," *European Sociological Review* 9 (1993): 125–138; M. Pasquale, "Child Care Leave and its Impact on Fertility and Retention in the Firm for Married Women Employees in Japan," mimeo, Columbia University (1995); J. Waldfogel, "The Family Gap for Young Women in the United States and Britain: Can Maternity Leave Make a Difference?" *Journal of Labor Economics* 16, no.3 (1998): 505–545.

54. A. George and J. Hancock, "Reducing Pediatric Burn Pain with Parent Participation," *Journal of Burn Care and Rehabilitation* 14 (1993): 104–7; P. A. LaRosa Nash and J. M. Murphy, "An Approach to Pediatric Perioperative Care: Parent-Present Induction," *Nursing Clinics of North America* 32 (1997): 183–99; G. Van der Schyff, "The Role of Parents During Their Child's Hospitalization," *Australian Nurses Journal* 8 (1979): 57–61; S. J. Palmer, "Care of Sick Children by Parents: A Meaningful Role," *Journal of Advanced Nursing* 18 (1993): 185; M.R.H. Taylor and P. O'Connor, "Resident Parents and Shorter Hospital Stay," *Archives of Disease in Childhood* 64 (1989): 274–76; I. Kristensson-Hallstron, G. Elander, and G. Malmfors, "Increased Parental Participation on a Pediatric Surgical Daycare Unit," *Journal of Clinical Nursing* 6 (1997): 297–302; T. A. Waugh and D. L. Kjos, "Parental Involvement and the Effectiveness of an Adolescent Day Treatment Program," *Journal of Youth and Adolescence* 21 (1992): 487–97; C.P.Q. Sainsbury, O. P. Gray, J. Cleary, M. M. Davies, and P. H. Rowlandson, "Care by Parents of Their Children in Hospital," *Archives of Disease in Childhood* 61 (1986): 612–15; T. McGraw, "Preparing Children for the Operating Room: Psychological Issues," *Canadian Journal of Anaethesia* 41, no. 11 (1994): 1094–103; J. Cleary, O. P. Gray, D. J. Hall, P. H. Rowlandson, C. P. Sainsbury, and M. M. Davies, "Parental Involvement in the Lives of Children in Hospitals," *Archives of Disease in Childhood* 61, no. 8 (1986): 779–87; M. W. Gauderer, J. L. Lorig, and D. W. Eastwood, "Is There a Place for Parents in the Operating Room?" *Journal of Pediatric Surgery* 24, no. 7 (1989): 705–6; R. S. Hannallah and J. K. Rosales, "Experience with Parents' Presence During Anesthesia Induction in Children," *Canadian Anesthetists Society Journal* 30, no. 3, pt. 1 (1983): 286–89.

55. C. L. Hanson, M. J. DeGuire, A. M. Schinkel, S. W. Henggeler, and G. A. Burghen, "Comparing Social Learning and Family Systems Correlates of Adaptation in Youths with IDDM," *Journal of Pediatric Psychology* 17, no. 5 (1992): 555–72; S. Carlton-Ford, R. Miller, M. Brown, N. Nealeigh, and P. Jennings, "Epilepsy and Children's Social and Psychological Adjustment," *Journal of Health and Social Behavior* 36, no. 3 (1995): 285–301; K. W. Hamlett, D. S. Pellegrini, and K. S. Katz, "Childhood Chronic Illness as a Family Stressor," *Journal of Pediatric Psychology* 17, no. 1 (1992): 33–47; A. M. LaGreca, W. F. Auslander, P. Greco, D. Spetter, E. B. Fisher, and

J. V. Santiago, "I Get By with a Little Help from My Family and Friends: Adolescents' Support for Diabetes Care," *Journal of Pediatric Psychology* 20, no. 4 (1995): 449–76; B. J. Anderson, J. P. Miller, W. F. Auslander, and J. V. Santiago, "Family Characteristics of Diabetic Adolescents: Relationship to Metabolic Control," *Diabetes Care* 4, no. 6 (1981): 586–94; K. Johnson, "Children with Special Health Needs: Ensuring Appropriate Coverage and Care Under Health Care Reform," *Health Policy and Child Health* 1, no. 3 (1994): 1–5; E. W. Holden, D. Chimielewski, C. C. Nelson, V. A. Kager, and L. Foltz, "Controlling for General and Disease-Specific Effects in Child and Family Adjustment to Chronic Childhood Illness," *Journal of Pediatric Psychology* 22, no. 1 (1997): 15–27; S. T. Hauser, A. M. Jacobson, P. Lavori, et al., "Adherence Among Children and Adolescents with Insulin-Dependent Diabetes Mellitus over a Four-Year Longitudinal Follow-up: II. Immediate and Long-Term Linkages with the Family Milieu," *Journal of Pediatric Psychology* 15, no. 4 (1990): 527–42.

56. M.R.H. Taylor and P. O'Connor, "Resident Parents and Shorter Hospital Stay," *Archives of Disease in Childhood* 64 (1989): 274–76.

57. S. J. Heymann, S. Toomey, and F. Furstenberg, "Working Parents: What Factors Are Involved in Their Ability to Take Time Off from Work When Their Children Are Sick?" *Archives of Pediatrics & Adolescent Medicine* 153 (1999): 870–74.

58. S. Woloshin, L. M. Schwartz, A.N.A. Tosteson, et al., "Perceived Adequacy of Tangible Social Support and Health Outcomes in Patients with Coronary Artery Disease," *Journal of General Internal Medicine* 12, no. 10 (1997): 613–18; K. Orth-Gomer, M. Horsten, S. P. Wamala, et al., "Social Relations and Extent and Severity of Coronary Artery Disease—The Stockholm Female Coronary Risk Study," *European Heart Journal* 19, no. 11 (1998): 1648–56; A. M. Karner, M. A. Dahlgren, and B. Bergdahl, "Rehabilitation After Coronary Heart Disease: Spouses' views of Support," *Journal of Advanced Nursing* 46 (2004): 204–11; A. Rantanen, M. Kaunonen, P. Astedt-Kurki, and M. T. Tarkka, "Coronary Artery Bypass Grafting: Social Support for Patients and Their Significant Others," *Journal of Clinical Nursing* 13 (2004): 158–66.

59. S. J. Bennett, "Relationships Among Selected Antecedent Variables and Coping Effectiveness in Postmyocardial Infarction Patients," *Research in Nursing & Health* 16, no. 2 (1993): 131–39; L. Gorkin, E. B. Schron, M. M. Brooks, et al., "Psychosocial Predictors of Mortality in the Cardiac-Arrhythmia Suppression Trial-1 (Cast-1)," *American Journal of Cardiology* 71, no. 4 (1993): 263–67.

60. E. Tsouna-Hadjis, K. N. Vemmos, N. Zakopoulos, and S. Stamatelopoulos, "First-Stroke Recovery Process: The Role of Family Social Support," *Archives of Physical Medicine and Rehabilitation* 81 (2000): 881–87.

61. T. E. Seeman, "Health Promoting Effects of Friends and Family on Health Outcomes in Older Adults," *American Journal of Health Promotion* 14, no. 6 (2000): 362–70; L. F. Berkman, "Role of Social-Relations in Health Promotion," *Psychosomatic Medicine* 57, no. 3 (1995): 245–54.

62. R. K. Salokangas, "Living Situation, Social Network and Outcome in Schizophrenia: A Five-Year Prospective Follow-up Study," *Acta Psychiatrica Scandinavica* 96 (1997): 459–68; M. Jubb and E. Shanley, "Family Involvement: The Key to Opening

Locked Wards and Closed Minds," *International Journal of Mental Health Nursing* 11 (2002): 47–53; V. Stanhope, "Culture, Control, and Family Involvement: A Comparison of Psychosocial Rehabilitation in India and the United States," *Psychiatric Rehabilitation Journal* 25 (2002): 273–80.

63. W. Martin and K. E. Maskus, "Core Labor Standards and Competitiveness: Implications for Global Trade Policy," *Review of International Economics* 9, no. 2 (2001): 317–28.

Chapter 4

1. IMSS covers private sector workers. The insurance programs and services are available to adults in Mexico regardless of income level. Enrollment requires that a set contribution to the pool be made either by both employer and employee together, with the employer paying a percentage and the employee contributing the remainder, or by the individual alone. Workers in the informal economy, self-employed workers, as well as those working for small firms in the formal economy are eligible, but they must pay 100 percent of the contribution required. See Instituto Mexicano del Seguro Social, http://www.imss.gob.mx (accessed March 2, 2009).

2. For details about the Project on Global Working Families, see S. J. Heymann, *Forgotten Families: Ending the Growing Crisis Confronting Children and Working Parents in the Global Economy* (New York: Oxford University Press, 2006) and the Institute for Health and Social Policy, McGill University, http://www.mcgill.ca/ihsp (accessed March 2, 2009).

3. Informal sector work is work that is not "recognised, regulated, or protected by existing legal or regulatory frameworks." Employment Sector, International Labour Office, *Women and Men in the Informal Economy: A Statistical Picture* (Geneva: ILO, 2002), 12. The informal economy includes employment in the informal sector and employment in the formal sector that is contingent, temporary, or precarious, such as employment that is not regular or stable, that lacks a secure contract, and that typically does not include worker benefits, legal protections, or social protections that are funded or administered through registered employers. Examples of jobs that would be considered part of the informal economy include domestic workers, day laborers in such industries as construction, unpaid family workers in informal enterprises, temporary or part-time administrative or office staff, self-employed workers who make and sell their products from their homes, street vendors, piece-rate workers, and service workers employed through subcontractors, such as custodians, house cleaners, and security guards.

4. Among those respondents working in the informal economy, 60 percent of workers who earned *at or above* $10 purchasing power parity–adjusted (PPP-adjusted) per day were able to take advantage of paid leave, versus 19 percent of those earning *less than* $10 PPP-adjusted per day. In the formal sector, 85 percent of those earning *at*

or above $10 PPP-adjusted per day were able to take paid leave, compared to 70 percent of those earning *less than* $10 PPP-adjusted per day.

5. Among those respondents working in the informal economy, 61 percent of workers who earned *at or above* $10 PPP-adjusted per day had access to center-based child care, versus 11 percent of those earning *less than* $10 PPP-adjusted per day. In the formal sector, 51 percent of those earning *at or above* $10 PPP-adjusted per day had access to center-based childcare, compared to 41 percent of those earning *less than* the $10 PPP-adjusted per day. See S. J. Heymann, *Forgotten Families: Ending the Growing Crisis Confronting Children and Working Parents in the Global Economy* (New York: Oxford University Press, 2006), fig. 5-14.

6. H. Sock, H. Chea, and B. Sik, *Cambodia's Annual Economic Review* (Phnom Penh: Cambodia Development Resource Institute, 2001).

7. K. Kolben, "Trade, Monitoring, and the ILO: Working to Improve Conditions in Cambodia's Garment Factories," *Yale Human Rights and Development Law Journal* 7 (2004): 79–107; Foreign Investment Advisory Service, *Cambodia: Corporate Social Responsibility in the Apparel Sector and Potential Implications for Other Industry Sectors* (Washington, DC: World Bank, 2005).

8. Better Factories Cambodia, Synthesis Report 11 (Phnom Penh: ILO, June 2005).

9. Reports containing the information on how the company performed were reviewed by members of the government, the company, and union leaders.

10. L. Sibbel, *Arbitration Council Review* (Phnom Penh: Labour Dispute Resolution Project, June 2005).

11. Ibid.

12. S. Polaski, "Combining Global and Local Forces: The Case of Labor Rights in Cambodia," *World Development* 34, no. 5 (2006): 919–32.

13. L. Sibbel, *Linking Trade with Labour Rights: The ILO Garment Sector Working Conditions Improvement Project in Cambodia* (Lund, Sweden: Lund University, 2004).

14. Foreign Investment Advisory Service, *Cambodia: Corporate Social Responsibility and the Apparel Buyer Survey Results* (Washington, DC: International Finance Corporation and the World Bank, 2004).

15. A. Wells-Dang, "Linking Textiles to Labor Standards: Prospects for Cambodia and Vietnam," *Foreign Policy in Focus* (June 2002); M. Falkus and S. Frost, "Labour Relations and Regulation in Cambodia: Theory and Practice" (Southeast Asia Research Centre of the City University of Hong Kong, Working Papers Series no. 28, November 2002); R. Abrami, *Worker Rights and Global Trade: The U.S.-Cambodia Bilateral Textile Trade Agreement* (Boston: Harvard Business School, 2004); Better Factories Cambodia, "Facts and Figures," http://www.betterfactories.org/content/documents/Facts%20and%20Figures.pdf (accessed February 26, 2009).

16. See, for example, Campaign for Labor Rights, http://www.clrlabor.org/alerts/1997/nikey001.html (accessed February 26, 2009); "Abuse Rife at Nike's Indonesia Plants: Reports of Worker Abuse at Nike Factories Are Outlined in a New Report," *CNN World News*, February 22, 2001.

17. See, for example, Vietnam Labor Watch, "Nike Labor Practices in Vietnam" (March 20, 1997), http://www.saigon.com/nike/reports/report1.html (accessed January 17, 2008).

18. Vietnam Labor Watch cites the following reports:

> In the June '96 issue of Life Magazine, Sydney Schanberg (author of *The Killing Fields*) documented child labor being used in Pakistan in the production of Nike soccer balls—for 60 cents a day. The March 16 edition of the *New York Times* carried a story on union busting by Nike shoe contractors in Indonesia. One worker was "locked in a room at the plant and interrogated for seven days by the military, which demanded to know more about his labor activities." The October 17 edition of the CBS program *48 Hours* had a segment on Nike's labor rights abuses in Vietnam, including: beatings, sexual harassment and forcing workers to kneel for extended periods with their arms held in the air. On November 3, an article by Australian labor scholar Anita Chan was published in the *Washington Post.* She described Chinese shoe factories—producing for Nike and other companies—where supervisors submit workers to a military boot camp style of control. On March 14 1997, Reuters had a report on a Nike factory, Pouchen in Dong Nai, forced 56 Vietnamese women workers to run around the factory's premise, 12 fainted and were taken to the hospital emergency room.

See Vietnam Labor Watch, http://www.saigon.com/nike/reports/report1.html (accessed January 17, 2008). For a list of media pieces, see Vietnam Labor Watch, "Nike in the News," http://www.saigon.com/nike/nike-news.htm (accessed January 17, 2008).

19. Campaign for Labor Rights, http://www.clrlabor.org/alerts/1997/nikey001.html (accessed January 17, 2008).

20. M. Tran, "Nike Toes the Line," *Guardian News Blog*, April 13, 2005, http://blogs.guardian.co.uk/news/2005/04/nike_toes_the_l.html (accessed February 26, 2009).

21. D. Marcouiller, "Formal Measures of the Informal-Sector Wage Gap in Mexico, El Salvador, and Peru," *Economic Development and Cultural Change* 45, no. 2 (1997): 367–92.

22. A. Henley, G. R. Arabsheibani, and F. G. Carneiro, "On Defining and Measuring the Informal Sector" (World Bank Policy Research Working Paper, 2006).

23. International Labour Office, "Report VI: Decent Work and the Informal Economy" (International Labour Conference, 90th Session, 2002), http://www.ilo.org/public/english/standards/relm/ilc/ilc90/pdf/rep-vi.pdf (accessed March 2, 2009).

24. J. L. Daza, "Informal Economy, Undeclared Work, and Labour Administration" (Geneva: Social Dialogue Labour Law and Labour Administration Department, ILO, 2005), http://www.ilo.org/public/english/dialogue/ifpdial/downloads/informal.pdf (accessed March 2, 2009).

25. D. Grubb, "Informal Employment and Promoting the Transition to a Salaried Economy," in *OECD Employment Outlook*, ed. R. Torres (Paris: Organisation for Economic Co-operation and Development, 2004), 225–91.

26. National Commission for Enterprises in the Unorganised Sector, "Report on the Conditions of Work and Promotion of Livelihoods in the Unorganised Sector" (New Delhi: Dolphin Printo Graphics, 2007).

27. J. Howell, "Good Practice Study in Shanghai on Employment Services for the Informal Economy," Working Paper on the Informal Economy (Geneva: Employment Sector, International Labour Office, 2002).

28. Seventy-five to 80 percent of workers in Australia are covered through the 2006 Australia Fair Pay and Conditions Standard, which guarantees ten days of paid sick leave. Those not covered through AFPCS are covered through state legislation. Institute for Health and Social Policy, *Australian Work, Family and Equity Index: Minimum Employment Standards Across Australia* (forthcoming).

29. Analysis of the Bureau of Labor Statistics' National Compensation Survey (March 2008) with adjustment for workers who have less than the average minimum tenure requirement, as reported in J. Heymann, H. J. Rho, J. Schmitt, and A. Earle, *Contagion Nation: A Comparison of Paid Sick Day Policies in 22 Countries* (Washington, DC: Center for Economic Policy Research, 2009), http://www.cepr.net/documents/publications/paid-sick-days-2009-05.pdf (accessed June 9, 2009).

30. V. Lovell, *No Time to Be Sick, Why Everyone Suffers When Workers Don't Have Paid Sick Leave* (Washington, DC: Institute for Women's Policy Research, 2004).

31. Calculations of the authors using the National Longitudinal Survey of Youth.

32. S. J. Heymann, A. Earle, and B. Egleston, "Parental Availability for the Care of Sick Children," *Pediatrics* 98, no. 2, pt. 1 (1996): 226–30; A. Earle and S. J. Heymann, "Work, Family, and Social Class," in *How Healthy Are We? A National Study of Well-Being at Midlife,* ed. O. G. Brimm, C. Ryff, and R. Kessler (Chicago: University of Chicago Press, 2004); Institute for Women's Policy Research analysis of the March 2006 National Compensation Survey, the November 2005 through October 2006 Current Employment Statistics, and the November 2005 through October 2006 Job Openings and Labor Turnover Survey, cited in H. I. Hartman, "The Healthy Families Act: Impacts on Workers, Businesses, the Economy, and Public Health," testimony before the U.S. Senate Committee on Health, Education, Labor, and Pensions Hearing on *The Healthy Families Act: Safeguarding Americans' Livelihood, Families and Health with Paid Sick Days* (February 13, 2007).

33. D. U. Himmelstein, E. Warren, D. Thorne, and S. Woolhandler, "Illness and Injury as Contributors to Bankruptcy," *Health Affairs* (February 2, 2005), http://content.healthaffairs.org/cgi/reprint/hlthaff.w5.63v1.pdf (accessed March 2, 2009).

34. The twenty-two European nations for which reliable, recent data exist are Austria, Belgium, Czech Republic, Denmark, Estonia, Finland, France, Germany, Hungary, Ireland, Italy, Luxembourg, Malta, Netherlands, Norway, Poland, Romania, Slovak Republic, Spain, Sweden, Switzerland, and the United Kingdom. Estimates of unionization rates for these countries are: 53 percent in Norway, 55 percent in Belgium, 70 percent in Denmark and Romania, 74 percent in Finland, and 78 percent in Sweden. In Luxembourg at least 30 percent of workers are in unions, 34 percent in Italy, 35 percent in Austria, Ireland, and Slovak Republic, and 40 percent in Malta. Ten nations have less than 30 percent of their workers in unions: 8 percent in France, at most 10 percent in Estonia, 15 percent in Poland, 16 percent in Spain, 18 percent in Switzerland, 20 percent in Hungary, 22 percent in the Netherlands, 23 percent in

Germany, 27 percent in the Czech Republic, and 29 percent in the United Kingdom. Data for all countries except Romania, Malta, and Estonia are from J. Visser, "Union Membership Statistics in 24 Countries," *Monthly Labor Review* (January 2006): 38–49, http://www.bls.gov/opub/mlr/2006/01/art3full.pdf (accessed March 7, 2008); Romania, Malta, and Estonia data are from European Industrial Relations Observatory On-Line, "Trade Union Membership 1993–2003" (European Foundation for Improving Living and Working Conditions, 2004), http://www.eurofound.europa.eu/eiro/2004/03/update/tn0403105u.htm (accessed February 26, 2009). Figures may underestimate unionization rates in countries where data are from administrative sources (such as France) because, for example, only the main confederations and labor unions report or register themselves, leaving unaffiliated, small, independent unions unaccounted for.

35. In Norway, the majority of workers receive twenty-five days of paid annual leave. In Denmark the average is thirty days, in Finland twenty-five days, and in Sweden thirty-three days. In Belgium, in addition to the twenty-day minimum, collective agreements often include an additional five days of leave for those meeting certain tenure requirements, and beyond that, additional days of leave are guaranteed to workers with high weekly hours. See European Industrial Relations Observatory On-Line, "Working Time Developments—2006" (European Foundation for Improving Living and Working Conditions, 2007), http://www.eurofound.europa.eu/eiro/studies/tn0705019s/tn0705019s.htm (accessed February 29, 2008).

36. Bureau of Labor Statistics, U.S. Department of Labor, "Vacations, Holidays and Personal Leave: Access, Quantity, Costs and Trends," *Perspectives* 2 (February 2009), chart 1, http://www.bls .gov/opub/perspectives/issue2.pdf (accessed June 9, 2009).

37. Calculations of the authors using the National Longitudinal Survey of Youth.

38. Bureau of Labor Statistics, U.S. Department of Labor, Economic News Release, "Table 6. Selected paid leave benefits: Access, National Compensation Survey, March 2008," http://www.bls.gov/news.release/ebs2.t06.htm (accessed June 1, 2009).

39. "2000 SHRM Benefit Survey," Society for Human Resource Management, cited in U.S. Office of Personnel Management, "Report to Congress on Paid Parental Leave," http://www.opm.gov/oca/Leave/HTML/ParentalReport.htm#IV.%20%20Parental%20Leave%20in%20Non-Federal%20Establishments (accessed February 29, 2008).

40. S. J. Heymann, *The Widening Gap: Why Working Families Are in Jeopardy and What Can Be Done About It* (New York: Basic Books, 2000); A. Earle, J. Z. Ayanian, and S. J. Heymann, "What Predicts Women's Ability to Return to Work After Newly Diagnosed Coronary Heart Disease: Findings on the Importance of Paid Leave," *Journal of Women's Health* 15, no. 4 (2006): 430–41; S. J. Heymann, K. Penrose, and A. Earle, "Meeting Children's Needs: How Does the U.S. Measure Up?" *Merrill-Palmer Quarterly* 52, no. 2 (2006): 189–216; S. J. Heymann, P. H. Vo, and C. A. Bergstrom, "Child Care Providers' Experiences Caring for Sick Children: Implications for Public Policy," *Early Child Development and Care* 172, no. 1 (2002): 1–8; A. Earle and S. J. Heymann,

"What Causes Job Loss Among Former Welfare Recipients? The Role of Family Health Problems," *Journal of American Medical Women's Association* 57 (2002): 5–10; S. J. Heymann and A. Earle, "The Impact of Parental Working Conditions on School-Age Children: The Case of Evening Work," *Community, Work and Family* 4, no. 3 (2001): 305–25; S. J. Heymann and A. Earle, "Low-Income Parents: How Do Working Conditions Affect Their Opportunity to Help School-Age Children at Risk?" *American Educational Research Journal* 37, no. 2 (2000): 833–48; S. J. Heymann, "What Happens During and After School: Conditions Faced by Working Parents Living in Poverty and Their School-age Children," *Journal of Children and Poverty* 6, no. 1 (2000): 5–20; S. J. Heymann, S. Toomey, and F. Furstenberg, "Working Parents: What Factors Are Involved in Their Ability to Take Time Off from Work When Their Children Are Sick?" *Archives of Pediatrics & Adolescent Medicine* 153, no. 8 (1999): 870–74; S. J. Heymann and A. Earle, "The Impact of Welfare Reform on Parents' Ability to Care for Their Children's Health," *American Journal of Public Health* 89, no. 4 (1999): 502–5; S. J. Heymann, A. Earle, and B. Egleston, "Parental Availability for the Care of Sick Children," *Pediatrics* 98, no. 2, pt. 1 (1996): 226–30; S. J. Heymann, "Inequalities at Work and at Home: Social Class and Gender Divides," in *Unfinished Work: Building Equality and Democracy in an Era of Working Families*, ed. S. J. Heymann and C. Beem (New York: New Press, 2004).

Chapter 5

1. International Labour Organization, "About the ILO: Origins and History," http://www.ilo.org/global/About_the_ILO/Origins_and_history/lang—en/index.htm (accessed February 26, 2009).

2. Interview with Johan Norberg, author of *In Defense of Global Capitalism* (Washington, DC: Cato Institute), cited in N. Gillespie, "Poor Man's Hero," *ReasonOnline* (December 2003), http://www.reason.com/news/show/28968.html (accessed February 26, 2009).

3. L. Armstrong, "Why Is Tokyo Tinkering with the Treadmill?" *Business Week* (September 28, 1987).

4. R. J. Rosoff, "Addressing Labor Rights Problems in China," *China Business Review*, http://www.chinabusi nessreview.com/public/0403/rosoff.html (accessed February 26, 2009).

5. P. Navarro, *The Coming China Wars: Where They Will Be Fought and How They Can Be Won* (Upper Saddle River, NJ: FinancialTimes Press, 2006).

6. P. Bardhan, "Does Globalization Help or Hurt the World's Poor?" *Scientific American* (April 2006), http://www.sciam.com/article.cfm?chanID=sa006&colID=1&articleID=0004B7FD-C4E6-1421-84E683414B7F0101 (accessed February 26, 2009).

7. Depending on the policy, the number of countries on which legislation and social insurance information was available varied. NATLEX, the primary database for

legislation, covers 189 countries, and SSPTW, the primary source for social insurance, includes 164 countries.

8. International Labour Organization, ILOLEX: Conventions, http://www.ilo.org/ilolex/english/convdisp1.htm (accessed February 26, 2009). Several additional ILO conventions have addressed work hours and the inclusion of a day of rest for specific occupational groups, such as: C30 Hours of Work (Commerce and Offices) Convention 1930; C57 Hours of Work and Manning (Sea) Convention 1936; and C153 Hours of Work and Rest Periods (Road Transport) Convention 1979.

9. Office of the High Commissioner for Human Rights, United Nations, "The Universal Declaration of Human Rights: A Magna Carta for All Humanity" (1997), http://www.unhchr.ch/udhr/miscinfo/carta.htm (accessed February 26, 2009).

10. Office of the High Commissioner for Human Rights, United Nations, "Article 24 of the Universal Declaration of Human Rights" (1948), http://www.unhchr.ch/udhr/lang/eng.htm (accessed February 26, 2009).

11. Office of the High Commissioner for Human Rights, United Nations, "International Covenant on Economic, Social and Cultural Rights" (1966), http://www.ohchr.org/english/bodies/icescr/ (accessed November 21, 2007).

12. Office of the High Commissioner for Human Rights, United Nations, "Status of Ratifications," http://www.ohchr.org/EN/HRBodies/Pages/ConventionStatusRatification.aspx (accessed February 26, 2009).

13. Our analyses use income categories developed by the World Bank, which defines low-income economies as those with a 2006 GNI per capita of $905 or less; lower-middle-income economies, between $906 and $3,595; upper-middle-income economies, between $3,596 and $11,115; and high-income-economies, $11,116 and above. See World Bank, *World Development Report 2008* (Washington, DC: World Bank, 2007).

14. While many countries stipulate an amount of time off for all workers, others describe a system in which the length of leave is determined by years or months of service or employment (where longer-term employees receive longer paid leaves). Figures described in the text refer to the minimum amount of leave guaranteed for the newest employee.

15. While only a small fraction of nations in South Asia provide paid annual leave, among those that do, two-thirds provide two weeks or more. In the Americas, as in the Middle East, North Africa, East Asia, and the Pacific, the most common length of paid leave is two to three weeks. In Sub-Saharan Africa, Europe, and Central Asia, the most common amount of guaranteed vacation time is four or more weeks.

16. G. Aronsson, K. Gustafsson, and M. Dallner, "Sick But Yet at Work: An Empirical Study of Sickness Presenteeism," *Journal of Epidemiology and Community Health* 54 (2000): 502–9; A. Grinyer and V. Singleton, "Sickness Absence as Risk-Taking Behaviour: A Study of Organizational and Cultural Factors in the Public Sector," *Health, Risk, & Society* 2 (2000): 7–21; G. Johannsson, "Work-Life Balance: The Case of Sweden in the 1990s," *Social Science Information* 41 (2002): 303–17.

17. S. D. Cauley, "The Time Price of Medical Care," *Review of Economics and Sta-*

tistics 69 (1987): 59–66; D. B. Gilleski, "A Dynamic Stochastic Model of Medical Care Use and Work Absence," *Econometrica* 66 (1998): 1–45.

18. Eighty-five percent of low-income countries guarantee paid sick leave, compared to 80 percent of lower-middle-income nations, 100 percent of upper-middle-income nations, and 93 percent of high-income nations. Thirty-nine percent of low-income nations guarantee six months or more of leave, as do 49 percent of lower-middle-income nations, 73 percent of upper-middle-income nations, and 62 percent of high-income nations. Also, in all regions except for Asia and the Pacific, the most common duration of paid sick leave is a guarantee of twenty-six weeks or until the worker has fully recovered.

19. Legislative definitions of "serious illness" range from illnesses that last more than a few days to illnesses that require hospitalization.

20. Office of the High Commissioner for Human Rights, United Nations, "Status of Ratifications," http://www.ohchr.org/EN/HRBodies/Pages/ConventionStatus Ratification.aspx (accessed February 26, 2009).

21. Division for the Advancement of Women, Department of Economic and Social Affairs, United Nations, "Convention on the Elimination of All Forms of Discrimination Against Women" (1979), http://www.un.org/womenwatch/daw/cedaw/text/econvention.htm (accessed August 5, 2003).

22. Office of the High Commissioner for Human Rights, The Committee on Economic, Social and Cultural Rights, United Nations, "Fact Sheet no. 16 (Rev. 1)" (1991), http://www.unhchr.ch/html/menu6/2/fs16.htm#3 (accessed February 26, 2009).

23. The likelihood of providing a very long leave of fifty-two weeks or more generally increases with income also. Six percent of low-income nations, 14 percent of lower-middle-income nations, 24 percent of upper-middle-income nations, and 22 percent of high-income nations guarantee fifty-two weeks or more of paid maternal leave.

24. Out of 190 countries studied, 177 provide paid leave for mothers, and four guarantee unpaid leave. The remaining nine countries include Bhutan, where legislation specifically guarantees maternity and paternity leave, although no pay rate or duration is specified; Liberia, Tuvalu, and Samoa, where labor codes have no mention of maternity leave; Sierra Leone, which has no maternity or parental leave according to SSPTW and ILO's Maternity Protection database; and the following nations that have no accessible legislation and no data in SSPTW or the Maternity Protection database: Bosnia-Herzegovina, Marshall Islands, Micronesia, and Suriname.

25. K. Dewey, M. Heinig, and L. Nommsen-Rivers, "Differences in Morbidity between Breastfed and Formula-fed Infants. Part 1," *Journal of Pediatrics* 126, no. 5 (1995): 696–702; R. G. Feachem and M. A. Koblinsky, "Interventions for the Control of Diarrhoeal Diseases Among Young Children: Promotion of Breast-feeding," *Bulletin of the World Health Organization* 62, no. 2 (1984): 271–91; P. Howie, J. Forsyth, S. Ogston, A. Clark, and C. Florey, "Protective Effect of Breast Feeding Against Infection," *British Medical Journal* 300, no. 6716 (1990): 11–16; P. Lepage, C. Munyakazi, and P. Hennart, "Breastfeeding and Hospital Mortality in Children in Rwanda," *Lancet* 1, no. 8268 (1982): 403.

26. M. Cerqueriro, P. Murtagh, A. Halac, M. Avila, and M. Weissenbacher, "Epidemiologic Risk Factors for Children with Acute Lower Respiratory Tract Infection in Buenos Aires, Argentina: A Matched Case-Control Study," *Reviews of Infectious Diseases* 12, suppl. 8 (1990): S1021-28; P. Howie, J. Forsyth, S. Ogston, A. Clark, and C. Florey, "Protective Effect of Breast Feeding Against Infection," *British Medical Journal* 300, no. 6716 (1990): 11–16; C. J. Watkins, S. R. Leeder, and R. T. Corkhill, "The Relationship Between Breast and Bottle Feeding and Respiratory Illness in the First Year of Life," *Journal of Epidemiology and Community Health* 33, no. 3 (1979): 180–82; A. Wright, C. Holberg, F. Martinez, W. Morgan, and L. Taussig, "Breast Feeding and Lower Respiratory Tract Illness in the First Year of Life," *British Medical Journal* 299, no. 6705 (1989): 946–49.

27. G. Aniansson, B. Alm, B. Andersson, A. Hakansson, P. Larsson, O. Nylen, H. Peterson, P. Rigner, M. Svanborg, and H. Sabharwal, "A Prospective Cohort Study on Breast-feeding and Otitis Media in Swedish Infants," *Pediatric Infectious Disease Journal* 13, no. 3 (1994): 183–88; B. Duncan, J. Ey, C. Holberg, A. Wright, F. Martinez, and L. Taussig, "Exclusive Breast-feeding for at Least 4 Months Protects Against Otitis Media," *Pediatrics* 91, no. 5 (1993): 867–72.

28. C. Arnold, S. Makintube, and G. Istre, "Daycare Attendance and Other Risk Factors for Invasive *Haemophilus influenzae* Type B Disease," *American Journal of Epidemiology* 138, no. 5 (1993): 333–40.

29. A. S. Cunningham, D. B. Jelliffee, and E.F.P. Jelliffee, "Breast-feeding and Health in the 1980s: A Global Epidemiologic Review," *Journal of Pediatrics* 118, no. 5 (1991): 659–66; R. G. Feachem and M. A. Koblinsky, "Interventions for the Control of Diarrhoeal Diseases Among Young Children: Promotion of Breast-feeding," *Bulletin of the World Health Organization* 62, no. 2 (1984): 271–91; A. J. Naylor and A. Morrow, eds., *Developmental Readiness of Normal Full Term Infants to Progress from Exclusive Breastfeeding to the Introduction of Complementary Foods: Reviews of the Relevant Literature Concerning Infant Immunologic, Gastrointestinal, Oral Motor and Maternal Reproductive and Lactational Development* (Washington, DC: Wellstart International and the LINKAGES Project/Academy for Educational Development, 2001).

30. R. G. Feachem and M. A. Koblinsky, "Interventions for the Control of Diarrhoeal Diseases Among Young Children: Promotion of Breast-feeding," *Bulletin of the World Health Organization* 62, no. 2 (1984): 271–91; J. P. Habicht, J. DaVanzo, and W. P. Butz, "Does Breastfeeding Really Save Lives, or Are Apparent Benefits Due to Biases?" *American Journal of Epidemiology* 123, no. 2 (1986): 279–90; J. N. Hobcraft, J. McDonald, and S. Rutstein, "Demographic Determinants of Infant and Early Child Mortality: A Comparative Analysis," *Population Studies* 39, no. 21 (1985): 363–85; J. Jason, P. Nieburg, and J. S. Marks, "Mortality and Infectious Disease Associated with Infant-Feeding Practice in Developing Countries, Part 2," *Pediatrics* 74, no. 4 (1984): 702–27.

31. M. S. Kramer, F. Aboud, E. Mironova, I. Vanilovich, R. W. Platt, L. Matush, S. Igumnov, et al., Promotion of Breastfeeding Intervention Trial (PROBIT) Study Group, "Breastfeeding and Child Cognitive Development: New Evidence from a Large

Randomized Trial," *Archives of General Psychiatry* 65, no. 5 (2008): 578–84; J. W. Anderson, B. M. Johnstone, and D. T. Remley, "Breast-feeding and Cognitive Development: A Meta-analysis," *American Journal of Clinical Nutrition* 70, no. 4 (1999): 525–35; E. L. Mortensen, K. F. Michaelsen, S. A. Sanders, and J. M. Reinisch, "The Association Between Duration of Breastfeeding and Adult Intelligence," *Journal of the American Medical Association* 287, no. 18 (2002): 2365–71.

32. S. Ip, M. Chung, G. Raman, et al., "Breastfeeding and Maternal and Infant Health Outcomes in Developed Countries," AHRQ Publication 07-E007 (Rockville, MD: Agency for Healthcare Research and Quality, April 2007); N. Leon-Cava, C. Lutter, J. Ross, and M. Luann, *Quantifying the Benefits of Breastfeeding: A Summary of the Evidence* (Washington, DC: Pan American Health Organization, 2002).

33. Office of the High Commissioner for Human Rights, United Nations, "Status of Ratifications," http://www.ohchr.org/EN/HRBodies/Pages/ConventionStatusRatification.aspx (accessed February 26, 2009); Office of the High Commissioner for Human Rights, United Nations, "Convention on the Rights of the Child" (1989), http://www.ohchr.org/english/law/pdf/crc.pdf (accessed April 10, 2007).

34. Division for the Advancement of Women, Department of Economic and Social Affairs, United Nations, "Convention on the Elimination of All Forms of Discrimination Against Women" (1979), http://www.un.org/womenwatch/daw/cedaw/text/econvention.htm (accessed February 26, 2003).

35. International Labour Organization, ILOLEX: Conventions, http://www.ilo.org/ilolex/english/convdisp1.htm (accessed February 26, 2009).

36. L. D. Lindberg, "Women's Decisions About Breastfeeding and Maternal Employment," *Journal of Marriage and the Family* 58, no. 1 (1996): 239–51; S. Noble, "Maternal Employment and the Initiation of Breastfeeding," *Acta Paediatrica* 90, no. 4 (2001): 423–28; V. Hight-Laukaran, S. O. Rutstein, A. E. Peterson, and M. H. Labbok, "The Use of Breast Milk Substitutes in Developing Countries: The Impact of Women's Employment," *American Journal of Public Health* 86, no. 9 (1996): 1235–40.

37. In May of 2001, an expert review panel reported to the Fifty-fourth World Health Assembly its conclusion that six months is the optimal minimum duration of breastfeeding, overturning the more flexible previous recommendation of "four to six months." See World Health Organization, "Global Strategy for Infant and Young Child Feeding" (Fifty-fourth World Health Assembly, May 1, 2001), http://ftp.who.int/gb/archive/pdf_files/WHA54/ea54id4.pdf (accessed March 2, 2009).

38. A. S. Cunningham, D. B. Jelliffee, and E.F.P. Jelliffee, "Breast-feeding and Health in the 1980s: A Global Epidemiologic Review," *Journal of Pediatrics* 118, no. 5 (1991): 659–66.

39. The Sadler Committee was convened by the British parliament in 1832 to investigate the accusations of appalling working conditions in the textile factories. Both factory owners and workers testified to the Committee, which made clear that industrial workers were being subjected to abominable working conditions in Britain. The Chair, Michael Sadler, worked tirelessly to pass limits on the workday for all persons under the age of eighteen. This investigation and the report paved the way to the

enactment of the Factories Act 1833, limiting hours of employment for women and children in textile work. Under the terms of the new act, it became illegal for children under nine to work in textile factories, and children between nine and thirteen could not be employed for more than eight hours a day.

40. A significant cause of discontent for the reformers was that under the provision of the Factories Act 1833, children over thirteen were allowed to work for up to twelve hours a day. Following Michael Sadler's defeat in the 1832 general election, Lord Ashley became the new leader of the factory reform movement in the House of Commons. In 1842 the report of Lord Ashley's Mines Commission was published, causing much public outcry. The majority of people in Britain were unaware that women and children were employed as miners. The Coal Mines Act of 1842 that resulted prohibited all women and all boys under thirteen from working underground in mines.

41. E. Chadwick, *Report on the Sanitary Condition of the Labouring Population of Great Britain*, ed. M. W. Flinn (Edinburgh: Edinburgh University Press, 1842).

42. P. Gaskell, *The Manufacturing Population of England* (London: Baldwin and Cradock, 1833), 202.

43. E. Hopkins, "Working Hours and Conditions During the Industrial Revolution: A Re-Appraisal," *Economic History Review New Series* 35, no. 1 (1982): 52–66.

44. J. Fielden, *The Curse of the Factory System* (London: A. Cobbett, 1836), 34–35.

45. R. Ray and J. Schmitt, *No Vacation Nation* (Washington, DC: Center for Economic and Policy Research, May 2007), http://www.cepr.net/documents/publications/NoVacationNation_asofSeptember07.pdf (accessed February 26, 2009).

46. S. J. Heymann, *The Widening Gap: Why Working Families Are in Jeopardy and What Can Be Done About It* (New York: Basic Books, 2000).

47. M. R. Vance, "Breastfeeding Legislation in the United States: A General Overview and Implications for Helping Mothers," *LEAVEN* 41, no. 3 (2005): 51–54, http://www.llli.org/llleaderweb/LV/LVJunJul05p51.html (accessed February 26, 2009).

48. J. T. Bond, E. Galinsky, S. Kim, and E. Brownfield, *National Study of Employers* (New York: Families and Work Institute, 2005).

49. Azerbaijan: 1999 Azerbaijan Labor Code; Benin: Code du travail 1998; China: China Labor Act 1994; India: 1948 Factories Act; Mexico: Ley Federal del Trabajo, Article 80 [Texto vigente al 1° de octubre de 1995]; Pakistan: 1934 Factories Act, as amended to 1997; Paraguay: Ley núm. 213 que establece el Código del Trabajo; Russian Federation: Labor Code 2001, Article, 114; Switzerland: 1911 Swiss Code d'obligations [Labor Code] revised as of 2005.

50. Brazil: Law no. 8.213, issued July 24, 1994 (updated December 27, 2000); Canada: Canada Labor Code Chapter L-2, http://laws.justice.gc.ca/en/L-2/text.html, updated to August 31, 2004, and SSPTW The Americas 2007; Cuba: Law 49 1984 Labor Code: Chapter VIII Work of Women, section IV Maternity Protection Law 234 of 2003; Finland: Employment Contracts Act (55/2001, amendments up to 456/2005 included) and SSPTW Europe 2006; India: ILO Maternity Protection Database and SSPTW Asia and the Pacific 2006; Malawi: Employment Act 1999 (no. 6 of 2000);

Mexico: Federal Labor Law, 1995 and SSPTW The Americas 2007;Mongolia: Labor Code, 1999 and UN World's Women, 2005; United Kingdom: SSPTW Europe 2006, The 2006 Work and Family Act, and Statutory Instrument 2002 no. 2788, The Paternity and Adoption Leave Regulations 2002, Statutory Instrument 2002 no. 2822, The Statutory Paternity Pay and Statutory Adoption Pay (General) Regulations 2002, Statutory Instrument 2002 No. 2789, The Maternity and Parental Leave (Amendment) Regulations 2002, Statutory Instrument 1999 no. 3312, The Maternity and Parental Leave etc. Regulations 1999; United States: The Family and Medical Leave Act of 1993.

51. Eritrea: Labor Proclamation of Eritrea (No. 118 of 2001); Guatemala: SSPTW The Americas 2007; Iceland: Act Respecting Labourers' Right to Advance Notice of Termination of Employment and to Wages on Account of Absence through Illness and Accidents, No. 19/1979, and SSPTW Europe 2008; Italy: SSPTW Europe 2004 & 2006; Mexico: SSPTW The Americas 2007; Seychelles: SSPTW Africa 2007; Spain: SSPTW Europe 2006; Sweden: SSPTW Europe 2006; Tanzania: Employment And Labor Relations Act, 2004; United States: The Family and Medical Leave Act of 1993. Public Law 103-3 Enacted February 5, 1993.

52. Belarus: ILO Maternity Protection Database, 1999 Labor Code of the Republic of Belarus §267; Dominican Republic: Ley núm. 16-92 que aprueba el Código de Trabajo, and Decreto núm. 258-93, regulamento para la aplicación del Código de Trabajo; India: Maternity Benefit Act 1961 (No. 53 of 1961) and Women's Alliance for Breastfeeding Awareness; Italy: ILO Maternity Protection Database, Decreto Legislativo 26 Marzo 2001, no. 151, Testo unico delle disposizioni legislative in materia di tutela e sostegno della maternità e della paternità, a norma dell' articolo 15 della legge 8 marzo 2000, n. 53:§(39); Mexico: Ley Federal del Trabajo [Texto vigente al 1.o de octubre de 1995]; Norway: Worker Protection and Working Environment Act as amended to 2004; Spain: Real decreto legislativo núm. 1/1995, de 24 de marzo, por el que se aprueba el texto refundido de la Ley del Estatuto de los Trabajadores and ILO Maternity Protection Database; Syria: Labor Code 1959; Jordan: Labor Code, Law No. 8 of 1996.

Chapter 6

1. The 165 to 220 million estimate is likely to be a lower bound of the true prevalence of global child disability. This estimate is calculated by multiplying the population of children globally by a conservative estimate of the fraction of children with a disability, or 10 percent. Estimates from developing countries based on national surveys of children age two to nine years of age (from UNICEF's Multiple Indicator Cluster Study, or MICS) are approximately half again as large (14 percent). Studies in individual countries using the same ten questions used in MICS support a similar estimate, 9 percent of six-to-nine year olds in Kenya, 11 percent of children in South Africa, and 20 percent of children in Pakistan. Other epidemiological surveys conducted in developing countries estimate that 20 percent of children have a mild dis-

ability (and 4.4 percent with a severe disability). For MICS data, see UNICEF, "Monitoring Child Disability in Developing Countries" (2008), http://www.childinfo.org/files/Monitoring_Child_Disability_in_Developing _Countries.pdf (accessed June 11, 2009). For an individual study in Kenya, see V. Mung'ala-Odera, R. Meehan, P. Njuguna, N. Mturi, K. J. Alcock, and C. Newton, "Prevalence and Risk Factors of Neurological Disability and Impairment in Children Living in Rural Kenya," *International Journal of Epidemiology* 35, no. 3 (2006): 683–88. For data from South Africa, see A. L. Christianson, M. E. Zwane, P. Manga, E. Rose, A. Venter, D. Downs, et al., "Children with Intellectual Disability in Rural South Africa: Prevalence and Associated Disability," *Journal of Intellectual Disability Research* 46, no. 2 (2002): 179–86. For data from Pakistan, see M. Yaqoob, A. Bashir, S. Zaman, H. Ferngren, U. von Dobeln, and K. H. Gustavson, "Mild Intellectual Disability in Children in Lahore, Pakistan: Aetiology and Risk Factors," *Journal of Intellectual Disability Research* 48, no. 7 (2004): 663–71. For other epidemiological studies, see M. S. Durkin, et al., "Validity of the Ten Questions Screen for Childhood Disability: Results from Population-Based Studies in Bangladesh, Jamaica and Pakistan," *Epidemiology* 5 (1994): 283–89; M. S. Durkin, et al., "Validity of the Ten Questions for Screening Serious Childhood Disability: Results from Urban Bangladesh," *International Journal of Epidemiology* 19, no. 3 (1990): 613–20.

2. While comparisons across countries must be done carefully because definitions and interpretations of similar survey questions vary, studies have found a higher prevalence of child disability among low-income nations and among low-income individuals. See A. Elwan, *Poverty and Disability: A Survey of the Literature*, SP Discussion Paper 9932 (Washington, DC: World Bank, December 1999).

3. Enrollment data are from the World Development Indicators. For 1960 figures, see World Bank, "World Development Indicators 2002" (CD-ROM, 2002); for 2005 figures, see World Bank, "World Development Indicators Online" (WDI Online), http://go.worldbank.org/6HAYAHG8H0 (accessed March 2, 2009).

4. For 1990 and 1997 figures, see UNESCO World Education Report 2000, "Table 8: Enrollment (millions) and gross enrollment ratios in tertiary education, 1990 and 1997"; for 1999–2004 figures, see UNESCO Institute for Statistics Data Centre, http://stats.uis.unesco.org (accessed February 25, 2009).

5. Ibid.

6. By *higher-income* countries, we refer to the World Bank's "high-income" and "upper-middle-income" countries, and by *lower-income* countries we refer to the World Bank's "low-income" and "lower-middle-income" countries. World Bank income classifications are from the World Development Report 2008. See World Bank, *World Development Report 2008* (Washington, DC: World Bank, 2007): 331–33. Enrollment data are from the World Development Indicators. For 1960 figures, see World Bank, "World Development Indicators 2002" (CD-ROM, 2002); for 2005 figures, see World Bank, World Development Indicators Online (WDI Online, 2002), http://go.worldbank.org/6HAYAHG8H0 (accessed March 2, 2009).

7. For 1960 figures, see World Bank, World Development Indicators 2002 (CD-ROM, 2002); for 2005 figures, see World Bank, World Development Indicators Online (WDI Online), http://go.worldbank.org/6HAYAHG8H0 (accessed March 2, 2009).

8. The UN's regional classifications are used here except where subregional patterns differ from the overall regional pattern, in which case the subregions are described separately. See United Nations Statistics Division, "Composition of Macro Geographical (Continental) Regions, Geographical Sub-Regions, and Selected Economic and Other Groupings" (2008), http://unstats.un.org/unsd/methods/m49/m49regin.htm (accessed February 25, 2009). Two patterns can be seen: (1) regions where the ratio of the percentage of enrolled females to enrolled males rose significantly from 1960 to 2005; (2) regions where the ratio was high early on and has stayed high. The experiences in the regions of Africa (except for primary school enrollment in the subregion of Southern Africa), Oceania, and Asia all follow the first pattern of marked movement toward equity for both primary and secondary school enrollment. Central and South America and the subregions of Southern Europe show the same pattern, but for secondary school enrollment only. In Africa, the ratio of the percentage of females to males enrolled in primary school rose from .54 in 1960 to .89 in 2005, and in secondary school from .41 to .82. In Oceania, the ratio rose from .87 to .99 in primary school enrollment, and from .89 to .98 in secondary school enrollment. In Asia overall, girls' secondary school enrollment relative to boys' increased dramatically from .41 in 1960 to .92 in 2005, and from .60 to .96 for primary enrollment. In Southern Europe the gender parity measure in secondary school rose from .64 in 1960 to 1.02 in 2005. In Central America the gains for girls in secondary school were significant: the relative share of girls enrolled in secondary school to boys rose from .64 to 1.06 from 1960 to 2005. Similarly in South America, the secondary school ratio rose from .91 to 1.07.

The entire region of Europe—except for secondary school enrollment in Southern Europe—and the subregion of Southern Africa followed the second pattern. Girls in Southern Africa were near parity in primary school in 1960, ratio of .95, and stayed high at .99 in 2005, while girls in all parts of Europe were at or above parity in primary school in 1960 and have stayed there. The Americas experienced similar trajectories in terms of primary school enrollment: girls' primary school enrollment has stayed at near 1.0 over the last forty-five years. In secondary school enrollment, North America and the Caribbean follow this same pattern, but as noted above, Central and South America saw increases in gender equity in secondary school only. Enrollment data come from the World Development Indicators. See World Bank, World Development Indicators Online (WDI Online), http://go.worldbank.org/6HAYAHG8H0 (accessed March 2, 2009).

9. In low-income nations, there was a slight decline from 38 percent to 35 percent, and in lower-middle-income countries an equally small increase from 39 percent to 42 percent. (On average, these lower-income countries had little change.) For 1960 figures, see World Bank, World Development Indicators 2002 (CD-ROM, 2002); for

2006 figures, see World Bank, World Development Indicators Online (WDI Online), http://go.worldbank.org/6HAYAHG8H0 (accessed March 2, 2009).

10. Female share of the labor force data are from the World Development Indicators. For 1960 figures, see World Bank, "World Development Indicators 2002" (CD-ROM, 2002); for 2006 figures, see World Bank, World Development Indicators Online (WDI Online), http://go.worldbank.org/6HAYAHG8H0 (accessed March 2, 2009).

11. Ibid. The UN's regional classifications were used. See United Nations Statistics Division, "Composition of Macro Geographical (Continental) Regions, Geographical Sub-Regions, and Selected Economic and Other Groupings" (2008), http://unstats.un.org/unsd/methods/m49/m49regin.htm (accessed February 25, 2009).

12. D. Hernandez, "Children's Changing Access to Resources: A Historical Perspective," in *Families in the U.S.: Kinship and Domestic Politics,* ed. K. Hansen and A. Garey (Philadelphia: Temple University Press, 1998), 201–15.

13. D. Hernandez and D. Myers, *America's Children: Resources from Family, Government, and the Economy* (New York: Russell Sage Foundation, 1993).

14. D. Hernandez, "Children's Changing Access to Resources: A Historical Perspective," in *Families in the U.S.: Kinship and Domestic Politics,* ed. K. Hansen and A. Garey (Philadelphia: Temple University Press, 1998), 201–15.

15. S. J. Heymann, *Forgotten Families: Ending the Growing Crisis Confronting Children and Working Parents in the Global Economy* (New York: Oxford University Press, 2006). This figure is based on an estimate of the number of children aged zero to fourteen who are living in households where all adults are in the paid labor force. To calculate this figure, detailed household survey information was used from a sample of widely divergent countries.

16. Ibid. These figures are based on our analysis of the Botswana Multiple Indicator Survey; Russia Longitudinal Monitoring Survey; Vietnam Household Living Standards; Brazil Living Standards Survey (Pesquisa sobre Padrões de Vida); and Mexico's Encuesta Nacional de Ingresos y Gastos de los Hogares (ENIGH) 1996.

17. Population data are from United Nations Population Division, *World Population Prospects: 2006 Revision,* Population Database, http://www.un.org/esa/population/publications/wpp2006/2006wup.htm (accessed February 27, 2009).

18. Income categories are from the World Bank. Population data are from United Nations Population Division, *World Population Prospects: 2006 Revision,* Population Database, http://www.un.org/esa/population/publications/wpp2006/2006wpp.htm (accessed February 27, 2009) and United Nations Department of Economic and Social Affairs, Population Division, "Population Estimates and Projections Sections, Fact Sheet" (Series A, March 7, 2007), http://www.un.org/esa/population/unpop.htm (accessed February 25, 2009). Full report: *World Population Prospects: The 2006 Revision,* United Nations Population Division, DESA.

19. H. E. Restrepo and M. Rozental, "The Social Impact of Aging Populations: Some Major Issues," *Social Science & Medicine* 39, no. 9 (1994): 1323–38; A. J. Davis, I. Martinson, L. C. Gan, et al., "Home Care for the Urban Chronically Ill Elderly in the People's Republic of China," *International Journal of Aging & Human Development* 41,

no. 4 (1995): 345–58; P. B. Doress-Worters, "Adding Elder Care to Women's Multiple Roles: A Critical Review of the Caregiver Stress and Multiple Roles Literatures," *Sex Roles* 31, no. 9–10 (1994): 597–616; Y. Hashizume, "Gender Issues and Japanese Family-Centered Caregiving for Frail Elderly Parents or Parents-in-Law in Modern Japan: From the Sociocultural and Historical Perspectives," *Public Health Nursing* 17, no. 1 (2000): 25–31; B. Ineichen, "Influences on the Care of Demented Elderly People in the People's Republic of China," *International Journal of Geriatric Psychiatry* 13, no. 2 (1998): 122–26; S. O. Long and P. B. Harris, "Gender and Elder Care: Social Change and the Role of the Caregiver in Japan," *Social Science Japan Journal* 3, no. 1 (2000): 21–36; S. Medjuck, J. M. Keefe, and P. J. Fancey, "Available But Not Accessible: An Examination of the Use of Workplace Policies for Caregivers of Elderly Kin," *Journal of Family Issues* 19, no. 3 (1998): 274–99; J. M. Rawlins, "Caring for the Chronically Ill Elderly in Trinidad: The Informal Situation," *West Indian Medical Journal* 50, no. 2 (2001): 133–36.

20. P. Arnsberger, P. Fox, X. Zhang, and S. Gui, "Population Aging and the Need for Long Term Care: A Comparison of the United States and the People's Republic of China," *Journal of Cross-Cultural Gerontology* 15, no. 3 (2000): 207–27; C. Ikels, "Aging and Disability in China: Cultural Issues in Measurement and Interpretation," *Social Science & Medicine* 32, no. 6 (1991): 649–65.

21. V. Kumar, "Aging in India—An Overview," *Indian Journal of Medical Research* 106 (1997): 257–64.

22. I. K. Kim, "Population Aging in Korea: Social Problems and Solutions," *Journal of Sociology & Social Welfare* 26, no. 1 (1999): 107–23.

23. P. C. Chen, "Psychosocial Factors and the Health of the Elderly Malaysian," *Annals of the Academy of Medicine, Singapore* 16, no. 1 (1987): 110–14.

24. B. B. Niraula, "Old-Age Security and Inheritance in Nepal—Motives Versus Means," *Journal of Biosocial Science* 27, no. 1 (1995): 71–78.

25. Y.I.L. Shyu, H. C. Lee, and M. L. Chen, "Development and Testing of the Family Caregiving Consequences Inventory for Home Nursing Assessment in Taiwan," *Journal of Advanced Nursing* 30, no. 3 (1999): 646–54.

26. J. M. Rawlins, "Confronting Ageing as a Caribbean Reality," *Journal of Sociology & Social Welfare* 26, no. 1 (1999): 143–53; W. J. Serow and M. E. Cowart, "Demographic Transition and Population Aging with Caribbean Nation States," *Journal of Cross-Cultural Gerontology* 13 (1998): 201–13.

27. M. H. Mufti, "Status of Long Term Care in Saudi Arabia," *Saudi Medical Journal* 19, no. 4 (1998): 367–69.

28. I. A. Aytac, "Intergenerational Living Arrangements in Turkey," *Journal of Cross-Cultural Gerontology* 13, no. 3 (1998): 241–64.

29. F. Clausen, E. Sandberg, B. Ingstad, and P. Hjortdahl, "Morbidity and Health Care Utilisation Among Elderly People in Mmankgodi Village, Botswana," *Journal of Epidemiology and Community Health* 54, no. 1 (2000): 58–63; P. Draper and J. Keith, "Cultural Contexts of Care—Family Caregiving for Elderly in America and Africa," *Journal of Aging Studies* 6, no. 2 (1992): 113–34.

30. J. Jensen and S. Jacobzone, "The Intensification of Work in Europe," *OECD Labour Market and Social Policy Occasional Papers*, no. 41 (2001); S. Hardy and N. Adnett, "The Parental Leave Directive: Towards a 'Family-Friendly' Social Europe?" *European Journal of Industrial Relations* 8, no. 2 (2002): 151–72.

31. National Alliance for Caregiving and the American Association of Retired People, "Caregiving in the U.S." (NAC and AARP, 2004), http://www.caregiving.org/data/04finalreport.pdf (accessed February 27, 2009).

32. A. Riedmann, H. Bielenski, T. Szczurowska, and A. Wagner, "Working Time and Work-Life Balance in European Companies, Establishment Survey on Working Time 2004–2005" (Dublin: European Foundation for the Improvement of Living and Working Conditions, 2006), http:/www.eurofound.europa.eu/pubdocs/2006/27/en/1/ef0627en.pdf (accessed February 27, 2009).

33. Bureau of Labor Statistics, U.S. Deptartment of Labor, "Table 5: Shift usually worked: Full-time wage and salary workers by occupation and industry" (May 2004), http://www.bls.gov/news.release/flex.t05.htm (accessed February 25, 2009).

34. H. Presser, *Working in a 24/7 Economy: Challenges for American Families* (New York: Russell Sage Foundation, 2003).

35. S. J. Heymann, S. Toomey, and F. Furstenberg, "Working Parents: What Factors Are Involved in Their Ability to Take Time Off from Work When Their Children Are Sick?" *Archives of Pediatric and Adolescent Medicine* 153 (August 1999): 870–74; S. J. Heymann, *The Widening Gap: Why America's Working Families Are in Jeopardy and What Can Be Done About It* (New York: Basic Books, 2000).

36. A. George and J. Hancock, "Reducing Pediatric Burn Pain with Parent Participation," *Journal of Burn Care and Rehabilitation* 14 (1993): 104–7; P. A. LaRosa Nash and J. M. Murphy, "An Approach to Pediatric Perioperative Care: Parent-Present Induction," *Nursing Clinics of North America* 32 (1997): 183–99; G. Van der Schyff, "The Role of Parents During Their Child's Hospitalization," *Australian Nurses Journal* 8 (1979): 57–61; S. J. Palmer, "Care of Sick Children by Parents: A Meaningful Role," *Journal of Advanced Nursing* 18 (1993): 185; P. Mahaffy, "The Effects of Hospitalization on Children Admitted for Tonsillectomy and Adenoidectomy," *Nursing Review* 14 (1965): 12–19.

37. I. Kristensson-Hallstron, G. Elander, and G. Malmfors, "Increased Parental Participation on a Pediatric Surgical Daycare Unit," *Journal of Clinical Nursing* 6 (1997): 297–302.

38. M.R.H. Taylor and P. O'Connor, "Resident Parents and Shorter Hospital Stay," *Archives of Disease in Childhood* 64 (1989): 274–76.

39. J. Bowlby, *Child Care and the Growth of Love* (London: Pelican, 1964); J. Robertson, *Young Children in Hospital* (London: Tavistock, 1970); T. McGraw, "Preparing Children for the Operating Room: Psychological Issues," *Canadian Journal of Anaesthesia* 41 (1994): 1094–103.

40. C. Wolman, M. D. Resnick, L. J. Harris, and R. W. Blum, "Emotional Well-Being Among Adolescents With and Without Chronic Conditions," *Adolescent Medicine* 15, no. 3 (1994): 199–204; C. L. Hanson, M. J. DeGuire, A. M. Schinkel, S. W. Henggeler,

and G. A. Burghen, "Comparing Social Learning and Family Systems Correlates of Adaptation in Youths with IDDM," *Journal of Pediatric Psychology* 17, no. 5 (1992): 555–72.

41. S. Carlton-Ford, R. Miller, M. Brown, N. Nealeigh, and P. Jennings, "Epilepsy and Children's Social and Psychological Adjustment," *Journal of Health and Social Behavior* 36, no. 3 (1995): 285–301.

42. K. W. Hamlett, D. S. Pellegrini, and K. S. Katz, "Childhood Chronic Illness as a Family Stressor," *Journal of Pediatric Psychology* 17, no. 1 (1992): 33–47.

43. A. M. LaGreca, W. F. Auslander, P. Greco, D. Spetter, E. B. Fisher, and J. V. Santiago, "I Get By with a Little Help from My Family and Friends: Adolescents' Support for Diabetes Care," *Journal of Pediatric Psychology* 20, no. 4 (1995): 449–76; B. J. Anderson, J. P. Miller, W. F. Auslander, and J. V. Santiago, "Family Characteristics of Diabetic Adolescents: Relationship to Metabolic Control," *Diabetes Care* 4, no. 6 (1981): 586–94.

44. J. Cleary, O. P. Gray, D. J. Hall, P. H. Rowlandson, C. P. Sainsbury, and M. M. Davies, "Parental Involvement in the Lives of Children in Hospital," *Archives of Disease in Childhood* 61 (1986): 779–87; C.P.Q. Sainsbury, O. P. Gray, J. Cleary, M. M. Davies, and P. H. Rowlandson, "Care by Parents of Their Children in Hospital," *Archives of Disease in Childhood* 61 (1986): 612–15; M. W. Gauderer, J. L. Lorig, and D. W. Eastwood, "Is There a Place for Parents in the Operating Room?" *Journal of Pediatric Surgery* 24 (1989): 705–6.

45. C. Wolman, M. D. Resnick, L. J. Harris, and R. W. Blum, "Emotional Well-Being Among Adolescents With and Without Chronic Conditions," *Adolescent Medicine* 15, no. 3 (1994): 199–204; K. W. Hamlett, D. S. Pellegrini, and K. S. Katz, "Childhood Chronic Illness as a Family Stressor," *Journal of Pediatric Psychology* 17, no. 1 (1992): 33–47.

46. S. T. Hauser, A. M. Jacobson, P. Lavori, et al. "Adherence Among Children and Adolescents with Insulin-Dependent Diabetes Mellitus over a Four-Year Longitudinal Follow-up: II. Immediate and Long-Term Linkages with the Family Milieu," *Journal of Pediatric Psychology* 15, no. 4 (1990): 527–42; E. W. Holden, D. Chimielewski, C. C. Nelson, V. A. Kager, and L. Foltz, "Controlling for General and Disease-Specific Effects in Child and Family Adjustment to Chronic Childhood Illness," *Journal of Pediatric Psychology* 22, no. 1 (1997): 15–27.

47. T. A. Waugh and D. L. Kjos, "Parental Involvement and the Effectiveness of an Adolescent Day Treatment Program," *Journal of Youth and Adolescence* 21 (1992): 487–97.

48. P. A. LaRosa Nash and J. M. Murphy, "An Approach to Pediatric Perioperative Care: Parent-Present Induction," *Nursing Clinics of North America* 32 (1997): 183–99; A. George and J. Hancock, "Reducing Pediatric Burn Pain with Parent Participation," *Journal of Burn Care and Rehabilitation* 14 (1993): 104–7.

49. World Health Organization, "Measuring Child Mortality," http://www.who.int/child_adolescent_health/data/child/en/index.htm (accessed August 10, 2009); J. Bryce, C. Boscho-Pinto, K. Shibuya, and R. E. Black, "WHO Estimates of the Causes of Death in Children," *The Lancet* 365, bo. 9465 (2005): 1147–1152.

50. Centers for Disease Control and Prevention (CDC), National Immunization Program, "Estimated Vaccination Coverage with Individual Vaccines and Selected Vaccination Series Among Children Nineteen to Thirty-Five Months-of-Age by State," (Atlanta, GA: CDC, 2001); World Health Organization (WHO), *WHO Vaccine Preventable Diseases: Monitoring System* (Geneva: WHO, Department of Vaccines and Biologicals, 2000).

51. J. E. Fielding, W. G. Cumberland, and L. Pettitt, "Immunization Status of Children of Employees in a Large Corporation," *Journal of the American Medical Association* 271, no. 7 (1994): 525–30.

52. J. Coreil, A. Augustin, N. A. Halsey, and E. Holt, "Social and Psychological Costs of Preventive Child Health- Services in Haiti," *Social Science and Medicine* 38, no. 2 (1994): 231–38.

53. K. Streatfield and M. Singarimbun, "Social Factors Affecting the Use of Immunization in Indonesia," *Social Science and Medicine* 27, no. 11 (1988): 1237–45.

54. L. K. McCormick, L. K. Bartholomew, M. J. Lewis, M. W. Brown, and I. C. Hanson, "Parental Perceptions of Barriers to Childhood Immunization: Results of Focus Groups Conducted in an Urban Population," *Health Education Research* 12, no. 3 (1997): 355–62; C. Lannon, V. Brack, J. Stuart, M. Caplow, A. McNeill, W. C. Bordley, and P. Margolis, "What Mothers Say About Why Poor Children Fall Behind on Immunizations—a Summary of Focus Groups in North Carolina," *Archives of Pediatrics and Adolescent Medicine* 149, no. 10 (1995): 1070–75.

55. M. Mottonen and M. Uhari, "Absences for Sickness Among Children in Day Care," *Acta Paediatrica* 81 (1992): 929.

56. F. A. Loda, W. P. Glezen, and W. A. Clyde, Jr., "Respiratory Disease in Group Day Care," *Pediatrics* 49 (1972): 428–37; K. Strangert, "Respiratory Illness in Preschool Children with Different Forms of Day Care," *Pediatrics* 57 (1976): 191; A. B. Doyle, "Incidence of Illness in Early Group and Family Day Care," *Pediatrics* 58 (1976): 607.

57. R. Haskins and J. Kotch, "Day Care and Illness: Evidence, Costs, and Public Policy," *Pediatrics* 77, Suppl. 6, (1986): 951–80.

58. P. Sullivan, W. E. Woodward, L. K. Pickering, and H. L. Dupont, "Longitudinal Study of Occurrence of Diarrheal Disease in Day Care Centers," *American Journal of Public Health* 80 (1984): 436; M. A. Oyediran and A. Bamisaiye, "A Study of the Child-Care Arrangements and the Health Status of Pre-school Children of Employed Women in Lagos," *Public Health* 97 (1983): 267; S. D. Hillis, C. M. Miranda, M. McCann, D. Bender, and K. Weigle, "Day Care Center Attendance and Diarrheal Morbidity in Colombia," *Pediatrics* 90 (1992): 582.

59. S. J. Heymann, S. Toomey, and F. Furstenberg, "Working Parents: What Factors Are Involved in Their Ability to Take Time Off from Work When Their Children Are Sick?" *Archives of Pediatrics & Adolescent Medicine* 153 (1999): 870–74; S. J. Heymann, *The Widening Gap: Why America's Working Families Are in Jeopardy and What Can Be Done About It* (New York: Basic Books, 2000).

60. H. Joshi, P. Paci, and J. Waldfogel, "The Wages of Motherhood: Better or Worse?" *Cambridge Journal of Economics* 23 (1999): 543–64; National Alliance for

Caregiving and American Association of Retired People, "Caregiving in the U.S." (2004), http://www.caregiving.org/data/04finalreport.pdf (accessed March 2, 2009); S. J. Heymann, *The Widening Gap: Why America's Working Families Are in Jeopardy and What Can Be Done About It* (New York: Basic Books, 2000).

61. A. Earle and S. J. Heymann, "What Causes Job Loss Among Former Welfare Recipients? The Role of Family Health Problems," *Journal of the American Medical Women's Association* 57 (2002): 5–10.

62. Thirty nations offered paid sick leave at a fixed wage-replacement rate. In some countries these rates varied according to years of employment, length of the leave, severity of the illness, or age of the child. Among countries with fixed wage-replacement rates, the modal rate of replacement was 100 percent of wages.

63. T. E. Seeman, "Health Promoting Effects of Friends and Family on Health Outcomes in Older Adults," *American Journal of Health Promotion* 14, no. 6 (2000): 362–70; L. F. Berkman, "Role of Social-Relations in Health Promotion," *Psychosomatic Medicine* 57, no. 3 (1995): 245–54.

64. L. Gorkin, E. B. Schron, M. M. Brooks, et al., "Psychosocial Predictors of Mortality in the Cardiac-Arrhythmia Suppression Trial-1 (Cast-1)," *American Journal of Cardiology* 71, no. 4 (1993): 263–67; S. J. Bennett, "Relationships Among Selected Antecedent Variables and Coping Effectiveness in Postmyocardial Infarction Patients," *Research in Nursing & Health* 16, no. 2 (1993): 131–39; S. Woloshin, L. M. Schwartz, A.N.A. Tosteson, et al., "Perceived Adequacy of Tangible Social Support and Health Outcomes in Patients with Coronary Artery Disease," *Journal of General Internal Medicine* 12, no. 10 (1997): 613–18; K. Orth-Gomer, M. Horsten, S. P. Wamala, et al., "Social Relations and Extent and Severity of Coronary Artery Disease—The Stockholm Female Coronary Risk Study," *European Heart Journal* 19, no. 11 (1998): 1648–56.

65. E. Tsouna-Hadjis, K. Vemmos, N. Zakopoulos, and S. Stamatelopoulos, "First–Stroke Recovery Process: The Role of Family Social Support," *Archives of Physical Medicine and Rehabilitation* 81 (2000): 881–87.

66. R.K.R. Salokangas, "Living Situation, Social Network and Outcome in Schizophrenia: A Five-Year Prospective Follow-up Study," *Acta Psychiatrica Scandinavica* 96 (1997): 459–68; M. Jubb and E. Shanley, "Family Involvement: The Key to Opening Locked Wards and Closed Minds," *International Journal of Mental Health Nursing* 11 (2002): 47–53; V. Stanhope, "Culture, Control, and Family Involvement: A Comparison of Psychosocial Rehabilitation in India and the United States," *Psychiatric Rehabilitation Journal* 25, no. 3 (2002): 273–80.

67. G. K. Baruch, L. Biener, and R. C. Barnett, "Women and Gender in Research on Work and Family Stress," *American Psychologist* 42, no. 2 (1987): 130–36; D. Jamuna, "Stress Dimensions Among Caregivers of the Elderly," *Indian Journal of Medical Research* 106 (1997): 381–88; D. L. Hoyert and M. M. Seltzer, "Factors Related to the Well-Being and Life Activities of Family Caregivers," *Family Relations* 41, no. 1 (1992): 74–81; M. E. Starrels, B. Ingersoll-Dayton, D. W. Dowler, and M. B. Neal, "The Stress of Caring for a Parent: Effects of the Elder's Impairment on an Employed, Adult

Child," *Journal of Marriage and the Family* 59, no. 4 (1997): 860–72; M. R. Haug, A. B. Ford, K. C. Stange, L. S. Noelker, and A. D. Gaines, "Effects of Giving Care on Caregivers' Health," *Research on Aging* 21, no. 4 (1999): 515–38; S. O. Long and P. B. Harris, "Gender and Elder Care: Social Change and the Role of the Caregiver in Japan," *Social Science Japan Journal* 3, no. 1 (2000): 21–36; C. Ikels, "Aging and Disability in China: Cultural Issues in Measurement and Interpretation," *Social Science & Medicine* 32, no. 6 (1991): 649–65; Y. Hashizume, "Gender Issues and Japanese Family-Centered Caregiving for Frail Elderly Parents or Parents-in-Law in Modern Japan: From the Sociocultural and Historical Perspectives," *Public Health Nursing* 17, no. 1 (2000): 25–31; S. L. Lee, G. A. Colditz, L. F. Berkman, and I. Kawachi, "Caregiving and Risk of Coronary Heart Disease in U.S. Women: A Prospective Study," *American Journal of Preventive Medicine* 24, no. 2 (2003): 113–19.

68. B. Murphy, H. Schofield, J. Nankervis, S. Bloch, H. Herrman, and B. Singh, "Women with Multiple Roles: The Emotional Impact of Caring for Ageing Parents," *Ageing and Society* 17, no. 3 (1997): 277–91.

69. Part-time parity refers to a concept where part-time workers receive the same wage or salary per unit of time as full-time workers and the same benefits accrue at a rate proportional to the percentage of time worked. For example, a half-time worker would accrue half of the number of days of sick leave per month or annual leave as a full-time worker.

70. S. J. Heymann, S. Toomey, and F. Furstenberg, "Working Parents: What Factors Are Involved in Their Ability to Take Time Off from Work When Their Children Are Sick?" *Archives of Pediatrics & Adolescent Medicine* 153, no. 8 (1999): 870–74.

71. The duration of paid leave to care for elderly and disabled family members ranges from two days to two years. Some provide leave for a fixed period of time per case and others have a maximum number of days per month that can be taken. Most leave durations are between seven and ten days. Among countries that provide paid leave, wages are replaced at rates anywhere between 40 percent and 100 percent.

72. R. B. Iverson, G. Brownlee, and H. Walberg, "Parent-Teacher Contacts and Student Learning," *Journal of Educational Research* 74 (1981): 394–96; D. Stevenson and D. Baker, "The Family-School Relation and the Child's School Performance," *Child Development* 58 (1987): 1348–57.

73. C. Desforges and A. Abouchaar, "The Impact of Parental Involvement, Parental Support, and Family Education on Pupil Achievement and Adjustment: A Literature Review" (DFES Research Report 433, Ed. Department for Education and Skills, UK, 2003), http://publications.dcsf.gov.uk/eOrderingDownload/RR433.pdf (accessed February 24, 2009); A. Reynolds, "A Structural Model of First Grade Outcomes for an Urban, Low-Socioeconomic Status, Minority Population," *Journal of Educational Psychology* 81, no. 4 (1989): 594–603; A. Reynolds, "Early Schooling of Children at Risk," *American Educational Research Journal* 28, no. 2 (1991): 392–422.

74. K. Callahan, J. Rademacher, and B. Hildreth, "The Effect of Parent Participation in Strategies to Improve the Homework Performance of Students Who Are at Risk," *Remedial and Special Education* 19, no. 3 (1998): 131–41; T. Keith, P. Keith,

G. Troutman, P. Bickley, P. Trivette, and K. Singh, "Does Parental Involvement Affect Eighth-Grade Student Achievement? Structural Analysis of National Data," *School Psychology Review* 22 (1993): 474–76.

75. P. Fehrmann, T. Keith, and T. Reimers, "Home Influences on School Learning: Direct and Indirect Effects of Parental Involvement on High School Grades," *Journal of Educational Research* 80, no. 6 (1987): 330–37.

76. L. Feinstein and J. Symons, "Attainment in Secondary School," *Oxford Economic Papers* 51, no. 2 (1999): 300–21; A. Reynolds, "Comparing Measures of Parental Involvement and Their Effects on Academic Achievement," *Early Childhood Research Quarterly* 7, no. 3 (1992): 441–62; J. Griffith, "Relation of Parental Involvement, Empowerment, and School Traits to Student Academic Performance," *Journal of Educational Research* 90, no. 1 (1996): 33–41; S. Christenson, T. Rounds, and D. Gorney, "Family Factors and Student Achievement: An Avenue to Increase Students' Success," *School Psychology Quarterly* 7 (1992): 178–206; D. Miller and M. Kelley, "Interventions for Improving Homework Performance: A Critical Review," *School Psychology Quarterly* 6: 174–85 (1991); J. Comer, "Home-School Relationships as They Affect the Academic Success of Children," *Education and Urban Society* 16 (1984): 323–37; J. Fantuzzo, G. Davis, and M. Ginsburg, "Effects of Parental Involvement in Isolation or in Combination with Peer Tutoring on Student Self–Concept and Mathematics Achievement," *Journal of Educational Psychology* 87, no. 2 (1995): 272–81.

77. J. Comer and N. Haynes, "Parent Involvement in Schools: An Ecological Approach," *Elementary School Journal* 91, no. 3 (1991): 271–77; J. Griffith, "Relation of Parental Involvement, Empowerment, and School Traits to Student Academic Performance," *Journal of Educational Research* 90, no. 1 (1996): 33–41; A. Reynolds, N. Mavrogenes, N. Vezruczko, and M. Hagemann, "Cognitive and Family-Support Mediators in Preschool Effectiveness: A Confirmatory Analysis," *Child Development* 67 (1996): 1119–40.

78. T. Frigo, et al., "Australian Young People, Their Families and Post-School Plans: A Research Review" (Australian Council for Educational Research, 2007), http://www.thesmithfamily.com.au/webdata/resources/files/Acer_Report_2007WEB1.pdf (accessed February 25, 2009).

79. B. Iverson, G. Brownlee, and H. Walberg, "Parent-Teacher Contacts and Student Learning," *Journal of Educational Research* 74 (1981): 394–96; D. Stevenson and D. Baker, "The Family-School Relation and the Child's School Performance," *Child Development* 58 (1987): 1348–57; G. Van der Werf, B. Creemers, and H. Guldemond, "Improving Parental Involvement in Primary Education in Indonesia: Implementation, Effects, and Costs," *School Effectiveness & School Improvement* 12, no. 4 (2001): 447–66; World Bank, *Priorities and Strategies for Education: A World Bank Review*, Development in Practice Series (Washington, DC: World Bank, 1995); L. Barraza, "Environmental Attitudes Start at Home: Parents and Their Role in the Development of Values," *International Journal of Environmental Education & Information* 20, no. 4 (2001): 239–56.

80. National Center for Education Statistics, *Fathers' Involvement in the Children's Schools* (NCES 98-091) (Washington, DC: U.S. Department of Education, 1997);

C. W. Nord, D. Brimhall, and J. West, "Dads' Involvement in Their Kids' Schools," *Education Digest* (March 29–35, 1998); M. E. Lamb, "The Emergent American Father," in *The Father's Role: Cross-Cultural Perspectives*, ed. M. E. Lamb (Hillsdale, NY: Lawrence Erlbaum, 1987).

81. C. Benson, E. Medrich, and S. Buckley, "The New View of School Efficiency: Household Time Contributions to School Achievement," in *School Finance Policies and Practices: 1980's Decade of Conflict*, ed. J. Guthrie (Cambridge, MA: Ballinger, 1980); R. Clark, "Why Disadvantaged Students Succeed: What Happens Outside Schools' Critical Period," *Public Welfare* (Spring 1990): 17–23.

82. J. Epstein, "Parent Involvement: What Research Says to Administrators," *Education in Urban Society* 19 (1987): 119–36.

83. D. Leach and S. Siddall, "Parental Involvement in the Teaching of Reading: A Comparison of Hearing Reading, Paired Reading, Pause, Prompt, Praise, and Direct Instruction Methods," *British Journal of Educational Psychology* 60, no. 3 (1990): 349–55; R. Wilkes and V. Clarke, "Training Versus Nontraining of Mothers as Home Reading Tutors," *Perceptual and Motor Skills* 67 (1988): 135–42; United Nations Children's Fund (UNICEF), *The State of the World's Children 2001* (New York: UNICEF, 2001), http://www.unicef.org/sowc01/ (accessed March 3, 2009); R. Myers, *The Twelve Who Survive: Strengthening Programmes of Early Childhood Development in the Third World* (London and New York: Routledge, in cooperation with UNESCO for the Consultative Group on Early Childhood Care and Development, 1992).

84. H. Cooper and B. Nye, "Homework for Students with Learning Disabilities: The Implications of Research for Policy and Practice," *Journal of Learning Disabilities* 27, no. 8 (1994): 470–79; L. Fitton and G. Gredler, "Parental Involvement in Reading Remediation with Young Children," *Psychology in the Schools* 33, no. 4 (1996): 325–32.

85. L. Thurston and K. Dasta, "An Analysis of In-home Parent Tutoring Procedures: Effects on Children's Academic Behavior at Home and in School and on Parents' Tutoring Behaviors," *RASE Remedial and Special Education* 11 (1990): 41–52.

86. C. Vinograd-Bausell, R. Bausell, W. Proctor, and B. Chandler, "Impact of Unsupervised Parent Tutors on Word Recognition Skills," *Journal of Special Education* 20 (1986): 83–90.

87. J. Hewison, "The Long-Term Effectiveness of Parental Involvement in Reading: A Follow-up to the Haringey Reading Project," *British Journal of Educational Psychology* 58 (1988): 184–90; J. Tizard, W. Schofield, and J. Hewison, "Collaboration Between Teachers and Parents in Assisting Children's Reading," *British Journal of Educational Psychology* 52 (1982): 1–15.

88. J. Austin, "Homework Research in Mathematics," *School Science and Mathematics* 79 (1979): 115–21.

89. F. Davis, "Understanding Underachievers," *American Education* 20, no. 10 (1984): 12–14; M. Gajria and S. Salend, "Homework Practices of Students With and Without Learning Disabilities: A Comparison," *Journal of Learning Disabilities* 28 (1995): 291–96; S. Salend and J. Schliff, "An Examination of the Homework Practices

of Teachers of Students with Learning Disabilities," *Journal of Learning Disabilities* 22 (1989): 621–23.

90. H. Cooper and B. Nye, "Homework for Students with Learning Disabilities: The Implications of Research for Policy and Practice," *Journal of Learning Disabilities* 27, no. 8 (1994): 470–79; S. Salend and M. Gajria, "Increasing the Homework Completion Rates of Students with Mild Disabilities," *Remedial and Special Education* 16 (1995): 271–78.

91. S. J. Heymann and A. Earle, "The Impact of Parental Working Conditions on School-Age Children: The Case of Evening Work," *Community, Work and Family* 4, no. 3 (2001): 305–25; S. J. Heymann, *The Widening Gap: Why America's Working Families Are in Jeopardy and What Can Be Done About It* (New York: Basic Books, 2000).

92. S. J. Heymann, *The Widening Gap: Why America's Working Families Are in Jeopardy and What Can Be Done About It* (New York: Basic Books, 2000).

93. S. J. Heymann, A. Earle, and B. Egleston, "Parental Availability for the Care of Sick Children," *Pediatrics* 98, no. 2, pt. 1 (1996): 226–30.

94. L. Feinstein and J. Symons, "Attainment in Secondary School," *Oxford Economic Papers* 51, no. 2 (1999): 300–21.

95. S. J. Heymann, "What Happens During and After School: Conditions Faced by Working Parents Living in Poverty and their School-Age Children," *Journal of Children and Poverty* 6, no. 1 (2000): 5–20.

96. S. J. Heymann and A. Earle, "Low-Income Parents: How Do Working Conditions Affect Their Opportunity to Help School-Age Children at Risk?" *American Educational Research Journal* 37, no. 4 (2000): 833–48.

97. Decades of research have examined the formation of bonds between parents and infants and their impact on children's psychosocial development. See M. E. Avery, "A 50-Year Overview of Perinatal Medicine," *Early Human Development* 29, no. 1–3 (1992): 43–50; M. Crouch and L. Manderson, "The Social Life of Bonding Theory," *Social Science & Medicine* 41, no. 6 (1995): 837–44. In particular, a wealth of research has focused on the development of relationships between mothers and newborns, describing the development of feelings of attachment and affection and a sense of security—see C. K. Johnson, M. D. Gilbert, and G. H. Herdt, "Implications for Adult Roles from Differential Styles of Mother-Infant Bonding: An Ethological Study," *Journal of Nervous & Mental Disease* 167, no. 1 (1979): 29–37; E. Anisfeld and E. Lipper, "Early Contact, Social Support, and Mother-Infant Bonding," *Pediatrics* 72, no. 1 (1983): 79–83—exploring the implications of bonding on a child's later development—see M. E. Lamb, "Early Contact and Maternal-Infant Bonding: One Decade Later," *Pediatrics* 70, no. 5 (1982): 763–68; P. G. Mertin, "Maternal-Infant Attachment: A Developmental Perspective," *Australian & New Zealand Journal of Obstetrics & Gynaecology* 26, no. 4 (1986): 280–83—as well as the negative consequences of extended separation or neglect—see J. P. Henry and S. Wang, "Effects of Early Stress on Adult Affiliative Behavior," *Psychoneuroendocrinology* 23, no. 8 (1998): 863–75. The impact of the bond between fathers and infants has been a growing area of research in recent years. See A. M. Taubenheim, "Paternal-Infant Bonding in the First-Time

Father," *JOGN Nursing* 10, no. 4 (1981): 261–64; P. Nettelbladt, "Father/Son Relationship During the Preschool Years; An Integrative Review with Special Reference to Recent Swedish Findings," *Acta Psychiatrica Scandinavica* 68, no. 6 (1983): 399–407. While the bulk of the literature to date has focused on the bonds between mothers and infants, there is no evidence to suggest that bonding with fathers is any less significant to children.

98. R. Feldman, A. L. Sussman, and E. Zigler, "Parental Leave and Work Adaptation at the Transition to Parenthood: Individual, Marital and Social Correlates," *Applied Developmental Psychology* 25 (2004): 459–79.

99. C. E. Coutrona and B. R. Troutman, "Social Support, Infant Temperament and Parenting Self-Efficacy: A Mediational Model of Post-Partum Depression," *Child Development* 57 (1986): 1507–18.

100. B. Brandth and E. Kvande, "Flexible Work and Flexible Fathers," *Work, Employment & Society* 15, no. 2 (2001): 251–67.

101. R. R. Seward, D. E. Yeatts, and L. K. Zottarelli, "Parental Leave and Father Involvement in Child Care: Sweden and the United States," *Journal of Comparative Family Studies* 33, no. 3 (2002): 387–99; B. Brandth and E. Kvande, "Flexible Work and Flexible Fathers," *Work, Employment & Society* 15, no. 2 (2001): 251–67. While "use it or lose it" policies have led to increased uptake by fathers, they have not erased the gender inequalities and high penalties at work for the adult who does most of the parenting. To argue that the glass is half full, one could note that Finnish fathers increased their use by 50 percent; conversely, to claim that it is half empty, one could note that the absolute increase was minimal, from fathers using 11 percent of their available parental leave in 1994 to 17 percent in 2003. See A. Crittenden, *The Price of Motherhood: Why The Most Important Job In the World Is Still the Least Valued* (New York: H. Holt, 2002); OECD, *Babies and Bosses: Reconciling Work and Family Life*, vol. 4. (Paris: OECD, 2005).

102. While the United States lags far behind most of the world even in unpaid leave, it is not alone. At thirteen and fourteen weeks of unpaid leave, Cyprus and Ireland provide little more than the United States.

103. H. P. Presser, "Nonstandard Work Schedules and Marital Instability," *Journal of Marriage and the Family* 62, no. 1 (2000): 93–110.

Chapter 7

1. D. Luff, "Bankruptcies Heading for a Record Year," *The Adelaide Advertiser*, January 8, 1999.

2. D. Himmelstein, E. Warren, D. Thorne, and S. Woolhandler, "Illness and Injury as Contributors To Bankruptcy," *Health Affairs* 24 (January 2005): 63–73.

3. A. Earle and S. J. Heymann, "What Causes Job Loss Among Former Welfare Recipients? The Role of Family Health Problems," *Journal of American Medical Women's Association* 57 (2002): 5–10. Research using large-scale labor force data from the United States confirms that the birth of children is associated with lower

rates of employment and higher rates of discrimination, particularly for mothers. See A. Leibowitz and J. Klerman, "Explaining Changes in Married Mothers' Employment Over Time," *Demography* 32 (August 1995): 365–78; A. Nakamura and M. Nakamura, "Predicting Female Labor Supply: Effects of Children and Recent Work Experience," *Journal of Human Resources* 29, no. 2 (1994): 304–27. Trend data from 1987 to 2004 on parents' employment and the amount of time off taken after the birth of a newborn show that women continue to take longer periods of leave than men; this has been hypothesized to lead to or perpetuate lower rates of employment and discrimination in the hiring of women. See W. Han, C. Ruhm, and J. Waldfogel, "Parental Leave Policies and Parents' Employment and Leave-Taking" (National Bureau of Economic Research Working Paper no. W13697, December 2007).

4. J. Waldfogel, Y. Higuchi, and M. Abe, "Maternity Leave Policies and Women's Employment After Childbirth: Evidence from the United States, Britain, and Japan" (Centre for Analysis of Social Exclusion [CASE] Paper 3, London School of Economics, 1998), http://sticerd.lse.ac.uk/dps/case/cp/Paper3.pdf (accessed March 3, 2009).

5. S. Harkness and J. Waldfogel, "The Family Gap in Pay: Evidence from Seven Industrialised Countries" (LSE STICERD Research Paper no. CASE030, Working Paper Series, 1999).

6. Social Security Administration, "Social Security: A Brief History" (SSA Publication no. 21-059, ICN 440000, October 2007), http://www.ssa.gov/history/pdf/2007historybooklet.pdf (accessed February 24, 2009); Social Security Online, "History, Social Security Administration" (2003), http://www.ssa.gov/history/briefhistory 3.html (accessed February 24, 2009).

7. Social Security Online, "Presidential Statement Signing the Social Security Act—August 14, 1935," Presidential Statements: Franklin D. Roosevelt, Social Security Administration, http://www.ssa.gov/history/fdrstmts.html#message2 (accessed February 24, 2009).

8. W. J. Nordlund, *The Quest for a Living Wage: The History of the Federal Minimum Wage Program* (Westport, CT: Greenwood Press, 1997).

9. J. J. McGill, "The Minimum Wage and Its Proposed Application in the Dominion of Canada" (Economics, Master of Commerce diss., McGill University, 1936); International Labour Organization, *Minimum Wages in Latin America: ILO Studies and Reports* (Geneva: ILO, 1954).

10. J. R. Pichetto, "The Present State of Social Legislation in the Argentine Republic," *International Labour Review* 46, no. 4 (1942): 383–419; Social Security Programs Throughout the World (SSPTW), http://www.ssa.gov/policy/docs/progdesc/ssptw/ (accessed February 24, 2009); NATLEX, International Labour Organization, http://www.ilo.org/dyn/natlex/natlex_browse.home (accessed February 24, 2009).

11. E. D. Owen, "Paid Vacations in Latin America," *Monthly Labor Review* 50, no. 5 (1940): 1128–39; MLR, "Paid Vacations in Latin America," *Monthly Labor Review* 46, no. 2 (1938): 378–82; F. Green and M. Potepan, "Vacation Time and Unionism in the US and Europe," *Industrial Relations* 27, no. 2 (1988): 180–94.

12. P. Lindert, *Growing Public: Social Spending and Economic Growth Since the*

Eighteenth Century (New York: Cambridge University Press, 2004); L. Mishel, J. Bernstein, and S. Allegretto, *The State of Working America 2004–2005* (Ithaca, NY: Cornell University Press, 2005).

13. M. E. Porter, *On Competition*, updated and expanded edition (Boston: Harvard Business School Press, 2008).

14. A. Hochschild, *Bury the Chains: Prophets and Rebels in the Fight to Free an Empire's Slaves* (New York: Houghton Mifflin, 2005).

15. Margaret Mead (1901–1978), U.S. anthropologist. See The Institute for Intercultural Studies, "Frequently Asked Questions About Mead/Bateson," http://www.interculturalstudies.org/faq.html (accessed February 24, 2009).

16. Grameen Bank, "Grameen Bank at a Glance" (2009), http://www.grameen-info.org/index.php?option=com_content&task=view&id=26&Itemid=175 (accessed February 24, 2009).

17. Environmental policy surrounding the potentially devastating effects of global climate change is just one recent example. In 1998, all of the world's countries reached an agreement in Kyoto to take steps on this issue. As the world's largest economy, the United States is an enormous contributor to emissions. Although the United States initially signed the Kyoto agreement under the Clinton administration, along with all other major countries, the Bush administration subsequently refused to ratify it, thereby undermining hope of progress. This did not, however, impede the actions of individuals and small communities. People began walking or biking to work and forming programs to support others in doing the same. Increased consumer demands gave companies additional incentives to produce hybrid and other fuel-efficient vehicles. Despite the national government's failure to act, subnational governments, cities, and states in the United States made commitments to lower fuel consumption. Beginning with a few dozen individuals, the movement against climate change grew to include hundreds, then thousands, and then millions of people around the world. Governments, including the Bush administration, began to pay attention again.

18. National surveys that are conducted and completed in a setting outside of the workplace have the potential to ensure greater privacy and confidentiality and therefore allow respondents to provide more accurate answers.

19. When conducted on-site, it is particularly important to structure these interviews in such a way as to avoid risking any penalty to workers for participating or for providing honest answers.

20. The 2002 Agreement on Labor Cooperation between the Government of Canada and the Government of Costa Rica and the 1997 agreement between Canada and Chile are two examples. In order to increase enforcement of labor standards, these agreements state that the involved nations will: (1) put in place a program that includes, among other components, seminars and training sessions on the contents of the labor standards and methods of implementation; joint research projects to evaluate the extent and effectiveness of implementation; technical assistance on carrying out enforcement measures, and (2) set up a process that allows individuals in one nation to raise concerns about the effective implementation of labor law in the other

country. If evidence of inadequate enforcement is brought forward, ministerial consultation or an external review by an uninvolved body can result.

21. N. Keresztesi, "Linking Labor Rights and International Trade: Evaluating the NAALC Model," in *The Auto Pact: Investment, Labor and the WTO*, ed. Maureen Irish (The Hague: Kluwer Law International, 2004), 197–241. There are trade agreements linking trade and labor standards, but not specifically linking trade and the ILO Principles. With the exception of the North American Agreement on Labor Cooperation, however, these agreements are between very unequal trading partners, in which one party is a relatively small nation that lacks real negotiating power and/or already has good labor standards.

22. When asked, the overwhelming majority of people around the world agreed that it was the responsibility of the state to take care of the very poor, including 96 percent of people living in Spain; 94 percent of those in Lebanon; 93 percent in Bulgaria, Kuwait, Bangladesh, Malaysia, Indonesia, and Tanzania; 90 percent or more of those living in Brazil, Chile, Germany, Britain, Morocco, Israel, India, China, Senegal, and Nigeria; 80 percent or more in Canada, Argentina, Peru, Venezuela, Mexico, Sweden, Italy, France, Poland, The Czech Republic, Ukraine, Russia, Slovakia, the Palestinian Territories, Turkey, South Korea, Pakistan, Mali, Kenya, Ethiopia, South Africa, and Uganda; and 70 percent or more in the United States, Bolivia, and Ghana. The only countries in which less than 70 percent of people agreed nonetheless showed a majority in favor of governments' involvement: two-thirds in Egypt and Jordan, and 59 percent in Japan. See The Pew Global Attitudes Project, "47-Nation Pew Global Attitudes Survey," Pew Research Center (October 2007), http://pewglobal.org/reports/display.php?ReportID=258 (accessed February 23, 2009).

Appendix

1. The number of UN nations about which at least one of our primary sources, NATLEX and SSPTW, had collected data is 190. NATLEX provided data on 189 UN nations, and SSPTW provided data on 164.

2. NATLEX is available online: see ILO, NATLEX, http://www.ilo.org/dyn/natlex/natlex_browse.home (accessed February 23, 2009).

3. We did not include legislation that referred only to a specific region of a country. Similarly, we did not include legislation that referred only to a specific sector of industry (e.g. legislation defining maximum hours of work per week for food services, or laws that referred only to public-sector employees). Rather than creating a longitudinal record of labor legislation, we sought to capture the most up-to-date regulations relating to the Index items for each country. In cases where there were multiple, overlapping amendments to previous legislation, we sought to identify legislation that consolidated the amendments, or we included the most recent amendments, but not those that had been overridden by subsequent legislation.

4. World Bank, "Doing Business Law Library," http://www.doingbusiness.org/LawLibrary/Default.aspx (accessed March 4, 2009).

5. Lexadin, "The World Law Guide," http://www.lexadin.nl/wlg/ (accessed February 23, 2009).

6. World Legal Information Institute, WorldLII Databases, http://www.worldlii.org/ (accessed February 23, 2009).

7. U.S. Social Security Administration, "Social Security Programs Throughout the World": Africa, 2007; Europe, 2006; Asia and the Pacific, 2006; and The Americas, 2007, http://www.ssa.gov/policy/docs/progdesc/ssptw/ (accessed February 23, 2009).

8. SSPTW reports the percentage of wages paid by social security during periods of leave, employer contributions as a percentage of payroll, and employee or insured contributions as a percentage of earnings. The SSPTW sometimes includes the minimum and maximum amount of pay or benefits stipulated in a country's laws.

9. ILO, "Working Time Database," Conditions of Work and Employment Programme (TRAVAIL), http://www.ilo.org/travaildatabase/servlet/workingtime (accessed March 2, 2009).

10. ILO, "Maternity Protection Database," Conditions of Work and Employment Programme (TRAVAIL), http://www.ilo.org/travaildatabase/servlet/maternityprotection (accessed March 2, 2009).

11. World Alliance for Breastfeeding Action, "Status of Maternity Protection by Country" (2006), http://www.waba.org.my/whatwedo/womenandwork/pdf/MaternityProtectionChart21May2006.pdf (accessed March 3, 2009).

12. European Industrial Relations Observatory Online (EIRO), http://eiro.eurofound.europa.eu (accessed March 4, 2009).

13. M. Moss and M. O'Brien, eds., "International Review of Leave Policies and Related Research 2006" (Employment Relations Research Series no. 57, UK Department of Trade and Industry, 2006), http://www.dti.gov.uk/files/file31948.pdf (accessed March 2, 2009).

14. OECD, Social Policy Division, Directorate for Employment, Labor and Social Affairs (2008): "Report PF9: Additional Leave Entitlements for Working Parents," http://www.oecd.org/dataoecd/53/58/41927359.pdf and "Report PF7: Key Characteristics of Parental Leave Policies," http://www.oecd.org/dataoecd/45/26/37864482.pdf (both accessed March 2, 2009); OECD, "Babies and Bosses: Reconciling Work and Family Life (vol. 1): Australia, Denmark and the Netherlands" (2002), http://www.oecd.org/document/32/0,3343,en_2649_34819_30652384_1_1_1_1,00.html; (vol. 2): "Austria, Ireland and Japan" (2003), http://www.oecd.org/document/37/0,3343,en_2649_34819_28932069_1_1_1_1,00.html; (vol. 3): "New Zealand, Portugal and Switzerland" (2004), http://www.oecd.org/document/63/0,3343,en_2649_34819_31588543_1_1_1_1,00.html; (vol. 4): "Canada, Finland, Sweden and the United Kingdom" (2005), http://www.oecd.org/document/35/0,3343,en_2649_34819_34905443_1_1_1_1,00.html (sites accessed March 2, 2009).

15. R. Ray and J. Schmitt, *No Vacation Nation* (Washington, DC: Center for Economic and Policy Research—CEPR, 2007), http://www.cepr.net/documents/publications/2007-05-no-vacation-nation.pdf (accessed March 4, 2009); R. Ray, *A Detailed Look At Parental Leave Policies in 21 OECD Countries* (Washington, DC: Center

for Economic and Policy Research, 2008), http://www.cepr.net/documents/publications/parental-app_2008_09.pdf (accessed March 5, 2009); R. Ray, J. C. Gornick, and J. Schmitt, *Parental Leave Policies in 21 Countries: Assessing Generosity and Gender Equality* (Washington, DC: Center for Economic and Policy Research, 2008), http://www.cepr.net/documents/publications/parental_2008_09.pdf (accessed March 5, 2009).

16. Clearinghouse on International Developments in Child, Youth and Family Policies, "Comparative Policies, Section 1: Comparative Child, Youth and Family Policies and Programs: Benefits and Services" (Institute for Child and Family Policy, Columbia University), http://www.childpolicyintl.org/ (accessed March 2, 2009).

17. Country reports consulted include ILO, "Facts and Figures on Gender Equality: Lithuania" (2005), http://www.ilo.org/public/english/region/eurpro/budapest/download/gender/lithuania.pdf (accessed March 2, 2009); United Nations, "Contextual Database of the Generations and Gender Program," Population Activities Unit, UN Commission of Europe, http://www.demogr.mpg.de/cgi-bin/databases/cdb/cdb.php (accessed March 2, 2009); T. Rostgaard, "Family Support Policy in Central and Eastern Europe—A Decade and a Half of Transition," Early Childhood and Family Policy Series, No. 8-2004 (synthesis report prepared for Consultation Meeting on Family Support Policy in Central and Eastern Europe, UNESCO, 2004), http://unesdoc.unesco.org/images/0013/001337/133733e.pdf (accessed March 2, 2009); Council of Europe, European Committee of Social Rights, "Conclusions 2007 (Albania)," "European Social Charter (revised)" (2007), http://www.coe.int/t/dghl/monitoring/socialcharter/conclusions/State/Albania2007_en.pdf (accessed March 2, 2009); Council of Europe, European Committee of Social Rights, "Conclusions 2007 (Armenia)," "European Social Charter" (2007), http://www.coe.int/t/dghl/monitoring/socialcharter/conclusions/State/Armenia2007_en.pdf (accessed March 2, 2009); Belarus, "Belarus: Country Report (Users)" (Working Paper no. 1, Statistical Commission and Economic Commission for Europe, Conference of European Statisticians, Joint ECE/UNDP Workshop for Gender Statistics and Policy Monitoring and Benchmarking, Orvieto, Italy, 2000), http://www.unece.org/stats/documents/2000/10/gender.workshop/1.e.pdf (accessed March 2, 2009); ILO, "Dialogue: Social Dialogue, Labour Law and Labour Administration," National Labour Law Profile: Republic of Finland, http://www.oit.org/public/english/dialogue/ifpdial/info/national/fin.htm#ole (accessed March 2, 2009); Belgium, European Trade Union Institute, "Clés pour le travail et la maternité," Service Public Fédéral Emploi, Travail et Concertation Sociale (Brussels: SPF Emploi, Travail et Concertation Sociale, 2002), http://www.labourline.org/Record.htm?idlist=1&record=19122358124919405309 (accessed March 2, 2009).

18. World Bank, World Development Indicators Online (WDI Online), http://go.worldbank.org/6HAYAHG8H0 (accessed March 5, 2009).

19. The Standardised Unemployment rates (SURs) for all thirty OECD nations are drawn from the OECD's Main Economic Indicator's Labour Force Statistics (LFS) database. OECD, "OECD Labour Force Statistics: 1987-2007, 2008 Edition," http://

www.oecd.org/document/46/0,3343,en_2649_34251_2023214_1_1_1_1,00.html (accessed June 12, 2009).

20. The data used in the Competitiveness Reports is obtained through a global network of 104 research institutions and academics that partner and collaborate with WEF, as well as data from a survey of 11,000 business leaders from 131 nations. See WEF, "Our Organization," http://www.weforum.org/en/about/Our%20Organization/index.htm and WEF, "Frequently Asked Questions: The Organization," http://www.weforum.org/en/about/FAQs/index.htm (both accessed March 2, 2009).

21. World Bank, *World Development Report 2008* (Washington, DC: World Bank, 2007), http://siteresources.worldbank.org/INTWDR2008/Resources/2795087-1192111580172/WDROver2008-ENG.pdf (accessed March 2, 2009).

Index